Plain Talk

AND

Common Sense

FROM

the Black Avenger

KEN HAMBLIN

Simon & Schuster

SIMON & SCHUSTER
Rockefeller Center
1230 Avenue of the Americas
New York, NY 10020

Ken Hamblin is a columnist for
the New York Times Syndicate.

Designed by Edith Fowler
Manufactured in the United States of America

10   9   8   7   6   5   4   3   2   1

Library of Congress Cataloging-in-Publication Data
is available.

ISBN 0-684-80756-4

This book is dedicated to my grandchildren,
Olivia Christine Hamblin and Rayce Ricardo Denton,
for they represent the hope of my race
and the future of our nation.

Contents

Introduction

I'm fortunate to be able to combine my voice as a syndicated talk-radio host with the power of the quill to lend credence to the opinions I have about the complicated world we live in today.

Initially, the opportunity fell into my lap when an invitation was extended to me by Chuck Green, formerly editorial-page editor of the *Denver Post*. Five years ago, I started writing also for the New York Times Syndicate.

When I asked Green, "Why me?," he said it was because he thought I had a lot of opinions about a great many things—something many of my friends and family would readily confirm. But the fact remained that I certainly never thought of myself as a newspaper essayist.

And that's an opinion many of my detractors still share after more than a decade of my holding their feet to the fire with my views on social and political issues that confront our nation today.

"But what if I fail?" I asked Green, when he asked if I was interested in writing on his page. "What if I'm not good as a writer?"

He chuckled, then said, "Then I'll fire you."

And thus, resolute not to flop, I accepted the challenge.

It's been a heady experience and very rewarding. It's been a profoundly eye-opening experience, that of watching liberals squirm when my count of one-plus-one on matters of quotas and affirmative-action policies failed to tally the same as theirs.

Over the years, I've been blessed, though, to meet a lot of folks who've paid me some very wonderful compliments:

"I have your column posted on the refrigerator."

"I clip and send your columns out to California, or back to New York, to our son."

"We have all your columns. You should put them in a book someday."

Thanks to that challenge from Green and all the encouragement I've received over the years, someday is now.

I chose to title this book "Plain Talk and Common Sense" because that's what I have always sought to bring to the three essays I write each week—two for the *Post* and the one for the Times Syndicate.

As you will read on these pages, I've written about many of the social taboos that the twin evils of runaway liberalism and political correctness have inhibited my colleagues in the fourth estate to grapple with.

I touch upon crime. Upon our nation's collective victory over institutional racism and the incongruous emergence of black-on-white bigotry. Upon what I consider to be the failure of the African-American political machine to deliver the basics of the American Dream to its xenophobic inner-city constituency. On the corruption of mainstream American politics as it is exemplified in our time by the moral failure of President William Jefferson Clinton.

Plain Talk and Common Sense is dedicated to the values I'd like to be remembered for one hundred years from now. The values I'd want my granddaughter Olivia Christine Hamblin and my grandson Rayce Ricardo Denton to pass along to their children when they are born.

But this book also is dedicated to every American in our great nation. Be they Christian or Jew. Rich or poor. Black or white. So long as they reflect the heritage and the values of our great nation.

These are difficult times, and I foresee difficult times ahead for Americans such as ourselves, who trust in such things as God, honor and patriotism. The essays in this book reflect my vested interest in the principles and the values that make America great today and that will see her through many more tomorrows if we don't abandon them now.

ONE

The American Dream

Doing the Right Thing
Pays Off

First published July 1996

Recently I performed a ritual that parents, who have been blessed with the luxury, the joy and the wonderment of holding their children's children, have enjoyed since the dawn of humankind. I traveled across the fruited plains of Kansas on a pilgrimage to behold my firstborn grandson.

Rayce Ricardo Denton II isn't my first grandbaby. No, sir. That honor belongs to his cousin Olivia Christine Hamblin, who came to us like a gift from heaven five years ago.

To be honest, after sixty months of doting over a little girl—whom I cuddled when she was just forty-five minutes old—I was curious whether my new grandson would rip and tug at my heartstrings the way Olivia had.

Don't get me wrong about little Rayce. I was definitely overflowing with joy and pride when the news of his birth reached me by cellular telephone. I remember the exact moment. It was about 4:45 in the afternoon of May 31, and I was stuck in southbound traffic on I-25 in Denver.

My phone rang, and at the other end of the line was Grandma Sue announcing to me that it was a boy. We had a grandson. I was so delighted after her call that I punched the "end" button, rolled down the window on the passenger side of my car and announced the arrival of my grandson to the first face that came into view in the traffic.

The face belonged to a white guy about thirty-five or forty years old driving a service truck. He looked hot and cranky from trying to stretch his neck long enough to see what the traffic delay was all about.

"Hey," I shouted.

He threw an impatient look to me, as he took another draw on his cigarette.

"It's a boy," I said.

"What?" the trucker said, irritably.

"It's a boy. My wife just called to say I've got a new grandson."

In that moment, without any hesitation, the expression on his face changed from one of a man trapped in slow-moving Colorado traffic to one that appeared to send nothing but great joy and happiness for me.

He flashed a wide smile my way, followed by a supportive thumbs-up.

"That's great, buddy. That's really great. Good luck with him."

"Thanks," I said. And the enchanted moment that two strangers happened to share because of the birth of a baby—my grandson—became a pleasant imprint as we went about our separate ways.

Before long, Grandma Sue and I were headed east across the eternal plains of Kansas. During the long ride, my head was filled with a million pointless questions.

Would I like him?

Of course, you'll like him, I answered myself.

You're going to love him and you know it.

Grandma and Grandpa live in Colorado and he's way across the country in Missouri, I thought. What's that going to be like? Will we really get to know each other? Or will our relationship become one of the millions of long-distance telephone relationships that I've heard so many other grandparents bemoan.

Needless to say, in that nine-hour motorcar trip from Denver to Kansas City, I did a lot of thinking about my grandson. I thought about stocks and other financial investments I would make for him as a means to secure his financial future.

I wondered whether he would follow in the hardworking, talented footsteps of my daughter, his mother, who had scrapped her way to a television anchor position in Kansas City.

I wondered whether he would be a sports geek like his dad.

Finally on Saturday morning, after a short night's sleep in Salina, Kansas, the nose of our car turned in to the baby's driveway. Grandma reached over and honked the horn excitedly. As if on cue, a door in the garage opened, and there he was—no bigger than a ten-pound bag of sugar, swaddled in his father's arms.

Hugs and kisses were exchanged and finally I was introduced to little Rayce. He squirmed in my arms, and as he did so, the pride of being his grandpa washed over me like a tidal wave.

I felt like he was my ultimate reward for being brave and not yielding to the misfortune and dead end of poverty, for not buckling and giving up on the belief that I and my children had an inherent right to the American Dream.

Today, I have two rewards for doing the right thing in my two grandbabies—one from a son and the other from a daughter, neither of whom ever wavered from following their father's advice to chase ideals founded in pride, character and self-respect.

Doing the right thing has paid off for me, and it's paid off for them. And as I held my grandson for the first time, I knew without a doubt that those principles would pay off for him too.

Pick a Better Country

First published July 1996

I've taken a lot of criticism from affirmative-action-and-quota-prone blacks because of my deeply held beliefs about the merits of the American Dream.

What's amazing to me is why I'm chastised for believing in a dream that promises that any man—no matter his color—who works diligently and stays the course of right instead of wrong is destined eventually to prevail. That dream certainly beats the alternative of facing a lifetime of wretched poverty and dependency on the kindness of strangers and the dole.

Perhaps I've given more thought than usual these days to the benefits of the American Dream and what it promises, because of late I've been buffeted by an assortment of modern-day pseudo–black revolutionaries calling my radio show to denounce me for escaping the ghetto and prospering like a lot of other mainstream Americans.

Sometimes the voices of my detractors haunt me at night just before I drift off to sleep.

"No, you ain't right. You is ah Uncle Tom."

"You don't believe in nothing, except the money the white man is paying you to run the brothers down."

The best denunciation of them all is: "You ain't black no mo'. You done forgot where you come from."

It's remarkable once you've decided not to be any man's nigger how easy it is to muster your pride and your self-respect in the face of such criticism. I think about that a lot at night when I'm in bed, the house is still and the only sound I hear is the wind rustling through the pine trees.

About that time, I feel a smile creeping across my face. Then I'm able to turn off the voices in my head, because I'm reassured, as I approach the final third of my life, that I have made the right choices.

Choices that catapulted me away from the mean streets of Brooklyn, New York, where I grew up. Decisions that ultimately meant that my children and my children's children wouldn't live in a world where they were overcome by the culture of bottom-feeding black trash. I know that whatever they become, I fought the good fight so they too saw that they had choices.

Like other successful men and women, I doubt whether it ever will be possible for me to forget my roots or my road traveled, as my critics claim I have. I will always be aware of just how far both America and I have come in my lifetime.

After my own life of struggle and the difficulty I and others faced to forge the America of opportunity for all that we know today, I find it quite paradoxical to be denounced by the new wave of politically correct hyphenated African-Americans.

If, as they contend, the U.S. is a doomed nation, I think she is doomed because she suffers from a mega-dose of forgetfulness concerning her rich historical past. Too many have forgotten the opportunity she has always provided for all—albeit an opportunity for change during her ugliest days of racism and hatefulness.

Pick a better country.

Name a greater nation where people of color, who still today have little hope or opportunity in their native land, can get a better opportunity to be all that they can be. I defy you.

It definitely wouldn't be on the African continent, where in countries like Mauritania in the northwest portion of the continent, black Africans still today are being captured and sold as slaves.

The opportunities this new generation of African-Americans turn away from in the States can't be found in Kenya either, where a rapid expansion of the population and a shortage of welfare programs—as ghetto blacks in the U.S. know them—have put a strain on limited health facilities and social services in that black nation.

Nor would it be in Zimbabwe, where 70 percent of the black African population—the population so romanticized by African-Americans—struggles to scratch out a meager living.

Nope. When you get right down to it, the good old U.S. of A.—warts and all—remains the best place on earth as far as this American is concerned. If you work hard for a better opportunity for yourself and your children, you can't do better than America.

And I, for one, think it's amazing how many minorities denounce that basic truth every day God chooses to splash his benevolent grace across our land.

The Liberals Wage War on Capitalism

First published February 1995

There is a grand myth concerning the integrity of all minimum-wage workers which is being fostered by socialist Democrats eager to worm their way back into the hearts of the American people.

The myth is that every minimum-wage employee hired punches the employer's time clock tan, fit and ready to work.

The scenario suggests that while this unassuming proletariat shows up with the strongest of work ethics, fully eager to deliver an honorable day of work, the minimum wage of $4.25 an hour smacks of exploitation by their capitalist employers.

If only that tale were factual.

As the co-owner of two gourmet sandwich shops in predominantly white, middle-class localities in Colorado, my wife and I have learned from firsthand experience just how inept, surly and, in some instances, totally worthless some entry-level minimum-wage employees are.

They are a far cry from the president's depiction of them as poor underpaid workers struggling in desperation to pull themselves up the ladder of affluence.

Our experience, and the experience of many small-business owners we meet, is one of hiring young people—and in some cases older workers—who simply don't want to work. They consider it an imposition if our managers ask them to clean or prep for the next day during slow periods. They treat customers as interruptions in their social time with other like-minded workers.

And they never grasp—though we tell them over and over—that the slightest sign of interest they might show in their job would mean an almost immediate increase in their starting minimum wage.

Meanwhile, Clinton and the Democratic rabble defeated in the 1994 "November Revolution" are searching for a way to fill in the moat they have dug between themselves and the American people.

So they have created the fantasy that the minimum wage should be increased to a level that would allow every employee, no matter his or her commitment, to raise a family and make a down payment on a little bungalow.

Well, most of us know that success in the American scenario doesn't work like that.

It's clear to me, and maybe that's why I'm a success, that the entry-level salary was never meant to be a stopping point. Rather, it was a launch pad from which to begin the journey to a higher wage—ultimately a wage that would afford me and my family access to the American Dream.

Think about your own first job. Mine paid $1.25 an hour. I couldn't join the middle class on that salary.

But my wife and I worked. We saved. I moved to a higher-paying job after I could claim "experience" on my job application.

And after a while, I found I could compete for yet a higher-paying job that got me well on the road to fulfilling my ambitions. I could legitimately demand, because of my worth to the employer, higher pay.

That's the same system of supply and demand for good workers that is at work today.

As a matter of fact, competition in the marketplace, not a government minimum, determines what the entry-level wage is in many areas today.

For example, the opening salary for an inexperienced employee at one of my sandwich shops is $6 an hour. That figure wasn't established by the government or by unions. The businesses in the area didn't get together and agree to pay almost $2 higher than the minimum wage out of the goodness of our hearts.

That starting wage was determined by the relatively small size of the entry-level labor pool in that particular region—a traditional capitalist concept of supply and demand.

But none of these real-world facts matter when you are trying to ignite class warfare or fuel a war against capitalism—against too much prosperity—as I believe the White House is.

America is a country where the work ethic still pays off, eventually.

Old-fashioned values like not getting pregnant in your teens, studying diligently to get an education and developing a salable skill are the real keys to economic success in our American system—not a guaranteed house payment your first day on the job.

You Can Give a Man a House, but Not a Home

First published September 1996

A socialist government may be able to give a man or a woman a house, but it cannot transform that house into a home.

Homes are the stuff of dreams and youthful ambition. They are the illusions of optimistic young people aspiring—sometimes against the odds—to a bright future.

I have repeated my house-and-home distinction on dozens of occasions while trying to address America's socialist political faction that is seeking to level the playing field by attempting to legislate and subsidize personal success.

My directness on this seemingly obvious truth has not afforded me much popularity among the petty politicos—many of whom I classify as poverty pimps. Perhaps it is because they are intent on peddling the notion to their constituents that America should guarantee success for any and all.

Why are some people poor? Why do some manage to claw their way out of the worst kind of deprivation, while others go with the flow like dead fish? What makes some men and women eternal losers, while others remain determined to struggle to their last breath?

Those may well be the $64,000 questions of my generation.

But if I am certain of anything at all, it is that billions of American taxpayer dollars have been consumed seeking these answers with little success.

Perhaps that's why I took special notice when I happened across an article recently concerning the efforts of media mogul Oprah Winfrey to achieve that which the collective wealth of American taxpayers has failed to accomplish—the demise of poverty in America, particularly in black America.

According to a recent article in the *Chicago Tribune*, Winfrey decided to tackle poverty head-on in 1994.

During a Chicago press conference that winter more than two years ago, Winfrey announced that she would "finance a program to move a hundred families out of public housing, off public aid and into better lives."

The program was designed to exclude drug users, alcoholics and those who lacked motivation.

A remarkable plan, indeed. Possibly Winfrey was motivated by, perhaps even feeling a bit guilty about, the fact that America had given her so much while others had been given so little.

Whatever. According to the article in the *Tribune*, Winfrey committed a portion of her own sizable fortune to the program, lovingly tagged "Families for a Better Life."

The *Chicago Tribune*, in a lofty editorialization, noted that no other program had a better chance to succeed than this one.

Well, no matter how noble Winfrey's goal and despite two years of screening and $1.3 million ($843,000 contributed by Winfrey), the program has ended up a miserable flop.

Why?

Because of the fundamental truth that dreams are born in the hearts of men and women. They cannot be constructed by a charitable hand where none exists.

Only five of the one hundred families managed to complete the program, and at least one of those still receives public aid.

The officials administering the program told the *Tribune*: "The original plan of putting 100 families through the program was too ambitious."

Furthermore, they noted something that I have always said, that the welfare mentality—the belief that poor people are simply victims of society and thus entitled to restitution from society—remained a formidable obstacle to the program's success.

"We had to keep emphasizing that this is not about what you get. This is about what you do," the program officials told the *Tribune*.

Has Oprah Winfrey learned that no amount of money can implant desire where none exists? One would hope so, but I doubt it.

Welfare Snuffs Out
Survival Skills

First published March 1996

Like the unfolding of an airtight murder case, evidence continues to mount against the socialist policies of the liberal Democrats.

Despite the repeated failures of the welfare state promoted in the name of their lofty socialist notions, these liberals are unwavering in their insistence that the quality of people's lives is enriched when the government assumes responsibility for them.

But case after case shows otherwise.

A pathetic example is embodied in a *New York Times* report about the results of a study concerning the impact of public assistance on 790 Atlanta-area welfare families. The study was conducted by Child Trends Inc., a nonprofit research group working for the Department of Health and Human Services.

The children in the study group were between three and five years old, and almost all of them were black. Test results concluded that these children were likely to have trouble when they started school.

According to the *Times*, the study revealed that "On average, the children . . . correctly answered only slightly more than half the questions in a test of concepts and skills—such as shapes, colors and understanding relationships like 'under' or 'behind'—needed for school readiness."

As I would have predicted, these welfare babies of ghetto mothers scored lower on vocabulary tests than did a national sample of black children.

Even though the study indicated that the longer a family stayed on welfare, the lower the children tested, some liberal-minded pundits who responded in the article to the study refused to address these data as a clear measure of the obvious negative effects of welfare.

Instead, people like Nancy Ebb, senior staff lawyer for the Washington-based Children's Defense Fund, used the test results as ammunition to argue that higher-quality child care be made available to welfare families. In essence, calling for more welfare, more of the same.

I grew up on the dole. And I contend, from firsthand experience, that it is impossible to live on welfare for years at a time without losing your drive and your ambition. Welfare makes it impossible to provide cognitive stimulation and emotional support to children, the kind of support the study showed was lacking in these welfare families.

Even when I was growing up on welfare forty to fifty years ago in New York, there were poor people around me, conditioned by welfare, who always had a lot of reasons why it was irrational for me to even think about trying to compete outside the boundaries of the ghetto.

The human brain may be designed with an inherent thirst for knowledge, experience and information, but I'm convinced we deaden that brain activity when we have a guarantee of survival tied to a regular welfare check.

I view the people subject to today's liberal folly of welfare as robots—people living a mechanical existence, lost souls mandated by their liberal lords to dwell eternally in ignorance brought about by a lack of stimulation and, thus, drive.

Today I see American ghettos full of such people, languishing in the shadow of society, never daring to reach for the fruits of success that are available to everyone in America.

By continuing to offer up constantly improved government assistance by way of more conveniently delivered welfare checks and broader and better social programs, the liberals have managed to all but snuff out the basic survival skills in poor people. They have deadened even the survival instincts they need to pass on to their children.

But despite all the visible shortcomings of the expanding welfare state, the liberal socialists continue shamelessly to ignore the facts and promote the supposed benefits.

I have said it in the past, and I'll say it again. The only compassionate way to save the poor children in America—whether they are black, Hispanic or white—is to kill the American welfare system as we know it. Shoot it squarely between the eyes.

Lower Taxes, Less Government, and Reinvestment in the American Dream

First published September 1996

I received a letter from a woman who chose to take issue with my stance that the individual, and not the government, is ultimately responsible for nurturing his or her own dreams, for mustering the courage to reach for the stars.

By this woman's logic: "A person needs to have time available in order to dream and help to make that dream come true.

"Many people are so busy just trying to survive that they never have the time or energy to dream. These people work full-time at one or two or maybe even three jobs just to get enough money to provide the basic essentials for themselves and their families. Any time left over is spent taking care of those families."

After reading her words—words in total opposition to everything I have ever been taught or encouraged to believe in—I concluded that they were spoken like a true liberal social worker. They contained all the common traits of the liberal socialist ideal.

They dampened the ambition that most of us Americans like to think is second nature to the American spirit.

I marveled at the defeatism imparted in her words because although I grew up poor, raised by women on public assistance in a household where every day was a fight to survive, the ideal of "yes, you can do it" was deeply implanted in me.

Learning responsibility and how to do for myself wasn't over-shadowed by an intellectual philosophy that deemed the government morally obligated to care for me.

It was a hard lesson about life. Taking responsibility for yourself is tough, and doubly so if you are poor. But maybe that's why and how I managed to survive. I saw poverty as the ordeal I had to over-come, and the only resources available to help me do it were my own inner resources and energy.

Success, however long it took to come, was marked by breaking away from one's reliance on the government, not by becoming fur-ther dependent upon it.

As a result of my own experience, I am seldom shy when it con-cerns pressing my point that I am bullish on America. I talk about the ideals and principles of this great country every day on my syn-dicated radio show. I wrote a book entitled *Pick a Better Country*.

In spite of her shortcomings and her blatant warts, the United States is still the best bet when it comes to dreaming about building a future for your family.

In her letter, my critic told me about her dream of someday working with computers. She noted that it would take several years to achieve her goal, and that she spent one entire year taking a col-lege course, thanks to funds from the government.

She concluded: "Dreams are such fragile things. They also often take a lot of time to achieve."

What she failed to note, however, is that no matter how noble one's dreams may be, their fulfillment isn't guaranteed anywhere on God's earth. And despite all of the socialist nonsense frequently spouted by liberals, success isn't, nor should it be, guaranteed in the United States either.

By this woman's logic, however, everything—from a demand for self-reliance to welfare reform—is part of a dastardly capitalist plot "for large corporations to make money administering the new programs while taking money from poor people who need help to achieve their dreams."

I'm curious. Where and when did the poor and their spokespersons garner the authority to lay claim to more of the working man's income?

Approximately 54 cents of every dollar earned in the United States today is gobbled up by state and federal tax collectors, and apparently that still isn't enough to comfort, educate and nurture the dreams of the poor.

In closing her letter to me, my nemesis said: "Poor people may have a welfare mentality but rich people and large corporations also have the same welfare mentality that the government owes them and they are constantly trying to get more and more government money."

Could it be that the rich man's welfare she is sensing is really a growing demand from working people for lower taxes, less government and a reinvestment in the American Dream?

America Offers Lots of Safe Landings Beyond Welfare

First published February 1995

I have been thinking about how avoiding the pitfalls of poverty and piloting a single-engine airplane over the Rocky Mountains have a lot in common.

For one thing, it's always a good idea for a pilot traversing the craggy peaks of the mountains to keep both eyes peeled for a safe spot to put down in the event of an unscheduled emergency landing.

Just as a pilot flying high above a potentially hostile environment should be prepared for an emergency landing, I believe people should devise a strategy to help them survive in case an economic emergency should occur.

For instance, have you ever considered how you would support yourself if no one would hire you and you had to create your own gainful employment?

Could you create a job for yourself in today's society? Or would you, like so many others, wallow in your distress and eventually end up on the public dole?

How would you survive an unexpected economic catastrophe like the death of the breadwinner in your family?

Having begun my life in grinding poverty, I ponder questions like those all the time.

I still have the 35mm cameras I used as a professional photo-journalist in the 1960s. I keep them as sort of a safety net tucked away under my bed—as a hedge between me and the humbling chill of poverty.

The way I figure it, no matter what the future brings, as long as I have those cameras, I'll always be able to support myself. If necessary, I could market my photographic skills, make a living shooting pictures of babies or weddings.

What, you ask, if I were forced even to sell or pawn my Nikon and Leica cameras?

According to wisdom attributed to Jonathan Swift, "Necessity is the mother of invention."

It's obvious that like a hunter in the forest, I would have to become very imaginative very quickly if I expected to become an effective forager in our twentieth-century high-tech and service-oriented workplace.

I'm convinced, though, that if you are willing to work hard, there are jobs you could invent to earn an honest living and avoid living off welfare.

If you have a valid driver's license, I'll bet you could market your services to a world of people who detest taking their cars to the auto dealership for service to comply with the terms of the warranty.

I know how much people hate it, because I'm one of them. I'd be willing to pay a reasonable fee—say thirty bucks—for a dependable person to pick up and deliver my vehicle back to my office or my home.

There must be virtually dozens of services like that one that I'll bet working folks would be willing to hire reliable people to do. And a lot more services homebound folks would hire out.

Except in big cities like Los Angeles and New York, I bet there aren't enough people offering dog-walking services. And there's always a need for people willing to clean homes and offices.

If those jobs don't meet your fancy, or aptitude, how about a gourmet grocery service for folks too busy to shop? How about distributing fresh flowers regularly to the homes and offices in your area?

Trust me, every community has an overworked handyman. Maybe he needs an apprentice.

If you've ever tried to hire the services of a plumber, an electrician or a specialty repairman, you know it's practically impossible to get a quick response to your desperate call.

The chaos in those kinds of small businesses might also represent an employment opportunity.

With a little inventiveness, you might sell the overworked furnace repairman or the disorganized plumber on the notion that you could be the greatest appointment scheduler—not just another answering service.

Think about it. It could be a great little white-collar job, and you could work at home.

Once you put your mind to work, you'll find all it takes is a little initiative and the guts to sell yourself to land safely in an unscheduled emergency.

The best part is that no matter how hard you end up working, it's infinitely better than giving in to subsisting on the dole.

Three Young American Men

First published August 1994

While I was dining with a friend, the conversation turned to the lack of ambition among some people today and the plight of the homeless.

We concluded that being homeless today is a condition worn by many like a badge of honor.

In fact, being poor in America these days is even considered to be politically righteous, while the pursuit of economic security is sneered at by many liberals.

My buddy, the father of two boys, said something that I think was right on target:

"I remind my boys that poverty and wealth represent two opposing extremes of the social spectrum, and that you have to work very hard to reach either of them. For instance, you can work hard to get an A, or you can work just as hard to get an F in school."

Affluence, according to him, represents one extreme and poverty the other. When you consider the broad base of people in the middle class, a person has to work awfully hard to reach the top or to scrape bottom.

The scenario of three young men I know who once worked together in a Denver cinema came to mind.

The jobs they had in the theater were entry-level, low on the skill and pay scale. They all were smart enough to realize that making a career working there wasn't ever going to lead to a fulfilling future.

Consequently, two of them quit and enrolled in college, one after a stint in the U.S. Navy. The third quit too, but he sat on his tush waiting for opportunity to sneak up on him.

Today one of those men is the successful CEO of a thriving national corporation that recently went public. The second went to law school when he got out of the Navy and today is a successful corporate lawyer.

The third young man—while waiting for opportunity to reach out for him—tumbled far beyond the reach of his two prosperous friends and all of their endeavors to reach him.

Why couldn't they save him? There are probably many reasons.

I think the primary ingredient in the third man's recipe for failure was his own lack of a desire to succeed and a poor work ethic founded on the idea that whatever he wanted eventually would drift his way if he waited long enough.

I know a lot of people who think like that. They bemoan the fact that life hasn't been kind to them, and eventually many of them become destitute and homeless.

But the fact is, over the years, the third young man has worked just as hard to wallow in his misery based on his hard luck as the first two men did to make good "luck" for themselves.

What should society, in the name of the government, be obligated to do when it comes to the sticky task of saving human beings from themselves?

I'm beginning to think that the best and most instructive lesson of all—as cruel as it sounds—may be to write off most homeless adults, let them live with the results of their own poor choices in life.

And what of the children of the homeless? Confiscate and distribute the ones who are wanted to foster and adoptive homes. As for the unwanted ones, rearing them in state-supported orphanages isn't half as mean as leaving them to live in the back seats of motorcars and under railroad bridges, is it?

Harsh and ruthless? You bet it is.

But from the moment every creature draws its first breath, life is a competitive dog-eat-dog struggle to survive. And based on the growth of our homeless population, we haven't been doing too swell a job of getting that point across.

We might well lose some of the homeless to the grim reaper—especially those determined to die if it'll help them count coup against society.

Still, we just might impress some in the coming generation of lackadaisical young men and women that life is a very serious affair. And, most important, it takes just about as much energy to master the artistry of failure as it does to be a maestro of success.

Speaking Well
Is a Cornerstone
of Success in America

First published April 1995

When I was a young boy, my mother—who was my primary role model—never skimped when it came to telling me and my siblings what we needed to do to succeed in America.

Other members of my West Indian family were there to guide me as well.

On matters of power dressing and the fine points of a gentleman's wardrobe, I consider myself lucky to have had the guidance of my Uncle Roy's good taste and style.

He was an artist, a jazz musician and a male role model who impressed me with the fundamental truth that it was important for a gentleman to be well groomed.

From him, I learned a number of lifelong lessons.

For example, I learned that it was okay for a man to sew in order to perform preventive maintenance on his wardrobe. And I learned that a man wasn't well dressed if his cuff or the collar of his shirt exceeded a measured length below the sleeve of his jacket or above the collar of his jacket at the neck.

Uncle Roy taught me that a shine on my shoes and a crease in my slacks said a lot about my values and what I thought of myself.

The matter of the spoken word came under the domain of the heavily accented Barbadian women who assumed the collective responsibility of preparing me to speak in a manner befitting a successful American.

They tutored me on the importance of mastering the language along with the cultural traditions of our new country. Although we were poor and conspicuously black, poverty and race were never considered legitimate excuses for failure in the United States.

And to achieve the American Dream, they placed the importance of speaking proper English at the very top of their list.

Although we were surrounded in New York by a number of stereotypical poor, black dialects, mostly from the South, my siblings and I soon learned to take them for what they were—the language of the street, the language of black trash. The language that went right along with Saturday-night knife fights to settle a grudge.

In those days, Americans of color who sought success knew that the first thing they needed to get into the game was a reasonable mastery of the English language.

The United States is no different from any other country when it comes to absorbing immigrants. We require them to learn our language and something of our culture if they hope to prosper.

But all of that said, I think proof that political opportunism and collective ignorance know no bounds can be found in the liberal argument concerning the legitimacy of "black English" in the American mainstream.

Today, among a shallow group of blacks, a philosophy persists that inner-city kids' retarded ability to communicate is merely a sign of cultural distinction and should be accepted as a sign of racial pride.

According to this misguided perspective, the inability of some black youth to speak well in order to enhance their social and economic viability in the marketplace isn't the fault of the black teachers employed to educate them, or parents who fail to be role models.

Rather, they say, the only problem with black English lies with white racists in the mainstream who refuse to acknowledge the worth of this viable ghetto dialect.

Most thinking Americans—black and white—know that's silly.

Nonetheless, the argument is being put forth by dysfunctional blacks—whose pupils stand as monuments to their ignorance.

Black kids would do fine in the mainstream, they say, if white people would just accept Black English Vernacular (BEV) in the workplace.

According to the *Wisconsin State Journal,* a handful of blacks are trying to push the value of BEV in Madison. They want to change the way professionals, teachers and government view the lazy verbiage of the ghetto.

The group argues that black English is only different, not a disability.

I wholeheartedly disagree. I think merely promoting the legitimate concept of BEV exhibits dysfunctionalism—dysfunctionalism not so much among the students as among their African-American "leaders" and educators.

According to the pro-BEV pack, approximately 90 percent of blacks use some form of black English among family and friends.

Be that as it may, I don't believe that BEV has a place in the cockpit of a space shuttle, in a classroom at West Point or before the bench.

The sooner the BEV blacks accept that fact, the sooner they—and their children—will get their just rewards in America.

Ebonics Comes from Americans Suffering Fools

First published December 1996

I have written at length about the seemingly uncanny knack of liberal apologist blacks to dodge the bouncing ball when it concerns their own inabilities.

As is the case with their white liberal counterparts, liberal blacks look for any way possible to avoid certain political and social realities.

In particular, liberal blacks refuse to accept responsibility for the moral, social and political decline of their own downtrodden urban communities.

An excellent example of what I mean in this regard is the recent blustery debate sweeping the nation about Ebonics.

You won't find "Ebonics" listed in your dictionary because the word didn't exist until recently. "Ebonics" came about through the marriage of two words: "ebony," which means black, and "phonics," a method of teaching reading.

In plain talk, "Ebonics" is no more than African-American gutter slang.

The recent controversy arose because the Oakland, California, school board voted to legitimize Ebonics as a recognized second language, purportedly to reach the losers who use it in the classroom.

The "E" word was invented by the same black educators whose abilities I have questioned for a long time.

I have contended that this group of affirmative-action blacks in the classroom would use any means to try to avoid the truth that they aren't getting better results than the white teachers they conspired to expel from predominantly black classrooms in the 1960s and 1970s.

What's worse, despite their failures, evidenced by high dropout rates and low test scores, these "educators" will continue to use any ruse necessary to garner more supplementary federal funds for their failed ghetto schools—thus, paying their wages.

Despite all the recent Ebonics blather in the media, however, the "E" movement isn't a new one.

San Diego City School Trustee Shirley Weber has been pushing Ebonics as a legitimate second language among ghetto blacks since 1989. Weber, quoted in the *Los Angeles Times* in September 1992, argued: "That language, known as Ebonics, is recognized by most researchers as a separate oral language with its own rules of grammar and structure."

According to her, the answer always has been simply to legitimize Ebonics in the classroom.

The archives are replete with cure-alls like Ebonics from broadminded psychologists, administrators and unqualified public school teachers desperately seeking a new magic method to educate feral ghetto kids.

But to me, the solution never has been to give in to these kids. The real answer is enforcing respect and discipline in the classroom.

Those two standards always have been at the core of education, whether the student was a grunt suffering through military boot camp or a serious scholar at a prestigious medical school.

Unfortunately, though, the demand for affirmative action—the demand to saturate administrative and tutorial slots in inner-city schools at a time when qualified black academicians did not constitute large numbers—has resulted in the inevitable.

Academic achievement among some black students has fallen to a new, unimaginable low.

So now, instead of owning up to their academic shortcomings, African-Americans responsible for the Oakland public school system are trying to hide their mistakes with the introduction of Ebonics as a legitimate second language.

If Ebonics has any credibility at all, it is as the dialect of the street—the dialect of the pimp, the idiom of the gang-banger and the street thug, the jargon of the school dropout, a form of pidgin English that reeks of African-American failure.

Ebonics is what results when we Americans, black and white, suffer fools too easily too long. And it represents the extreme to which opportunistic adults will go to stay in power.

In essence, Ebonics is the ultimate residue, the greasy ring around the social bathtub, which I predicted would come about when a society succumbs to a lesser set of rules for some of its people.

As far as this American is concerned, the black phonics movement is just one more step in the wrong direction for inner-city, xenophobic African-Americans. I parallel it to a people dowsing themselves in gasoline and then playing with matches.

Flippin' Burgers Can Open Door to American Dream

First published July 1995

Had I a buck for the number of occasions I have listened to compassionate white liberals and apologetic minorities proclaim that people shouldn't have to work at menial occupations for the minimum wage of $4.25 an hour because they can't ever get ahead, I'd be pretty well heeled by now.

Liberal Democrats in Congress are renowned for making such statements in an effort to try to justify the endless number of young men and women—especially blacks and Hispanics—who supposedly languish in unemployment lines.

President Clinton's position is that low-income Americans ought to be educated, then given public assistance for two years and finally be subject to work requirements—if they are able.

But he also seems to think that they should be able instantly to attain the status of middle-class Americans.

Historically, blacks and Hispanics have suffered higher unemployment rates than their white counterparts. And the minority propagandists, of course, attribute the differences to the existence of institutional racism.

But many of the unskilled and unemployed blacks and Hispanics themselves say that the entry-level jobs available to them are far beneath the image they have of themselves.

"Yo, I ain't gonna flip no burgers at Ronald McDonald's fo' no chump change when I kin make fifteen hundred dollars a day selling drugs."

Interestingly enough, though, the new wave of immigrants to America who are determined to make a life for themselves here don't seem to have any of those hang-ups.

Perhaps that's why a recent story in the *New York Times,* "Dead-End Jobs? Not for These Three," caught my eye. The three featured were Mark Ishaya from Iraq, Zdenka Bulic from Bosnia and David Nunez from Mexico.

Each of them came to America to make their fortune and a better life for their family, and all three ended up in management jobs overseeing other up-and-coming immigrants at McDonald's in Chicago. Their salaries today range from $25,000 to $45,000 plus benefits.

Barnaby J. Feder noted in his article: "Their achievement testifies to the energy and talent of immigrants who use 'burger flipping' jobs that most Americans deride as dead ends to lift themselves to modest prosperity and many of the trappings of middle-class American life."

In essence, Feder confirmed that for folks who are willing to work hard when the opportunity presents itself, the American Dream is still healthy and alive in the U.S.A.

Feder noted that the starting hourly pay for McDonald's part-time crew members is usually only a little above $4.25 an hour and fringe benefits are "meager." Keeping employees is such a problem that McDonald's and its franchisees will hire well over a half million new employees this year alone to remain fully staffed.

Many of the new immigrants start at the restaurant chain with no skills—sometimes even unable to speak English. But they take advantage of training programs that McDonald's had to develop to build permanent staffs.

The key obviously is the immigrants' positive attitude and willingness to learn.

On the other hand, based on the attitude that "flipping burgers is for chumps," which persists among the adolescents languishing in housing projects like Chicago's Cabrini Green, it's unlikely that many of those jobs will be used by inner-city kids as employment springboards into the mainstream.

Any cowboy worth his wages will confirm that you can lead a horse to water, but you can't compel it to drink. The same certainly can be said of those people who after a three-decade expansion of the liberal welfare state have become a lot more accustomed to handouts than work—apparently at any pay rate.

McDonald's and other fast-food operations have shown that there is a pressing need for employees who are civil, ambitious and willing to work. A new wave of immigrants with names like Ishaya, Bulic and Nunez has proven that success is still attainable in America if you are willing to work for it.

It's time the American people brought pressure on white liberal and minority politicians to acknowledge that it's not the minimum wage or menial jobs standing in the way of progress for most welfare recipients. It just might be that the eternal helping hand of the welfare state is taking precedence over pursuing the virtue of ambition.

Exit Ramp Bums
Need Jobs, Not Alms

First published May 1998

It's that time of year, when my emotional well-being sails on high, parallel to the high of the equinox. It's a special time to me, a time when I am blessed to rouse to the sound of birds chirping their mating calls, clamorous lawn mowers and the heavy fragrance of fresh cut grass suspended in the air like an early-morning Appalachian fog.

It's spring—a time when most of us look to clear away the baggage of a long, confining winter spell. It's a season of renewal, ambition and hope, when many of us turn our thoughts to preening ourselves in a sleek new summer wardrobe and poking around at our favorite gardening emporium.

It's the time of the year when I dally along in the right lane—observing the speed limit for a change—my windows down, taking time to gaze at the greening mountains.

Unfortunately, it's also the time of year when the entrance and exit ramps that carry me onto the arteries I traverse to and from work are littered with human beings—people I have come to think of as the crabgrass of our society.

These are men and women who profess to be down on their luck, people who seem to be without bootstraps and thus not capable of freeing themselves from the dark hole of poverty. They seem to always be down on their luck, experiencing hard times.

The liberal socialists have taken pride in labeling these unproductive citizens "The Homeless."

That leaves working folks, conditioned to political correctness, drenched in guilt because of the success we have achieved by working. And it compels us to elevate the crabgrass people littering the exit ramps to a status of blessedness.

It's as if by paying alms to the exit-ramp bums we will be drawn a little bit closer to God, with the opportunity to cut a better deal when the bidding begins for admission to heaven.

I am not against helping a man who is down on his luck.

What I'm against is being hustled by hardcore professional panhandlers who seemingly haven't an ounce of guilt when it comes to dragging along little children for the express purpose of capitalizing on the early-morning suckers, A.M. chumps all too eager to respond to the hand-printed placards proclaiming, "Homeless, will work for food. Any penny will help."

I must have been stewing about a particular bum who has become a regular fixture at the exit near my radio studio while working my way through the checkout line at Safeway recently, because a clerk there said to me, "Take this. I know who you are."

She handed me a Safeway flyer headed "SAFEWAY CAREER AND JOB FAIR."

"Invite your friends and family to check us out!" it read. "Representatives will be available to answer questions about career options and benefits with Safeway. Applications for employment and on-site interviews will be available for people interested in working for Safeway. Great opportunities exist in all retail store departments, trucking, distribution center and supply plants."

Sorry, folks, call me jaded if you like. But now, more than ever, I'm just not amenable to allowing professional panhandlers, bums and beggars, whose only ambition seems to be living off the fat of the land, to browbeat me into offering up my hard-earned money for their daily bread.

Especially with a major employer like Safeway so desperate for employees it's resorted to leafleting its customers.

Willing to work?

Don't make me laugh.

Willing to perform at a minimum level for a tax-free income is more like it. I say, go get a real job. Clearly, opportunities for gainful employment abound all around you.

A Holiday Gift
of Self-Respect

First published December 1996

It's that time of year once more when hardworking Americans must come to grips with the traditions of our holiday gift-giving season.

It's a time when we suffer the hustle and bustle of customary Christmas giving, including cutting a swath through toy stores, shopping malls and the more than occasional impatient motorcar driver who, more often than not, may be mirror examples of ourselves.

Despite all the stress, like many other husbands, wives, grandmas and fathers, I nominate Christmas as my favorite time of year.

I like it because of the sound of nostalgic holiday music coming over the radio and piped through shopping malls. I enjoy the Christmas decorations and the sticky fingerprints of little kids pressed against plate-glass windows where they linger to indulge in their dreams about Christmas morning.

I have come to love gift-giving—even if it means throwing financial caution to the wind and overextending to purchase that extra-special item for my loved ones.

But in spite of my generally good holiday spirit, I'm not blind to the fact that the liberals notice my good cheer.

They are aware of it, and they don't hesitate to take advantage of it to try to instill social guilt and persuade me and other joyful souls into giving more to the less fortunate.

In the remaining days between now and December 25, I fully expect the liberal media to lead this manipulative goading.

They will bombard us with the typical images of the forlorn, the abandoned and the abused. They will insinuate that we should feel guilty and encourage us all to take time out from our selfish pursuit of excessive consumption to give more to the needy.

Don't let my tone mislead you. I have neither disdain for nor an ax to grind with the legitimately impoverished. I used to be one of them, and it's a trauma I have never forgotten.

But recently, I asked myself what the poor people have done for us—especially in this season of giving.

Now, after decades of socialist conditioning from liberals who use poor people mercilessly to further their own political cause, you may honestly wonder what a poor person could possibly do to help someone else.

But if you think about it, poor people—even those living on the public dole—can do a lot for working folks now and throughout the year.

For instance, with proper guidance and supervision, poor women could volunteer their time at temporary nurseries set up at department stores or malls to help harried shoppers.

Adolescent children of the poor and their parents could volunteer their services to charitable organizations dedicated to feeding the elderly. They could work as Salvation Army bell-ringers. They could take turns working in the soup kitchens where they themselves find sustenance.

As I said, I have no ax to grind with poor people. But why shouldn't we make demands of the poor to give like everyone else? If, as I believe and as my own life has shown, poverty can be a temporary situation, the worst such giving can do is ready the poor for the demands of success and affluence.

Furthermore, if giving makes us feel good, won't it make them feel good as well? Won't it add to their dignity and self-respect?

Best of all, I believe it would prepare them to overcome the liberal notion that their salvation only can come about when capitalism is vanquished by replacing it with the utopian dream of socialism.

Dignity and self-respect are keys to vesting poor people's future. And I think giving those qualities would make one heck of a gift exchange between hardworking Americans and poor people—a lot more lasting than a few bucks in the bell-ringer's bucket.

It's something to think about this holiday season when the liberals try to make you feel guilty for not giving enough.

This previously poor person certainly has given it some thought.

What Price
the American Dream?

First published February 1997

From the moment a Santa Monica civil jury determined that O.J. Simpson should pay $25 million in punitive damages to the estates of Nicole Brown Simpson and Ronald Goldman, the media has been in a tizzy about whether that sum was hefty enough to properly punish O.J.

The consensus of the media—and many Americans—has been that the $25 million in punitive damages, plus the $8.5 million in compensatory damages awarded the Goldmans previously, add up to a penalty large enough to get the attention of a wealthy Middle Eastern sheik—let alone a retired football player.

In the days following the trial, we watched live shots from TV news whirlybirds of O.J.'s Brentwood, California, estate, while reporters rattled on trying to evaluate the worth of the home, the contents within and O.J.'s pricey motorcars.

But it has dawned on me that O.J. Simpson—a tarnished American, an accused wife beater, a man believed by a majority of Americans to have brutally murdered his wife and her friend—may have been deprived of something much more valuable than the sum of $33.5 million.

It may be too early for him to comprehend, but the cruel trick the fates have played on O.J. Simpson is that despite his emancipation from a criminal conviction for murdering Nicole and Ron Goldman, he nonetheless has been condemned to the very prison that he and his manipulative team of lawyers sought to help him escape.

Put simply, O.J. Simpson may have cheated the hangman, but

ultimately the system has made him forfeit that which he has pursued all his life—the American Dream.

Liberals and disgruntled anti-capitalist socialists with an ax to grind against the free-enterprise system may dispute the validity or the value of the American Dream—particularly for Americans of color. But O.J. Simpson never wavered from his pursuit of it.

Even as a young thug growing up in Oakland, O.J. must have gotten the scent of what this great country could offer him. He understood that if he played his cards right and believed in the Dream, he could work his way out of the wretched poverty of the black ghetto.

He obviously sensed that if he diligently pursued the skills where he excelled—in the game of football—he would have a shot at the sweetest nectar the American Dream could offer.

O.J.—aka The Juice—did work hard, and ultimately he commanded the respect and the adulation of mainstream America. In addition to making a lot of money, his success meant being invited to all the best country clubs to play a casual round of golf and to socialize with men who were his equals. It meant never thinking twice about being offered the best table in the best restaurants or being invited to smoke a cigar or sip fine brandy with the Hollywood swells.

I have no bone to pick with the fact that a poor black kid achieved such a lifestyle. I don't begrudge any of the wealth he has amassed.

But now that he has been held responsible for murdering two people, I am also comfortable that O.J. has had the hopes of a better tomorrow—the essence of the American Dream—removed from his grasp.

No matter how much money he figures out how to make, a vigilant court will be in the wings to confiscate it. No matter how much respect and esteem he attempts to regain, a unanimous jury decision against him will stand in the way.

It's a harsh sentence and a heavy cross the fates have dealt O.J. For ultimately he has been condemned to subsist without hopes or aspirations among Americans whose warmth and respect he had grown to take for granted.

As far as I am concerned, the American system of justice has indeed worked in the case of O.J. Simpson.

African-American—
Pick One

First published November 1995

I received a fax from a frustrated listener to my syndicated radio talk show that read: "AFRICAN-AMERICAN (pick one)." I thought it was a pretty clever play on words. In fact, I liked it so much that I tacked it up on my studio wall.

I thought it would make a great bumper sticker because it challenges those American Negroes who have the desire to have their cake and eat it too.

They attempt to gobble up as many benefits of the American Dream as they possibly can, whether through aid to the poor, full employment or personal freedoms. All the while, they denounce America as an unfair, racist country and resist pledging any allegiances to our way of life.

I hear attitudes like the latter a lot from the blacker-than-black, purer-than-pure "African-Americans" who call me on the radio to berate me for the pride and the pleasure I take in being a first-generation American.

Running down America has become such a popular, usually liberal-minded thing to pursue that even some dusky Africans do it. In this instance, I am talking about contemporary native Africans.

Recently, a black African, who came here on a student visa, called to denounce me as a dupe of the white man. In his opinion, I was a sucker to cast my fortune with the United States today, because my ancestors had been brought to America as slaves.

The caller intrigued me for a couple of reasons.

Here was a guy from an obscure Third World black African nation living in my country, taking advantage of the benefits of the First Amendment, using them to insult me and my support of the American way of life. If he'd said those things about countries in many parts of the dark continent, it might well have gotten him killed.

The second reason he intrigued me was because he originally came to my country—which he denounced as a land of black persecution—to get an education to benefit the black people of his nation.

But interestingly, when he had completed his education, he neglected to go home.

I asked him why he had decided to remain in a country he regarded with disdain, but he became vague and evasive. With an air of superiority, he informed me that he didn't think I was so smart. He had a master's degree, which he had earned in the United States.

When I continued to pressure him for an answer, he said that since Americans lived in his country, he had a right to live here in the U.S.A.

He was not what I would consider to be a critical thinker.

But then, I don't have a master's degree—or any other degree, for that matter.

Where do people like him get their jaded ideas?

After all, it takes a lot of gall for some expatriate of a Third World country—a black African nation where the infrastructure has been in decline for the better part of this century and where concepts like political freedom and human rights don't even exist—to nurture the notion that America is a land of oppression for black people.

Well, listen up, my fellow Americans, because you're not going to like the answer I came up with.

I believe people like this disgruntled African get those notions from the minions of "African-Americans" who set the tone for their black-skinned brothers visiting our nation.

And they get those notions from the good Americans who remain silent in the face of this vocal contempt for our country.

Those notions come from the ease with which we seem to have abdicated our pride in America—pride in our culture, in our technology and in the opportunity this great nation affords every man and woman willing to roll with the punches for a chance to make a better life for themselves.

The signs of our abdication are all around us, starting in our schools, where we have allowed pledging allegiance to our republic to become optional. The signs of abdication are in the ongoing debate about whether it's okay for some disgruntled citizen to trash and burn our flag.

"African-American (pick one)." That fax kind of said it all.

I believe the moment is fast approaching when the Negroes who have prospered in the United States—as most of us have, and as all of us can—will have to decide whether they are Africans or Americans first.

And someday, perhaps sooner than they can imagine, they just might be forced to pick one.

The Dream of Flight

First published December 1998

After a very unscientific survey among my flying buddies, I must acknowledge the irrefutable fact that the marvel of punching out of rain or snow into a brilliant azure sky may be lost to a generation of pilots' children.

And, alas, my son and daughter are not the exception to that rule.

Although I have tried to ignore it, I am compelled to recognize that they are indeed indifferent to the adventure of general aviation. They seem likewise indifferent to the general aviation luxury of avoiding the indignities commonly inflicted on commercial air travelers.

Last year, for instance, during a trip aboard my airplane to the Caribbean, my son slept every mile of the way from Denver to the Bahamas. My daughter settled back and read a magazine when I ferried her from West Palm Beach over the turquoise-blue waters to our island destination.

My granddaughter, on the other hand, wouldn't think of missing a single sight during one of our family flying trips.

I thought her eyes would pop out when we flew over the sea and she spied her first glimpse of the Caribbean islands, their reefs and the tramp steamers pushing through choppy seas around them.

Actually, I realized early on that my granddaughter was an enthusiastic general aviation participant. Because of her boundless inquisitiveness, even at seven years of age, she has an elementary working knowledge of how the Global Positioning Satellite works.

I am thrilled when she pipes up to answer an inquiry of how long it'll be before we arrive at our destination.

"Twenty minutes," she'll say, pointing to the descending numbers on the instrument panel.

Until she came along, frankly, I had been forced to consider the probability that when I give up my wings to the inevitable march of time, it might be a long while before another Hamblin nurtured the aspiration to fly among the clouds.

But my concerns disappeared forever during a recent flight from Las Vegas to Denver, when I decided to treat my granddaughter to a bird's-eye view of the Grand Canyon, 15,000 feet below.

As she sat comfortably in her grandma's lap in the right seat of my Piper Seneca II, her headset impressively positioned over her ears and mouth, it dawned on me that my granddaughter had a thing for flying in little airplanes.

Between her questions and nods of understanding as her grandma explained she was looking at the Colorado River below, I realized for the first time that for her, little airplanes exist primarily to facilitate her expanded view of our world.

Before long, she had me dipping one wing, and then the other, so she could see in all directions.

It overwhelmed me when it dawned on me that in the big design of things, that's why I fly my family.

I fly to give that little girl the perspective on life that if she wishes and is determined, she can be anything she dares to dream.

High up in the sky on that day, I felt as though all the decades I've spent sharpening my flying skills ultimately were meant to bring me to that moment.

Eavesdropping on the chattering in the headset, I took comfort in hearing her enthusiasm and curiosity about the geography below.

Eventually, I cut in to say, "Olivia, I want to show you a game your papa and I use to play when he was about your age."

She looked at me. I could tell she was being polite and that she really wanted to get back to feasting her eyes on the Grand Canyon below.

"It's called astronaut," I persisted.

Then without another word, gradually I reduced the power to the engines and pulled back on the yoke to reduce our airspeed to a near stall.

Her interest increased when Grandma said, "You're going to like this."

When the Seneca was flying slowly enough, and I was sure it was safe, I gently pushed the yoke forward, and as the nose pointed toward the earth, my Olivia's eyes widened as she felt like she was floating in space.

Being the adventuresome kid she is, Olivia wanted to float like an astronaut again. I promised we would do it again soon, but now it was time to head for home.

Three days later, her mother told us Olivia had decided that, among other things, she wanted to be a pilot when she grew up. A medical doctor and a hairdresser were the other two career options on her current short list.

Like those of a lot of other pilots I know, my family may have skipped a generation of fliers. But on that day, I felt I had indeed finally passed along my dream to slip the surly bonds of earth.

TWO
Clinton

Bill and Hillary
Meet Their Match
in Monica

First published January 1998

"You know, I'm not sitting here like some little woman standing by my man like Tammy Wynette. I'm sitting here because I love him, and I respect him and I honor what he's been through and what we've been through together."

It was Super Bowl Sunday, six years ago, 1992. Hillary, speaking on CBS-TV's *60 Minutes*, stood by her man as Bill denied he had ever had an affair with Gennifer Flowers. Six years later, under oath, in a deposition in the Paula Jones sexual harassment case, Bill Clinton came clean and confessed what I already had suspected.

Flowers was vindicated.

Even back then, I'm certain Hillary was an old hand at cleaning up behind her man in these matters.

How could she suck up her pride and stand by her man in front of all of the Western world?

On that day in 1992 there was a tremendous amount of power at stake. In spite of all of his cheating, husband Bill, marital warts and all, was precariously perched in the portal of presidential power. And Hillary wasn't about to allow it all to slip through her hands.

That made it difficult for Hillary, liberated or otherwise, to hike her skirt like some little suburban housewife and waltz off to domestic court in defense of her feminine esteem.

I don't have any sympathy for the predictable predicament

Hillary Clinton finds herself in today. Maybe it's because, in my view, she put sipping from the golden chalice of power before her own dignity.

Still, I marvel at the seemingly poetic justice of both Bill and Hillary's plights today.

The irony I see in this latest Lewinsky affair is that Bill ran into a 1990s "liberated" woman of the ilk created by feminists like Hillary in the 1960s. Let me explain.

First, I believe Clinton, a supposedly sensitive liberal who is establishing himself as a sexual predator of the first order, is the kind of man who has a passion for the seemingly ordinary Paulas and prosaic Monicas of the world.

I have always believed that the pattern of sexual predators like Clinton is to make moves on average-looking females who they assume are desperate for attention and sex and who, because of that, aren't likely to divulge the details of a back alley affair.

He belongs to a generation of men who grew up believing that every sexual conquest they made came about because they seduced the woman.

And when the lust of the moment had passed, a moral girl was expected to weep the night away in shame.

Men on the make for that kind of sex aren't my favorite people.

But here is the irony: Preying on people for uncomplicated sex is not a sport limited to males these days.

In the liberated 1990s, sexual predators come in both genders. And with Monica Lewinsky, Clinton may have discovered that his good-old-boy days are long passed.

Now, the other irony enters—that of Hillary's contribution to the 1990s. Her brand of feminism has made today's little misses everything the feminist movement of the 1960s hoped to produce— women who are tough, sexually aggressive, competitive and just as assertive as the boys they romped with on campus.

And that's the beauty of the honey trap in which President Clinton has himself snared this time.

While it may serve Lewinsky's lawyers to present her to the world as "a doe caught in the headlights" and an innocent victim of

President Clinton's lust, I don't see Lewinsky as an innocent babe in the woods.

If anything, I see her a complement to her male counterpart.

I think in Bill Clinton, Lewinsky saw, seduced and conquered the biggest sexual trophy of her life.

And true to Hillary's brand of feminism, she felt no shame, and thus was not inclined to keep her conquest a secret.

Clinton's dilemma today is that unlike his situation with Flowers, the present situation finds most Americans still comfortable thinking of Lewinsky as a twenty-one-year-old casualty of a dirty old man. That means Clinton can't afford to trash her reputation as he tried to do with Flowers.

Meanwhile, deep in her heart, Hillary should know she is only reaping the feminist oats she sowed in Lewinsky's generation.

And both Bill and Hillary are politically astute enough to know that should this latest 1990s gal spill the beans, she has the power to propel them both right out of the White House.

Clinton Lowers the Bar on National Standards

First published February 1998

The often-idealized generation of Americans whom the media and marketeers have dubbed the baby boomers face quite a dilemma these days.

These proud moralists of the 1960s—led by "it takes a village to raise a child" Bill and Hillary Clinton—are struggling to explain away the foulness in the atmosphere hanging over 1600 Pennsylvania Avenue.

The boomers' dilemma is evident in the mixed messages they are sending through daily polls taken to assess the political impact of allegedly immoral antics attributed to the man currently occupying the Oval Office.

One recent poll revealed that the president's popularity had raced to an all-time high of 78 percent, despite continuing allegations—which many Americans say they believe—that Clinton had an affair with then–White House intern Monica Lewinsky, lied about it and urged her to do the same.

Of course, the greater legion of prestigious Beltway journalists, who derive their livelihood from getting along with the boys in the White House, are right there wondering at the amazing political prowess of Clinton, the Comeback Kid.

I have listened to man-on-the-street interviews and scanned an assortment of letters to newspaper editors on this topic. Almost all of them have a similar theme.

"No, I don't care about the president's (alleged) sexual escapades."

"What's the big deal? Roosevelt died with his mistress at his side, didn't he?"

"Leave the guy alone. He hasn't done anything President Kennedy didn't do."

"Didn't Eisenhower have another woman?"

My response is resoundingly in the affirmative to all of the above—but with the following qualifier.

We who remember the morality of those good old days all know how swiftly the disgraceful cold blanket of impeachment would have overcome and vanquished the presidencies of Roosevelt, Eisenhower and Kennedy had the American people known of their immoral lifestyles at the time.

There is a big difference between the media of their day, which tacitly agreed to keep a human indiscretion of a president off the front page for the good of the country and in order not to end his political career, and today's media, which pursues and ultimately publishes or broadcasts every hint of indiscretion.

Clinton is the last person who could use the "they did it too" defense, because he should be the first to know the workings of the modern-day media. After all, he manipulates it enough.

To me, his indiscretion in the face of today's reporting style is nothing less than a violation of our American trust in the ethical use of power.

I suppose what appalls me the most, however, is the public's seeming indifference to the long trail of scandal that has dogged the Clintons.

Who is more corrupt?

Bill Clinton, who knows exactly how hot the fire is with which he plays?

The Americans who worship Bill and Hillary blindly because the Clintons have promised to safeguard them from conservatives who want to put an end to the federal gravy train?

Or are the real culprits in the decline of character in the Oval Office—from Whitewater and illegal fund raising, to Travelgate and Filegate—the power brokers in the media?

Until this point, and perhaps even now, I believe the pundits in the media have sorted through the political dirt, not for the enlightenment of the American people and the good of our country, but rather to empower themselves as omnipotent information filters—experts best suited to determine not only what is reported, but how we should act on it.

Should Bill Clinton leave office in disgrace?

I say yes. Others say no.

Unfortunately, though, the American tragedy in this case is less about Clinton and his escapade of the moment. The real tragedy is how we, as a nation, have permitted an ethically challenged president and national press corps to lower the bar on our national standards.

Humiliation of Family in the Name of Politics

First published February 1998

Roy Romer, three-term Colorado governor, Democratic National Committee chairman and a bully defender of President Bill Clinton during his hour of need in the Monica Lewinsky crisis, recently was compelled to hold a press conference to speak to allegations of his own less than honorable behavior.

He was responding to an article published by *Insight*—the same conservative Washington, D.C., publication that exposed the undeserved burial of former Ambassador Larry Lawrence at Arlington National Cemetery.

The Romer article linked the governor with his former State House and DNC aide Betty Jane (B.J.) Thornberry in a long-term romantic affair. The magazine claimed to have photos and videotapes that documented the governor hugging and smooching Thornberry in D.C. as recently as 1995.

This allegation caused Romer to address a black cloud of dishonor suggesting disloyalty to his marriage, to his family, to the voters of Colorado and to Democratic Party faithful across this great land, who thought they had in him a man with qualities most Americans consider the cornerstone of family values.

Unlike Clinton—and reportedly against the advice of his staff—Romer, after carefully manipulating the first news stories about his supposed affair, came forward to face the music at a press conference at a general aviation airport in suburban Denver.

Looking and sounding like a very guilty politician attempting to put a spin on a smoking gun, here's how Roy came clean:

"Bea and I have been married forty-five years . . . and it's a very strong relationship. Solid. We have a very strong extended family. In the course of forty-five years, in many marriages in this country, different attitudes develop in a marriage. About fifty percent of them end up in divorce; they can't work it out.

"But in those who remain married there still are times in which there are different feelings, ah, and different, ah, interests, different, ah, ah, relationships. In the course of this marriage, about sixteen years ago, I began to work with, ah, a person who became a very close professional colleague and, ah, a very good personal friend. A supportive personal relationship.

"I've made statements about that in the press which you have all read and, ah, I was open with Bea and my family about that all that period of time. . . ."

Excuse me, but was Roy telling us that Bea Romer, his companion through forty-five years of marriage and the mother of his seven children, was a silent and willing partner in his "supportive personal" relationship with Thornberry?

Was he really telling us all that, with his wife and daughter standing there silently in the wings?

More important, did his confession succeed in getting rid of the black cloud concerning his morality?

I think not.

Nor, according to political insiders, did his supposedly honest admissions save his political future.

Party regulars say this widely rumored liaison already had ruined Romer's shot at vice president and his previously hoped-for cabinet appointment. He can consider all hope lost now.

"My marriage, our marriage was always first, this relationship was secondary. This relationship had limits. We knew what they were. Ah and that was a family matter, a private matter. . . ."

Not private any longer, Roy.

In this era of doublespeak, spin and carefully chosen words, I think Romer has proven to be no better than Clinton.

While Romer's long-standing, stable relationship with Thornberry doesn't cast him in the likeness of a roving tomcat on the prowl for easy action like Clinton, it does make him a man without honor.

Some may simply consider him a man in love. But I consider him a selfish man who lacked the courage to follow his heart.

In the days when Roy was a young man coming of age in the small farm town of Holly, Colorado, folks would have said that he needed to make an honest woman of Thornberry.

But that would have meant divorcing his wife, leaving his children and surely scuttling his political career—apparently too high a price to pay for this man with a beautiful relationship outside his marriage.

So instead he chose the low road.

Believing—correctly, I think—that voters with proof of his infidelity would look elsewhere for the moral leadership they sought from a governor and party leader, Romer consciously decided instead to humiliate his wife and family and boldly mislead the public for sixteen years.

Grassroots Feminists Challenge Clinton

First published March 1998

Several months ago—from the perspective some might consider my flawed male perspective—I had the audacity in one of my columns to ask the question:

Where, oh where are the feminists since the president has been accused of an unseemly sexual encounter with a young woman intern?

I noted that nary a peep had been uttered from the female feminist community about the plight of Monica Lewinsky caught in this maelstrom, save for one meek response from Eleanor Smeal, president of the Feminist Majority, who apparently was more disconcerted about being asked for comment than about the situation itself.

Predictably, my inquiring essay brought forth a wrath of mail directed at me from the sisterhood of rage. The women of the sisterhood were striving to sway my supposedly crude X and Y chromosome mentality to believe that the American feminist movement remained strong and intact.

They insisted that the right of free choice belonged to them in matters of what and whom they chose not to support—namely, Ms. Paula Jones and Ms. Monica Lewinsky.

If the hysteria I sensed in the electronic mail sailing my way influenced me at all, it confirmed that these feminists were twitching the most about being taken to task for their double standard. They didn't like my assertion that they applied a stricter standard to the foibles of liberal boys who misbehave sexually toward the girls than they did to the same behavior by conservative fellows.

Apparently, they were particularly moved by the closing observation in my essay that radical feminists, like it or not, would have to learn to live with the fact that, by their silence, they had achieved something that Jerry Falwell, the Moral Majority and the conservative movement had been unable to do:

They had reduced their movement to a silly joke.

Well, it seems that bitter pill may be taking effect for some in the cadre of radical feminist babes.

Recently, for instance, the *Wall Street Journal* reported that "an 80–member chapter of the National Organization for Women in Fairfax County, Virginia, has voted unanimously to call for the group's national leadership to resign for its 'hypocrisy' in not speaking out on President Clinton's alleged affair with Monica Lewinsky.

"For some time now, people have been asking, where are the feminists on the Lewinsky affair?"

Sound familiar, girls?

The *Journal* editorial also noted that the Virginia group said it had received support in its challenge to NOW leaders from many other NOW members. It said feminist chapters in Texas, Kansas, California and Florida also were fed up with the highly political feminist notion that liberal mashers are okay: just flirty men who don't mean women—vulnerable or not—any real harm.

NOW leaders like President Patricia Ireland can struggle as hard as they like to shelter President William Jefferson Clinton by drawing him close to their political bosoms. But in the end, I predict that the backlash from other feminists and the ongoing charges (like the new accusations from Kathleen Willey) eventually will do them in.

A good example of NOW's haughty attitude coming home to roost among average American women is Bonnie Perry, chairwoman of Character Does Count, an Arlington, Virginia, grassroots movement in opposition to double standards practiced by NOW and the pro-woman-yet-philandering Clinton.

Although most national news managers didn't deem the attendance of three hundred women chastising President Clinton worthy of mention in their daily dispatches, I talked with Perry on my syndicated talk radio show last week.

Perry said that she and several other women were frustrated by media polls that said character didn't count where Clinton was concerned—even though the same polls showed that 58 percent of the American people didn't believe he was telling the truth.

Perry believes—as most Americans do, I think—that part of the president's job is to be a role model for the nation.

Speaking on my show, Perry said, "We're not talking about an affair to remember, here. We're talking about serial sexual encounters of the strangest kind. We are talking about perversion in the Oval Office of the White House. This is a serial offender, and he is a sexual harasser."

Bonnie Perry doesn't have a long history of political activism. She is a Virginia grandma who has stepped in to pick up the slack while the so-called professional protectors of women's rights have chosen, for political expediency, to look the other way.

If you're a woman who feels abandoned by that expediency, you can drop Bonnie Perry a note at Character Does Count, Box 7131, Arlington, VA 22207.

Selling Out America for the Black Vote

First published March 1998

Bill Clinton—the same president many patriotic Americans eternally will consider a traitor because he protested American involvement in the war in Southeast Asia from foreign soil—seems unable to benefit from experience.

During his twelve-day, six-country tour of the African continent, the president once again has been moved to run down his country from afar. And true to form, the liberal lefties in our media are sopping it up like water-starved sponges.

According to dispatches from Uganda, the president spoke with a repentant tone as he reasoned that "the United States has not always done right by Africa. Perhaps the worst sin America ever committed about Africa was the sin of neglect and ignorance. We have never been involved with you."

Hold up there one minute, Mr. President. That's not exactly correct. Why are you trying to blue-sky the people in Uganda? They can't vote for you.

Then again, perhaps your words weren't meant for those poor miserable souls in darkest Africa. Maybe they were being spouted for the benefit of voters in the coming November elections back here in the good old U.S.A.

But regardless of the intended audience, the fact is this nation has been involved in one way or another with Africa for centuries.

For instance, what about our nation's support for black African despots like Mobutu Sese Seko?

From the extraction of human souls (readily contributed for a price) to provide cheap labor abroad to the exploitation of her natural resources, such as ivory, Africa has played an essential role in the expansion of European empires as well as the economic growth of our America.

Yes, Mr. President, slavery was wrong. But history will show that the experience hasn't been unique to black people. Nor have the exploiters of slavery always been white, let alone white Americans.

But Africa really isn't the issue. What we have here are unsophisticated black American constituents, an urbane white president manipulative in matters of stroking minorities and a cadre of dusky, sly African-American politicians—all working together to develop a powerful cloud of liberal propaganda designed to do two things quite apart from Africa's well-being.

First, to help dissipate the heat from the investigation of Whitewater and the Monica Lewinsky affair.

Second, to drive home the message that this president—and thus the Democratic Party—maintains an especially warm place in his heart for black people.

But true to his liberal heart, Bill got carried away. No doubt engulfed by the gullibility of the black mob of humanity swirling at his feet, he went so far as to pledge dollars to try to eliminate genocide among the predominantly tribal African people.

It must have been the heat. Because considering the historical rift between peoples like the Hutu and the Tutsi, most people with any worldly wisdom know it would be easier to make the water spilling over Victoria Falls run upward.

If Bill Clinton, the Reverend Jesse Jackson and Louis Farrakhan of the Nation of Islam were really concerned—if they truly wanted to have an impact on injustice in black Africa—they could make Clinton's trip useful, beyond his self-serving attempt to get out of Washington.

Instead of pussyfooting around with the past injustice of slavery in the United States, it would serve modern-day black Africans far better if President Bill were to turn the full authority of the Oval Office on Sudan and Mauritania, where it has been well documented by the *Baltimore Sun* and CBS television that black Africans still today are being captured by marauding followers of Islam and hawked into bondage.

If this president were as pious as he pretends, he would muster the strength of character and the political courage to raise his voice on behalf of Africans in opposition to the continuation of human servitude on their own continent of supposed milk and honey.

But I doubt anything is going to transmute Bill Clinton from the creature that he is.

Deep inside me, though, there continues to burn the lantern of hope that perhaps in my lifetime black Americans will arrive at some semblance of their senses to see Clinton, Jackson and Farrakhan for what they are—all descendants of men who counted their gold and looked the other way when the first European slave ships weighed anchor from African shores.

Bitter Remains
of Feminist Politics

First published April 1998

It's taken a while, but heat from the political Bunsen burner finally is being turned up on female politicians who sought to sell their feminist double standard to the American people by their lack of indignation over the lustful antics of Bill Clinton.

Last month, a *Washington Post* article began: "The sex and perjury allegations against President Clinton are causing awkwardness for three female Democrat senators who rode into office on Anita Hill's coattails six years ago."

The *Post* noted that Senators Barbara Boxer (a Democrat from California), Carol Moseley-Braun (a Democrat from Illinois) and Patty Murray (a Democrat from Washington State) today are concerned that the issue of sexual harassment "could work against them this year, with all three involved in tough re-election campaigns."

I should think so, especially after the U.S. feminist movement came together to lay down the moral law after Anita Hill tried to fillet Judge Clarence Thomas during his 1992 Supreme Court confirmation hearings.

Morality and ethics, in particular the rights of women, were pretty regular chants from a bevy of females who managed to sell the notion that they were bitter about women being abused as sexual objects by lustful dirty old men—especially in the workplace.

Of course, the American people never caught on to the truth that feminists didn't have any problem manipulating the so-called plight of working gals to further their own political agenda.

Nor were the American people savvy to the fact that while feminists were carping about equality and liberation of women from the clutches of sexual oppressors, their concern and crusade only applied to conservatives, whom they demonized as sexual predators of the first order.

Nonetheless, these female political opportunists benefited by developing an illusion sold to the girls back home that they were champions women could not afford to lose.

Okay, girls. Where are your champions now?

Recently, I posed that question to two attractive young women who are just beginning to make their way in the corporate world.

Their reply was one of great concern. They were troubled about the fact that District Circuit Court Judge Susan Webber Wright's decision not only may have set women's rights back but also appeared to leave them vulnerable to any male coworker who might take a notion to call them into his office, drop his pants and sexually proposition them.

Unlike former Democratic congresswoman Pat Schroeder and Patricia Ireland, the president of NOW, these women didn't seem to take heart in knowing that Clinton was a Democrat and thus one of their own.

I left them pondering what had become of the shield against indignities in the workplace which they always assumed would be there for them, courtesy of the feminist crusade.

As far as Boxer, Moseley-Braun and Murray are concerned, I consider them little more than political opportunists, no different from men who partake in the business of politics.

But Schroeder. Now she was a chilling politician. A liberal who never saw a welfare program she didn't like, and an ideologue who revealed her true commitment when she justified the full-blown military assault against the Branch Davidians in Waco, Texas, on the grounds that the siege was costing the government too much money.

In the final analysis, I guess you'd have to say liberal Democrats are as efficient at political expediency as any supposedly hard-nosed Republican.

From trumping the race card in an effort to recapture a majority in the House to overlooking the sexual indiscretions of William Jefferson Clinton, the Democrats have shown they are willing to do whatever it takes to try to gain—and maintain—political control.

The tragedy, though, is that long after the Clintons, the Irelands and the Schroeders have retired from public office, the scum from their brand of feminist politics is going to have to be scrubbed away by little girls who today are still playing with dolls.

Clinton's Denial
Creates Morality Crisis

First published August 1998

As I write this essay, all the president's men and women were still insisting that we the people were mostly uninterested in learning whether or not Bill Clinton frolicked beneath the undergarments of former White House intern Monica Lewinsky—or to be more exact, whether she frolicked beneath his.

Be that as it may, that lack of interest was hardly the case among the talking heads who anchored political news shows on the day before the president was to testify before a Washington, D.C., grand jury.

Perhaps that's because the newscasters and the pundits from both camps who were their guests had realized that the president's "private life" was not the issue. At stake was whether he lied and coerced others to hide its most seamy side.

Listening to the White House's pundits, who were determined to hear no evil, see no evil and speak no evil concerning President Clinton, I was reminded of the level of denial to which flawed people are capable of sinking when they have a vested interest in wealth and political power.

The Unabridged Random House Dictionary, second edition, defines denial as:

"Disbelief in the existence of the reality of a thing."

It defines "opportunism" as:

"The policy or practice, as in politics, business, or one's personal affairs, of adapting actions, decisions, etc., to expediency or effectiveness regardless of the sacrifice of ethical principles."

Human history is replete with examples of profound denial and opportunism walking hand-in-hand with each other to the benefit of people without regard to matters of principle.

Maybe I can't understand the depth of denial and opportunism required to win an election in Podunk, U.S.A., let alone to be elected the president of the United States.

I have never aspired to run for a political office, and I doubt that I ever will.

But I am not naive; I know that life isn't fair. I understand that you have to be tough and that the raunchy dog—not necessarily the best-groomed—frequently wins.

And yes, I know that all is supposedly fair in love and war.

But this Clinton crisis of morality brings us to seriously question what the American people should demand of a politician.

What should we do about a president of the United States, in this case, who, with all the traits of a pathological liar, finally painted himself into the corner where all liars inevitably end up?

I pondered this larger question as I listened to the partisan arguments from Clintonites who appeared pathetically desperate—still trying to stonewall in the hope that maybe God might intercede.

Determined to defend their man to the end, the Clintonites even attempted to telegraph a doomsday message to the Republican majority in the House.

Some insinuated that with the president's high ranking in the popularity polls, the GOP should beware of doing anything hasty, such as convening a Congressional committee to impeach the president. The GOP, they warned—not the Democrats who supported this immoral sham—would be compelled to pay the ultimate political price of defeat in the November elections.

Hold on there.

Buried in Clinton's popularity polls, there have always been a large number of Americans who take offense at the president's outright lies.

As one clearly anti-Clinton guest pointed out on the Sunday-morning news shows, "This is a man who raised his hand, took an oath and said he couldn't remember being alone with Monica Lewinsky."

Do you swear to tell the truth, the whole truth and nothing but the truth, so help you God? All Americans know the seriousness of that oath.

But it's beginning to look as though Clinton's lack of regard for the values of the American people may even have extended to belittling this sacred oath we take before God.

Which brings me back to the "D" word.

Once denial has been allowed to grow in the hearts of self-serving followers, reality is a hard pill to swallow—especially after you've chosen to blind yourself to the truth in favor of a promise of power.

Clintons Change Their Tune on Impeachment

First published October 1998

Disingenuous. Phony. Questionable.

Lots of words can be used to characterize the strategies employed in the moral double standard by which the Clintons are hoping to survive politically.

But seldom has such a brazen example of Bill and Hillary's moral bankruptcy and disregard for the honor of the president's office been revealed to the American people than as in the case of a document I recently came across. It concerned what the Democrats considered to be constitutional grounds for the impeachment of Richard M. Nixon.

It seems that in February of 1974 the staff associated with the Nixon impeachment inquiry issued a report prepared by a group of attorneys and researchers who had been charged with developing this scholarly memorandum to define the "Constitutional Grounds for Presidential Impeachment."

As the fates would have it, Hillary Rodham Clinton was a member of that esteemed group of lawyers and researchers.

Here are some of the key findings from that report:

- "Far from being above the laws, [the president] is amenable to them in his private character as a citizen, and in his public character by impeachment" (page 9, quoting James Wilson at the Pennsylvania ratification convention in 1787).
- Impeachment relates to "misconduct of public men, or, in other words, from the abuse or violation of some public trust" (page 13, quoting from Federalist No. 65, written by Alexander Hamilton).
- "Impeachment . . . applies to offenses of a political character . . . and reaches, what are aptly termed political offenses, growing out of personal misconduct" (page 16, quoting from Justice Joseph Story's *Commentaries on the Constitution*, which supports a broad interpretation of the phrase "high crimes and misdemeanors").
- Instances in which impeachment has been employed in our country's history in the past "placed little emphasis on criminal conduct." Instead, impeachment has been used to remove any public official who had "seriously undermined public confidence in his ability to perform his official functions" (page 21).

Today Hillary Rodham Clinton and the Democrats clearly have changed their tune as they rely on the strictest legal letters, not the spirit, of the laws of impeachment.

Is the first lady in deep denial?

Possibly so.

If one considers that as more of the grand jury testimony is made available to the American people, we are learning that Mrs. Clinton either was very gullible or indeed in deep denial.

For instance, it has been reported by AP that in the transcripts of secret grand jury testimony, White House adviser Sidney Blumenthal testified that he raised a question about Monica Lewinsky with the first lady some time before the scandal broke and was assured by her not to worry, because the president was only "ministering to a troubled young person."

Apparently determined not to face the fact that there has been a meltdown in her marriage, Hillary Rodham Clinton now is proceeding full steam ahead down the only path left open to her—that of dismissing the ethics she once asserted.

These ethics required that impeachment be the course of action when there was "corruption in office" and "damage to the state in such form as . . . betrayal of trust."

Obviously, now that she has sipped from the golden chalice of power, Hillary's youthful ideals about corruption in office, damage to the state and betrayal of trust have all been reduced to poor reasons to surrender that power.

Like President Nixon, both Clintons maintain that the president has done no wrong that merits impeachment.

Each day, the Clintons reveal to our nation that they are without shame or scruples, and that they intend to hang on to the Oval Office in the face of a preponderance of evidence that this president is morally unfit to lead our nation.

Inevitably, though, I predict, the Clintons and the Democratic National Committee will have to face the truth, just as President Nixon did when he couldn't escape the fact that he had become a political liability to the GOP.

And when that happens, another generation of Americans will experience, maybe even understand, just exactly how amazingly resilient our form of government actually is—even when the ethically challenged hold the highest power.

Senate Needs to Take
Its Place in History

First published January 1999

I spent the concluding days of 1998 on Abaco, a tropical island 162 miles southeast of the United States in the Bahamas, without access to television and outside the range of my cellular telephone.

I must admit, as a confirmed newshound, I did haul along a portable radio to attempt to keep in touch with the world beyond the coral-pocked waters that encircled my Bahamian paradise.

Every day at sunrise I stealthily tuned in a Miami station, from which I heard local news, such as a grisly drug-related Christmas double murder in that city.

I heard reports about a weather phenomenon that swept across much of our nation, including that the Dallas–Fort Worth Airport and other major air hubs were closed, stranding thousands of holiday travelers.

It was a phenomenon many Americans—particularly those confined to their homes without electrical power and those stranded at the nation's airports—surely will remember as the blizzard of 1999.

For the most part, though, there wasn't much news about the trials and tribulations of Bill Clinton, the second American president ever to be impeached.

Inevitably my two-week sabbatical from my syndicated talk radio show, my time on this island where the saying is "It's Better in the Bahamas . . . But Gooder in Guana Cay" came to an end. It was time to fly myself back to Colorado.

Once home, I was anxious to see and hear whether any genuine progress had been made in the ongoing Senate debate about how best to proceed with the case of impeachment against the president.

But it wasn't long before I learned that the would-be statesmen and stateswomen in Washington were making little if any news. They were still hard at work trying to reach some sort of deal that would result in a fraudulent settlement to get them off the political hook.

A deal that would allow President Clinton to stay in office after perjuring himself in a federal court and before a D.C. grand jury. A deal that would merely slap his hand for boldly assuring the American people that he "did not have sex with that woman," a.k.a. Monica Lewinsky.

The news—I should say the lack of it—irked me.

I suppose it shouldn't have surprised me to learn that the president's apologists still were striving to hawk the notion to the American people that perjury isn't—at least according to the new morality of the liberal left—an impeachable offense.

Nothing much had changed during my two weeks away.

The liberals were still in deep emotional denial about the truth that the president had been exposed for the immoral man he was.

Having lost their bid to bully the nation into embracing their bias that Clinton's tribulations were due mostly to a conspiracy hatched among the American right wing, all the president's men now were busy at work, on to phase two of their endeavor to free Slick Willie Clinton.

The Sunday I returned, Senator Joseph Lieberman (a Democrat from Connecticut), a smooth Clinton operative, spoke on NBC's *Meet the Press*.

Because this was a time of high Constitutional responsibility, he said, a plan had emerged between Republicans and Democrats in which a trial would go forward in the Senate, allowing both sides to make their arguments concerning facts and law against the president.

According to Lieberman, while assuming that all the facts against the president were as alleged, the Senate then would be given the option to decide if there was:

"A cause of action, a case, a Constitutional ground for convicting and removing the president of the United States.

"If two-thirds of the Senators don't vote yes on that, it will say to us that under the best of circumstances for the prosecution, there will not be conviction and removal.

"And it will raise for each of us the question of why to proceed and inflict on the nation, on the presidency and on the Senate as an institution a long trial."

Personally, I have more faith in the Senate than Lieberman appears to.

I can only hope that, similar to their counterparts in the House, when the senators are forced finally to belly up to the task of sorting through the seamy facts in Article I of the impeachment of William Jefferson Clinton, they will do the right thing.

Like the representatives in the House, I believe they too will realize that anything short of a full review of the charges against Bill Clinton in the Senate will, in the end, threaten their own desired places in history.

I predict—and hope—that reality will oblige the Senate to abandon any prospect of taking the lower road for political expediency.

In the end, and much to the displeasure of the Clintons, I think the U.S. Constitution will prevail. The law of the land will hold the feet of the U.S. Senate, in the matter of the impeachment of President Clinton, close to the fire of honor. And in so doing, it will compel them to preserve the decorum of the American presidency.

THREE

Newt

Saint Newt and the
Congressional Vampires

First published January 1995

Poor Newt.

The new speaker of the House, Representative Gingrich (Republican of Georgia), seems astonished by the ferociousness of opposition being focused on him by the liberals left in Congress.

I would have thought that the newly anointed speaker would have anticipated that the Democrats would rise from their coffins in the catacombs of the House to feed on him like a pack of delirious vampires.

After all, he's the one who declared himself the true protector of the American people, the one who stole the Democrats' euphoria built up over four decades of nearly limitless Congressional power.

He's the one who is threatening to cut off the flow of dollars to the Democrats' welfare state and their defunct War on Poverty.

Doesn't the speaker realize that there is a lot at stake in this power shift?

According to a *Washington Times* report on recent testimony from a Heritage Foundation analyst, today's welfare state is made up of some seventy-five programs that rake in $324 billion annually. The lucrative War on Poverty has tallied $5.3 trillion in spending since its inception under President Lyndon Johnson.

Those dollars, for the most part, go directly to the Democratic Party's constituency.

The Democrats have made a growth industry out of these taxpayer-supported programs, and it's only understandable that they will continue fighting using any and all means at their disposal to hold on to their legendary empire.

It shouldn't be surprising, then, that they are saying the Republicans—led by Newt—are just a bunch of mean-spirited rich guys who care nothing about poor starving colored babies.

What else could they do in their desperate state?

They certainly can't point to the success of their government spending. After more than thirty years, we still have rampant poverty in urban encampments, which have become minority reservations and breeding grounds for babies having babies.

But instead of standing pat as the legitimate elected voice of fed-up American taxpayers demanding that Democrats show results or disband their poverty industry, Speaker Gingrich has chosen to whine. He seems amazed that the Democrats—and their sidekicks in the media—are out to get him.

Even—dare I say it—out to get his mom.

There is, of course, some merit to his perceptions. I call the media's rash of new reports on poverty and the profiles of the unfortunate the "dead baby chronicles."

I warned my radio audience to watch for them—the graphic reports of poor children who would be left homeless and starving because of heartless Republican tax cuts to welfare.

But I truly thought Newt would draw strength from the November mandate, draw strength from the people's precious trust and deliver something other than politics as usual.

Newt hasn't been my only big disappointment in these first few weeks of new Republican control in Washington, though.

I'm just as appalled at how quickly his fellow Republicans have forsaken the commission from the people in order to engage in their own brand of politics as usual.

Apparently feeling cocky from the Republican sweep, they seem to be too busy vying for 1996 presidential starting positions in smoky back rooms to address the American people's agenda or to support Newt.

If Newt's policies—and the wishes of the American people—are to prevail, influential Republicans like Senator Bob Dole, Senator

Jack Kemp and former Secretary of Education Bill Bennett need to speak up.

Their first public message should be to tell Newt to stop the fuss and assume the task he was elected to perform.

Even as a card-carrying Democrat, I had always considered the Republicans to be no-nonsense, bottom-line guys who approached politics as the business of America.

But now they're forsaking their "CEO" Newt and ignoring their shareholder Americans with their ridiculous display of nouveau riche political power antics.

My advice: Get Newt to remember his mandate from the people and then back him up.

Because he seems to be the only guy with any hope of driving a wooden stake into the heart of the bloodsucking vampire Democrat cult in Congress.

Stop Whining, Newt!

First published January 1997

Last Sunday, as I was enjoying my weekend ritual propped up in bed perusing my *Denver Post* and sipping tea, I happened across a story from the *Los Angeles Times* that nearly spoiled my day.

The headline was "Gingrich Gripes Over Punishment."

According to the story, House Speaker Newt Gingrich finally had broken his long silence concerning the punishment handed him by his colleagues last week.

It noted that "a defiant House Speaker Newt Gingrich told his Georgia constituents . . . that he was singled out for an ethics investigation because he is a conservative."

His claim was, in all probability, true.

But I found his whining ironic, because he was using the same excuse mode as the habitual lawbreakers who flood our courts, overwhelming the American legal system.

Singled out because he was a conservative?

Come now, brother Newt. You sound like a minority thug. You know, the ones whom the liberals constantly try to absolve of their crimes because they are poor, have bad homes and aren't very bright. The ones who claim the only reason they spend so much time in jail is because they are black, tan or poor.

Both this group of thugs and Newt may be right about being singled out. But that doesn't make either less guilty of their crimes.

I have taken a lot of heat from my generally conservative radio and newspaper audiences lately for daring to hold Representative Gingrich accountable for his deeds—deeds that won him an unprecedented reprimand from his colleagues, both conservative and liberal, in the House.

But Newt Gingrich is no freshman representative from the great state of Georgia. He is a hard-nosed, seasoned politician who is well aware of the severity of political payback inside the Washington Beltway.

I guess Newt thought the rules didn't apply to him.

He told the *Los Angeles Times:* "Somehow, if you're on the left you can commingle everything and no one seems to notice. If you are a conservative and you hire a lawyer and you make a mistake, you had better prepare to be pilloried."

That's exactly right, Newt. And you knew it.

No true conservative—especially a guilty one—should ever expect a break from the opposition on the left. Anyone who does is either foolish or incredibly naive to think he can beat the odds and escape the liberal bloodhounds on his scent.

Newt's whining just doesn't wash with me.

As speaker of the House and a four-star general in the army of the conservative revolution, how can Newt ask his constituents in Georgia—and all the other folks like me who thought the world of his political potency, his intellect and character—to believe he didn't have a clue that there were liberals lying in wait to scuttle him and his political career?

After allowing himself to be nailed by these liberals bent on proving that all conservatives—especially white males—are crooked and corrupt, brother Newt wants those of us who trusted in him to believe that he just learned there was a double standard for Bill Clinton and him.

Well, I don't buy it. I'm one American who is deeply disappointed in Newt.

Newt Gingrich tried to have his cake and eat it too—unfortunately not unlike lots of other politicians in Washington.

Like a great many Americans, I have come to accept some degree of corruption from all of our politicians on Capitol Hill, but I surely can't stomach them whining when their enemies bring them down.

Get Off the Dole, Newt

First published April 1997

Again last week, I irked the conservative Republican Party regulars who call my radio show because I dared to criticize speaker of the House Newt Gingrich, who they apparently believe can do no wrong.

This time, I challenged the way Gingrich chose to handle his $300,000 fine outstanding to the House Ethics Committee by accepting a sweetheart loan from former GOP presidential candidate Bob Dole.

I dared to ask some obvious questions that I think a lot of Americans want answered.

For instance, I questioned where Dole got the money. Was it tobacco money, laundered through Dole, as some Democrats have suggested?

Was this the political payoff to assure that Gingrich didn't lobby against Libby Dole for president in 1998?

Perhaps the broader question to ponder is, How does Dole have that much money anyway? He just ran a national campaign in which he attempted to tug at our hearts with stories of his salt-of-the-earth roots in Russell, Kansas. He spent his entire lifetime—after the war—serving in Congress in Washington, D.C.

Philosophically speaking, when have the American people ever intended that our political agents should become rich serving us?

For the record, I think Newt Gingrich is a very bright and capable politician when he doesn't make ridiculous blunders like publicly taking a lot of money from another politician.

No one can deny that it was Gingrich's insight and tenacious dedication to formulating the Republican Contract with America that gave the GOP an articulate rallying cry to disrupt four decades of Democratic dominance in Congress.

But as of late, he appears to have a strong proclivity for shooting himself in the foot. It's as if his moon is out of phase.

And I, unlike some other conservative broadcasters and pundits, who seem unduly wed to the party line, find it necessary to call it like I see it.

Some months ago, I said that Gingrich had gotten himself into a snafu of his own doing after a couple of Democratic snoops caught him caucusing with his political cronies on a cellular phone. The Democrats immediately charged that the speaker had broken his word to the House Ethics Committee by trying to strategize the impact of the $300,000 fine the committee had just imposed on him.

I said then that whether the content of the phone call was outside the spirit or the letter of the law and whether taping the call was legal or illegal were not the issues.

The issue was that Gingrich, a seasoned champion of the conservative cause, had fallen right into the hands of his liberal enemies waiting to snare him into a position of public scrutiny and then use it to their advantage.

It's never been a case of the Democrats' being better or brighter. Gingrich has just foolishly underestimated how much they disliked him and his cause.

His complete lack of savvy regarding his enemies was what I first found necessary to speak out about. As long as Gingrich fails to measure them effectively, I predict, he will continue to provide the liberals with an opportunity to broaden their support at his expense.

And that brings me back to the latest matter of the speaker's seeming political naiveté in accepting the $300,000 from Bob Dole— the deal I insist is so sweet it would be fatal to a diabetic.

The loan carries an interest rate of 10 percent, but no principal or interest need be paid until the loan comes due in 2005. Early media reports varied as to whether Gingrich would even need collateral for the loan.

Dole reportedly considered the loan an investment in the future of America.

Maybe. But I can think of innumerable Americans who will never get an opportunity to take out such a loan, even though they undoubtedly would consider it an investment in their future in America.

If I were Newt—ever concerned about planting the notion of political impropriety—I would have outmaneuvered the Democrats by doing the right thing.

I would have marched right into a bank, like any other American in debt, and applied for the loan. If I couldn't get it on my own, maybe my rich political pals like Dole would have cosigned on my behalf.

The Problem Was Newt, Not His Contract

First published November 1998

Call it a foreboding insight, but the fact is I've dedicated a lot of time and space on the radio and in this column trying to understand the namby-pamby ways of Republican speaker of the House Newt Gingrich.

And I don't mind saying that as of this moment, I still haven't a clue what makes the representative from Georgia tick.

Some are calling him an egomaniac. Others are simply amazed

at this Republican who bided his time for four decades of Democrat dominance in the House only to seize power for his party and then put his big foot in his mouth, wasting opportunity while the Grand Old Party burned.

As unimaginable as it is to me, there even are some Republicans who are weeping in their milk because Newt is gone.

If there is anything to be learned from the Newt Gingrich era as speaker of the House, though, I say it is to motivate the survivors of his tenure as GOP leader to roll up their sleeves and set about rebuilding the ideological and moral ideals of the Contract with America.

I am fully aware that the Contract was an inspiration that sprang from the head of the white-haired professor from Georgia. Newt is, indeed, one of the brightest men—academically—in my time.

And the fact is there was nothing wrong with his Contract's ideals of liberty, patriotism, fiscal responsibility and personal honor.

Who among us, except for a liberal socialist Democrat, would dispute that Newt's political ideals constituted the very essence of the ideological American model of self-reliance? Who could argue with his principle that less instead of more government intrusion in our lives is preferable?

Newt's problem was that apparently the reality of life on the floor of the House was too far removed from posturing behind a lectern to bright-eyed college students doting on his political ideals.

That became apparent to me right after the Democrats, embittered by their 1994 Congressional defeat at the polls, began to rip apart Newt's revolutionary idea of a Contract with America.

The gentleman from Georgia lacked the street-fighting skill, and ultimately the spirit, to defend his turf and thus his political ideals.

But no more crying over spilt milk.

Although I believe Gingrich should have been put out with the cat long ago, today, in his tradition of voluntarily bailing out when things get tough, Newt Gingrich is toast. The question that remains is whether the new Republican Party will be bold enough to resurrect the best that Gingrich had to offer.

And that best, I still contend, is the Contract with America.

Obviously, its principles represent goals easier stated than accomplished.

But it never surprised me that ideas like accountability in government or trimming back the bureaucracy would have unnerved the professional politicians in Washington, D.C.—Republican and Democrat alike.

It did disappoint me, though, that when all was said and done, old-guard members of the Republican Party found themselves supported by a speaker who himself was unable to resist the seduction of political power.

Nonetheless, if the Republicans are serious about getting our nation back on track with the core principles they put their John Hancocks to prior to the 1994 election, they'd better begin building another bridge betwixt themselves and the American people.

And this time, they had better be willing to defend it from the Democrat jackals ever on the lookout to pilfer any political thought that plays well in the polls.

The new-era Republican leadership in the House have got to dust themselves and the true Contract with America off and begin preparing themselves for the presidential election in 2000.

To that end, I hope there are still enough Americans who believe in ideals such as:

- The fiscal-responsibility act.

The Republicans need to reclaim their theory that the American Dream has gone beyond the reach of working folks because of harsh tax laws. They can't allow liberals to respond, as they have before, that a tax cut for middle-class Americans, who have dedicated themselves to an eternity of working, represents a tax cut for the rich.

- The taking-back-of-our-streets act.

Republicans need to expose the shortsightedness of hiring one hundred thousand new cops with funding to last only until the next election.

- The personal-responsibility act.

I still think it is a worthy cause to denounce illegitimacy and teen pregnancy by curbing welfare to minor mothers and by denying more AFDC for young girls and women intent on breeding for dollars.

This time Republicans must be ready to counter the Democrat propaganda machine, which will find new ways to accuse them of being indifferent to impoverished children, particularly black and Hispanic Americans.

With the presidential election approaching in 2000, I seriously doubt it'll be any easier for the Republicans, especially now that the Democrats have gotten the scent of GOP political blood.

And now that Newt is out of the picture.

But the GOP mustn't shy away from a strong frontal attack, if indeed they hope to capture their political ideals and the power of working people back from the Democrats. On the bright side, the difficult times ahead in the next few weeks for the Grand Old Party could ultimately help them build the strength they will need if they have any hopes of a presidential victory in two years.

FOUR

Liberals

Challenge to Liberals: Pick a Better Country

First published October 1996

Although stumping across the country to promote my book is proving arduous, I believe in the end it will serve me well, because already it has brought me face-to-face with liberals—the extreme liberals whom I write about frequently in this column and whom I consider nothing less than enemies of America.

Our encounters during some media interviews and at book signings have made me even more committed in my efforts to expose these liberals as the foes who, if left unchallenged, would strip us of our heritage, particularly by denying the hope for a good life available to every American willing to pursue the tenets of the traditional American dream.

Last week, I first met these liberals at KPFK, a Los Angeles public radio station that is part of the Pacifica network of stations, stations generally considered even more liberal than those associated with the National Public Radio network.

I was engaged in a lively and rather pleasant exchange of ideas with Sam Brown, host of a program called *Beneath the Surface*, when one of the KPFK managers entered the studio to join us for a station pledge break.

As he began to plead with his listeners to send money to support station programming, he made reference to me and to my probable crusade to strip stations like his of the dollars they received from the U.S. government.

I responded that my main complaint with public radio and public television is that for the most part they voice only a liberal point of view.

Our discussion became quite heated as he attacked a wide range of evils—evils, according to him—ranging from U.S. capitalism to talk programs on corporate-supported commercial radio.

By the time I left, frankly, I was angry. I was mad that this guy seemed so oblivious to the fact that the government and the political system he takes issue with are precisely the same ones that protect—and even finance, in part—his First Amendment rights to denounce them.

But my liberal encounters were only beginning that day.

Later the same evening, at a book signing, I crossed foils with a couple of other people who vigorously challenged my stance and my book *Pick a Better Country*, which characterize the U.S. as a swell place to live.

One man said he was Canadian, and he tried to peddle Canada as a better country than the U.S. I reminded him that the French separatists had just last year nearly torn his country apart.

He switched to what he claimed was superior health care offered by his country's socialist-style health care system. I debated him point by point.

Ironically, just a couple of days later I picked up the *San Francisco Chronicle*, which carried an Associated Press article headlined "Ontario Sends Women to U.S. to Give Birth."

It told how a fight with Canadian doctors over health care funding was resulting in arrangements being made to ship pregnant women from Ontario, Canada's largest province, into the U.S. to get medical treatment.

"The dispute, so bitter that many Ontario doctors have threatened to stop taking new patients, is the latest sign that Canada's public health care system is in crisis," the article said.

"Hospitals across Canada are closing as provincial governments slash funding. Doctors are emigrating across the U.S. border in quest of higher salaries. And conservative politicians increasingly are raising the once-taboo possibility of revising the health care system to allow some private care."

On the night I met the champion of Canada's health care system, I finally asked why he was in this country if Canada was better. He claimed he was only visiting. I doubted that.

Then he and his friend, a woman who claimed to be a Harvard graduate who had visited England, began to sing the praises of that country over the U.S. They said, for one thing, crime was much lower in London than in many American cities.

I answered that the venerable British bobby has a petition before Scotland Yard asking for authorization for arms in light of an increased crime rate. In the meantime, I added, American cops are involved in a drive to collect hand-me-down body armor to send over to help keep the British bobby alive.

Pick a better country, I continue to challenge.

If I could, I would make that a homework assignment for every child in every American classroom. I'd paint it on the side of every public service and military vehicle. I'd print it on billboards along roads and chisel it above the portal of every building where our citizens work at the business of keeping America great.

Maybe if the challenge were made public and prominent, the liberals would be quieted—not by force, but by facts.

Culturally Diverse Sales Tips

First published October 1997

In a typical example of trying to have your cake and eat it too, several groups of ethnic and racial minorities are claiming that they have been slighted by AT&T in Portland, Oregon. The offense purportedly was committed in a memo which, its author says, was created merely to accommodate their particular cultural characteristics.

According to an Associated Press dispatch from the great

Northwest, AT&T was moved to apologize for what has been labeled an indiscretion by an apparently well-intentioned employee.

The three-page memo in question was authored by Korean-American saleswoman Julie Kim Wagner in AT&T's Los Angeles office. She said she never meant any harm and certainly never intended for her in-house memorandum to go beyond the two employees she sent it to by electronic mail.

But alas, the best-laid plans of mice, men—and in this case women—do sometimes go astray.

Among other ethnically enlightening tidbits, the memo advised the telephone company's salespeople never to refuse coffee or tea when it is offered by a Japanese customer.

It warned that wasting the time of Jewish customers is not advised, and that price is always the bottom line for the Chinese.

AT&T confirmed that Wagner's in-house message characterized six specific ethnic groups: Japanese, Chinese, Korean, Jewish, "Iranian or Armenian" and Middle Eastern.

As expected of big corporations in this age of multicultural hypersensitivity and irrationality, AT&T swiftly fielded an apologetic spokeswoman to say the company was sorry if anyone was offended by the Wagner memo.

Wagner, on the other hand, insists she meant no harm, adding that, "I don't have any credentials or expertise on different ethnic backgrounds, so I'm sorry if people got upset. It wasn't meant to be read by everybody."

Wagner said she based the contents of her maligned synopsis on her personal experience with approximately one hundred AT&T customers.

In my view, her memo should in actuality be perceived in the best tradition of multicultural sensitivity. It simply underlined the cultural manner in which she had experienced the above-mentioned groups as prospective customers.

Nonetheless, Robert Horenstein, a community relations director for the Jewish Federation of Portland, was compelled to comment, "I think most people would find this offensive."

Sorry, Horenstein. This minority American disagrees with

you—and obviously so does another minority American who wrote the memo.

I think the majority of rational businesspeople would take the Wagner memo for what it was worth—tips to close sales. They might appreciate being coached that it makes good business sense to accept an offering of coffee or tea from a Japanese customer when trying to reel in his or her account.

As I began this essay, I think concern about the Wagner memo is ridiculous and a classic example of wanting to have your cake and eat it too.

How can you protest the acknowledgment of cultural differences and at the same time be so adamant about demanding the institution of multiculturalism in corporate America?

How is Wagner's memo different from corporate-sponsored seminars to promote sensitivity to multiculturalism?

In the news media, in the cinema and in the television shows we watch, multiculturalism is the politically correct order of the day. To that end, the Wagner memo was right on target.

In fact, instead of being reprimanded, I think this AT&T employee ought to have an "atta-girl" affixed to her corporate dossier for her astute observations and her willingness to share them with the company sales team.

A Case of Money, Not Honor

First published March 1996

According to the liberal placaters, the "America sucks" gang and the "let's get along no matter what the consequences" crowd, it would appear that all is well that ends well so far as Mahmoud Abdul-Rauf is concerned.

By their logic, the newest African-American victim, Abdul-

Rauf, personifies all the best qualities of exercising dissent, a birthright of every American citizen.

I believe they are correct that Denver Nuggets basketball star Abdul-Rauf has a right not to stand for the National Anthem—but only if he quits the NBA.

What I am still seething about is Abdul-Rauf's real reason for his actions. While he first said it was because of his religion, later he said on ESPN that he would not honor a flag that stood for "oppression" and "tyranny."

And what I can't get over is the fact that many sportswriters tried to elevate this youngster's protest to the stature of the great black moral dissenters of the past.

Few writers and commentators—pardon me—called a spade a spade in this situation. Abdul-Rauf ended his controversy and now stands "in prayer" during the Anthem for one reason—money. He was losing more than $30,000 every time he didn't.

Just once in my life, I'd like to see the hallowed liberals in the media confess that they mistakenly have championed the twisted ideology of a sadly misguided minority.

Instead, like vultures swooping down on crippled prey, a good many liberal commentators on the radio and in newspaper sports columns mindlessly flocked to the defense of Abdul-Rauf.

Take for example, *Denver Rocky Mountain News* sportswriter Bob Kravitz. He quoted Dr. Martin Luther King in defense of Abdul-Rauf: "The ultimate measure of a man is not where he stands in moments of comfort and convenience, but where he stands at times of challenge and controversy."

Throwing Dr. King's name around may play well with Kravitz's pals in the sports department and the city room, and perhaps among the black sports jocks he writes about, but it doesn't cut it with me.

When it comes to convictions, this American remembers the spectacle of Dr. King being pelted, scorned and cursed by white racists in places like Cicero, Illinois, because they were infuriated that they couldn't loosen him from his righteous cause.

Dr. King's dream was founded upon a strength of conviction that the American Negro was every bit as worthy of the right of full citizenship and participation in the American Dream as his white brethren.

And on April 4, 1968, Dr. King died for his conviction when he was assassinated in Memphis.

A lifelong dissent ending in death is a far cry from the whimper of a self-indulgent basketball player in the heartland of America—who, by the way, was nothing short of adored by his fans.

In fairness, Kravitz wrote another column after Abdul-Rauf's protest crumbled, in which he took the player to task for being a "part-time conscientious objector."

But just when I thought some commentators got it, I happened to stumble across another essay written about Abdul-Rauf by Howard Kleinberg for Cox Newspapers.

He thought the solution to future outbursts from disgruntled African-American jocks might be to "stop playing it [the National Anthem] before games, and play something else patriotic that doesn't require standing."

I wonder what Kleinberg might consider appropriate? Since most dissatisfaction with U.S. culture seems to stem from African-American jocks, maybe the NBA and the NFL should start playing a little gangsta rap before each basketball and football game.

Kleinberg, as Kravitz had done in an earlier column, begged the question about the less-than-patriotic fans who also disrespect the National Anthem by refusing to stand and remove their hats.

Come on, guys, get real. That is where individual American rights apply.

Sports heroes worshiped by the public are the American gladiators of the twentieth century. And in appreciation for being granted the adoration of the overweight fan in the bleachers, the National Basketball Association has put it in their rules that these heroes must exemplify the best examples of American patriotism, including standing for the Anthem.

Abdul-Rauf could have regained his individual rights if he had stuck to his guns and quit playing basketball. Then he, like any other average Joe, could remain seated in the stands.

Meanwhile, what about the right of the people who believe in America to speak up and say what we think of this country? I think we have a right to tout our nation. We help the poor by spending billions to clothe, feed and shelter them. We support our economy by going to work every day. We send our boys to war, or to "peace missions," when called.

Obviously, Kleinberg and Kravitz fail to see this controversy from that point of view.

They're too busy wrapping themselves up in the rhetorical right to protest, on the grounds of Abdul-Rauf's unending religious faith in Islam and Allah, to realize that when all was said and done, Mahmoud Abdul-Rauf, like every other good capitalist before him, put his income ahead of his disdain for the Anthem in order to become a very rich black man.

But keep on trolling, guys, because I have it on good account that there are lots of other moronic African-American jocks out there impatient to make their stands, just so you can make anti-U.S. martyrs out of them.

Murder Deserves Justice, Not Politics

First published October 1998

There was a time in our nation when oppressed men decried injustice heaped upon them when that injustice was based on a premise that they were unlike every other man in the eyes of God and the law.

They insisted that they were equal humans despite the color of their skin, their culture or their sexual preference. They sought equal treatment of blind justice, not special treatment on account of their differences.

While the premise of their argument continues to be debated among bigots and idiots, most of the good people of America have become comfortable with this just principle of equality.

Which brings me to the matter of the recent brutal murder of Matthew Shepard, who expired in a coma several days after he was kidnapped, pistol-whipped and lashed to a fence post on the prairie outside Laramie, Wyoming.

According to local media accounts, Shepard, twenty-one, was discovered barely alive by a bicyclist in near-freezing temperatures.

Initially, authorities surmised that robbery was the most likely motive for the attack against him.

But when it was disclosed that Shepard was an out-of-the- closet homosexual, gays and lesbians saw the murder differently. They were inspired across the nation to try to manipulate the brutal beating and killing to further their political efforts to implement special anti–hate-crime legislation conceived to safeguard gays and lesbians.

I questioned a caller to my syndicated talk radio show—who said he was a homosexual—whether the beating and the death of Shepard were more meaningful because he was gay. And if that was the fact, whether it should take precedence over the simple truth that a man had been murdered in a most brutal and inhuman way.

The caller's myopic political view on special federal legislation on behalf of the gay community inhibited him from acknowledging that Matthew Shepard was a human being first and a homosexual second.

But whether the victim is gay or straight, black or white, I insist, the first priority of law-abiding people must be to punish Shepard's loathsome offenders for their clear crime. The priority should not be to transform his demise into political fodder to serve other people's agenda.

To paraphrase the words of Clint Eastwood, who played the role of a drunken, burned-out gunfighter and murderer in the Academy–Award winning movie *Unforgiven:*

"When you kill a man, you take everything he has, and everything he ever hoped to have."

In this case, a particularly brutal murder was committed against a fellow human. And as far I am concerned, it doesn't matter whether that person was a homosexual or a celibate heterosexual.

All that the Shepard family hoped their boy would be was stolen from them that chilly fall night. And there is law on the books all across our nation that stipulates there be a heavy price to pay by those found guilty of this crime.

It seems difficult for gay-rights activists to grasp it, but the fact is that truth, justice and the American way dictate that when a man is murdered, it is irrelevant whether he was gay or straight.

Murder is the issue, and what matters is that justice be served.

For me, justice will mean a trial, conviction and ultimately execution, as determined by the people of Wyoming.

Those of us who care about preserving the strength of our colorless, sexless American system of justice are committed to preventing this murder from being muddied by a politically correct agenda—an agenda that finds it easy to forget the man in pursuit of personal politics.

By reacting to the murder of Matthew Shepard with angry politics, we do our system of justice—and Shepard—an injustice.

And if by chance justice isn't found in this case by our neighbors in Wyoming—not that I doubt for a moment it will be—legislation already exists within the confines of the U.S. Department of Justice to take up the case and avenge Shepard's death.

Whether you're gay, lesbian, black, Hispanic or Asian or a middle-class white male or female, if you happen to be in the wrong place at the wrong time, you just might be at risk of being exposed to someone's hatred.

And no amount of liberal government legislation is likely to alter that fact.

Gay Beneficiaries Need to Give Something Back

First published December 1997

"A state child welfare worker who was demoted after taking an infant foster child from a lesbian couple has filed a grievance," the

Associated Press report began, "citing the state's law against homo-sexual conduct and her own opinion that gay couples make less than ideal parents."

Considering the degree to which political correctness has brow-beaten most of us into agreeing that homosexuals are no different from heterosexuals, I commend Texas Department of Protective and Regulatory Service's Rebecca Bledsoe for having the courage to stand up for what she thinks is best for the child.

As is frequently the case, however, defending one's principles has incurred a considerable price.

Bledsoe's decision, in her capacity as a supervisor, to remove the then three-month-old boy from his lesbian custodians resulted in her being demoted to caseworker. She remained at a supervisor's pay scale pending the outcome of her claim that she was being penalized for going against the department's support of the gay lifestyle.

Despite the fact that Texas law considers homosexual behavior a Class C misdemeanor, punishable by a fine of up to $500, Bledsoe was overruled by her superiors and chastised for abruptly removing the child from his home.

According to department spokeswoman Linda Edwards, there is no policy prohibiting the agency from placing children with single gays or lesbians who are licensed foster parents.

Seems to me, the Bledsoe case is another example of liberal so-cial do-gooders blatantly ignoring laws with which they happen to disagree.

Still, Bledsoe, a ten-year employee, is sticking to her ideal of what a good environment is for a child. She told reporters that she believed children were better off with married couples or single peo-ple than with homosexual couples.

To further complicate this particular situation, the baby is black. And Bledsoe also has questioned the wisdom of placing a black child with two white women—especially since the baby's uncle, who is black, wishes to adopt him.

Once again, I think Bledsoe is right. I think she did a courageous thing when she took her stance against this bulwark of political cor-rectness.

I have a racially mixed granddaughter—whom I lovingly call "my little Zebra." And I have given a lot of thought about the day when I and her parents and grandmother will try to explain to her who and what she is—that she is neither black nor white. But aside from her racial makeup, I'll make sure she knows that she is a treasure and a joy derived from the union of a man and a woman bonded together in love.

I am glad that I won't have to try to explain to her why she has two mothers or two daddies.

I am not a homophobe. I've said time and time again if you find love and it doesn't kill you, hang on to it.

But I insist on drawing lines when it comes to children.

Our children should not be the victims of practitioners of political correctness who use them to try to further their notions.

They should not be the victims of being raised by a village.

And they should not be victims of homosexuals who try to worm their way into the humdrum existence of heterosexuals by adopting our children—or caring for our children as foster parents.

Living with two mommies or daddies is not the norm in our society. And we should not willingly stigmatize a child with that abnormal baggage.

I believe that if you happen to be gay or lesbian, it is God's will. In my lifetime, I have witnessed the world advance a considerable distance in coping with people who are different from the majority, both in terms of race and sexuality, and I am glad about that.

But maybe the time has come for the beneficiaries of that advance of civilization—homosexuals and lesbians in this situation—to give something back. Maybe, in this instance, they should consider whether their gay liberation movement is focused on what is best for the children or just on making them feel good about themselves.

Moonbeams Don't Fall
on Navajo Alone

First published February 1998

The *Arizona Republic* reported that traditional members of the Navajo Nation were offended by the desire of the National Aeronautics and Space Administration to grant a lifelong wish of one Eugene Shoemaker.

Shoemaker, a NASA scientist, always dreamed of going into space, but he was prevented from doing so because of health problems.

So when he died, the boys at the Ames Research Center, located south of San Mateo, California, thought it would be a swell idea to grant Shoemaker's wish by launching approximately seven grams of his remains to the moon.

Who said scientists don't have hearts?

But it was inevitable that such kindhearted compassion would offend someone. In this instance, the offended were the traditional Navajo.

According to the *Republic*, the way scientists at NASA hoped to honor their fallen colleague was the equivalent of sacrilege to these sensitive Navajo people.

Indeed, tribal president Albert Hale—who, by the way, has since resigned to avoid indictment for a runaway expense account—informed NASA that such an act showed a "gross insensitivity to Native American religious values."

Now, let me get this straight.

Sounds to me as though, based on their religion, the traditional Navajo have laid claim to the moon—the only natural satellite of the earth, a heavenly body with a radius of 1,080 miles, one-quarter the size of the earth.

Hale not only put forth this claim with a straight face, but even scolded the insensitive scientists at the Ames Research Center, telling them that they and other folks at NASA should have known that the moon is a sacred place for many Native Americans.

I've got no ax to grind with Native Americans or their religious values—be they traditional or not. But making an exclusive grab for the moon based on those arcane religious notions seems a bit far-fetched to me.

Always the politicians, however, the bureaucrats at Ames Research Center put forth their public information officer, David Morse, who insisted that no offense was intended. After all, the gesture involved only a small amount of the mortal remains of Shoemaker contained in a lipstick-sized container, which was buried deep inside a Lunar prospector probe.

Morse said that in the future, NASA will try to be more "inclusive" when attempting to do a good deed.

What am I missing here?

Is this some sort of half-baked "This is your mind on drugs" gag being played on me and the rest of the world?

Is everyone in America too politically correct—or moonstruck—to speak out on behalf of plain old common sense? Well, I'm not.

This is the United States of America, and under our doctrine of religious freedom, the Navajo people—traditional or otherwise—can worship anyone or anything they care to in 'most any way they see fit.

But it's clearly gone too far when we are asked to oblige the notion of a single group of people who insist that, based on their personal religious grounds, they are entitled to the exclusive domain of the moon.

I think it's time Hale, his successor and the people they represent got a grip on reality. It's time they realized that they and their fellow tribesmen aren't the only people on earth who get a charge out of gazing up into the heavens.

I think the Navajo leaders would better serve their people by acknowledging that they aren't the only spiritually motivated people on the planet who are dazzled by earth's natural satellite.

Fact is, Old Man Moon shines on a lot of other people, places and kingdoms besides the universe of the traditional Navajo people.

Cry the Beloved Victim

First published October 1996

Terms like "poor people" and "all of you" are fairly descriptive phrases, and they shouldn't require an explanation to anyone with a working knowledge of our English language.

Ah, but alas.

It seems that some minorities, upon hearing these simple phrases, perceive themselves to be the victims of covert white racist operatives speaking in code.

As ridiculous as that may seem to a rational mind, *USA Today* reported that the Philadelphia Third Circuit Court of Appeals ruled that a jury should decide whether the use of terms such as "you people," "poor people" and "that one in there" not only might not be politically correct but is legitimate grounds to uphold a claim of employment discrimination.

The court decided there might be merit to a claim brought by Carol Aman, an African-American plaintiff and former credit manager at CORT, a New Jersey furniture-rental store. Aman insisted that "code words" used among her white co-workers had created such a hostile environment she was forced to quit her job.

According to the paper, the ruling has prompted debate about a new level of racial discrimination in the workplace—a new level some say requires mind reading.

Extremist minority rights advocates, who sometimes perceive even the sound of laughter among white people at the other end of a room as an insult, are delighted that the law of the land finally has given some credibility to their xenophobic racial fears.

I, however, see this ruling as just another nail in the coffin where racial harmony is concerned. Not to mention that it undoubtedly will escalate anxiety among some American blacks who believe that the odds for a fruitful life in the United States are against them.

Sadly, I am also forced to predict that the Philadelphia Circuit Court ruling could bring all black Americans another step closer to a backlash from the American mainstream.

Just as affirmative action has been pushed beyond the realm of common sense, so too can cries of discrimination be uttered much too freely.

The American people have a masterful understanding of right and wrong. And no flexing of muscle can override that innate sense.

Consider the time when black people held little or no Constitutional, economic or political authority in the United States. It was still impossible for racist whites to maintain their brutal hold on this country's colored people. Morality and right triumphed in America.

Likewise today, Americans will not sit still for claims of injustice where no injustice has been committed.

And so it's unreasonable for today's minority of black Americans who call themselves "African-Americans" to believe that, even with the aid of liberal urban judges, they can possibly force mainstream America to bend to their ill-founded claims of coded racism.

CORT denies that any form of discrimination exists in its furniture company and has instructed its lawyers to appeal the decision all the way to the Supreme Court, if necessary.

The company's legal beagles predict that, in the interim, civil rights groups bent on broadening their numerical and political base could use the Philadelphia court decision to foster an atmosphere of suspicion and animosity among the nation's workers.

To me, all the Philadelphia court ruling will serve to do is to lend credibility to the African-Americans who insist on conjuring up images of white racists blocking their every opportunity to get ahead.

These African-Americans with victim mentalities do exist. I know because I grapple with them on my radio show every day. I have listened to their irrational tangents about how whitey hates black people—always has and always will.

I've been colored for more than a half century, and I haven't been able to reason with them, so I doubt that white America will be able to find common ground.

One thing is certain, though. I refuse to surrender to their irrational demands—demands that injustices against black people before them give them the right to glean retribution, simply because they happen to share the same complexion.

Libertarians Moving in on Democrat Territory

First published April 1998

Belong to a stick-in-the-mud, ineffectual American political party? An organization that can't seem to get its political act together?

Are you, like a growing number of voters frustrated with the political antics of the Democrats and Republicans, considering the Libertarian Party's box as the alternate receptacle to deposit your November election ballot?

But according to this latest news flash, the party seems to be mobilizing in the best tradition of the liberal socialist government agenda by setting a new course directly for the harbor of sociopolitical victimization.

Here is what Steve Dasbach, the party's national chairman, said in the release:

"The government cheats African-Americans out of their Social Security payments, routinely harasses them for DWB (Driving While Black); and disproportionately arrests them as part of the War on Drugs. Government policies keep black Americans poor, afraid and in jail."

The Libertarian dispatch refers to a study by the Washington-based conservative Heritage Foundation, which states that "the average black man actually earns a negative rate of return on his lifetime of Social Security payments." In essence, he gets back less than he paid in.

Why?

Because African-Americans have a lower life expectancy than white Americans.

The party quotes *USA Today:* "By dying at such a young age, the average black man essentially transfers $10,000 of wealth to white women (who live much longer)." The article quoted Congressman Mark Sanford (a Republican from South Carolina): "The average black male pays into the system for his entire life, collects eight months, and dies."

Frankly, the entire Libertarian press release seemed wacky to me.

But in principle it reflected the instability of which I have long accused the Libertarian Party. I've been suspicious of Libertarians for years, ever since I had a conversation with one of their spokesmen, who informed me of the party's stand for the abolishment of every government edict, ordinance and decree.

I thought their stance was silly back then, and I think it even more absurd today—especially since the anarchistic sociopolitical views this ineffectual party depicts already are reflected in the very ghetto communities they seem to be playing up to.

Arrests for Driving While Black. A fleeting life span compared with the rest of mainstream America. A higher percentage of blacks arrested on drug charges. These statistics all can be confirmed.

But what is the reason?

I contend it is the very anarchy the Libertarians promote.

To naive Americans and immature would-be revolutionaries the word "anarchy" has a romantic and passionate ring to it. They imagine a society without rules to govern, without laws to protect capitalism, with no pig cops and no government regulators to hassle you.

Libertarians and political day-trippers can bury their heads as deep into the sands of reality as they like, but the fact is anarchy—a state of society without government or law—is precisely the environment in the ghetto that contributes to the shorter life span and higher arrest rate of its black residents.

Since its inauguration in 1972, the Libertarian Party has never

scored enough votes to become a political influence, although its can-
didates have run for political office, including the presidency, in
every state of the union.

Could it be that now the party is placing its hopes for a grassroots groundswell on championing the cause of poor victim blacks?

Well, forget it, boys.

The liberal socialist Democrats have got a lock on that crusade.
As for the African-Americans you're courting, you can forget them
too. They may vote for you to liberate them from the squeeze of a
racist Uncle Sam. But in the end, they'll just want you to vote in a
bigger chunk of the public allowance. And that's more, not less, government any way you cut it.

Tax Dollars for
the "Tattoo-Challenged"

First published May 1996

Seldom has the term "tax-and-spend liberal" been better applied
than in the case of Ray Belgard.

Belgard is a Santa Cruz County, California, supervisor who, according to a recent article in the *San Jose Mercury News,* is brooding
about the fact that former gang members in his district have taken
themselves out of the job market by sporting tattoos that turn off
potential employers.

And what do you imagine the supervisor in the joyously liberal
land of California would like to do about that?

If your wildest guess was that the supervisor would like to create and fund—with tax dollars, of course—a program to refurbish
the tattoo-splattered physiques of recovering gang members in his
district, give yourself a pat on the back. You get the prize for hitting
the nail squarely on the head.

According to the *Mercury News,* Belgard has backed legislation,

SB 1956, introduced in Sacramento by State Senator Henry Mello, a Democrat from Watsonville, to create tattoo-removal pilot programs in Santa Cruz, Fresno and San Bernardino Counties.

Just when I thought it was impossible for another liberal idea to get a rise out of me, SB 1956, in true liberal jargon, notes that it is "in the interest of all Californians to correct these employment difficulties through tattoo-removal programs that include skill development and employment services."

Tattooing, or body marking, has been a human tradition for a long while. Traditionally tattooing has been used to mark the rank and the status of a person, as well as the group he or she belongs to—in this case, gangs.

Belgard—who represents the Watsonville area on the board of supervisors—told the *Mercury News* Mello's bill is a swell notion because it will "expand employment opportunities for former gang members."

The newspaper noted that gangs have been a problem in Watsonville and in the surrounding area.

Of course, gangs and juvenile crime in general are problems almost everywhere in the U.S.

According to data from the Bureau of Justice Statistics, in 1991, U.S. juvenile courts processed some 260,300 delinquency cases and offenses against persons, up 40 percent from the number in 1987.

Between 1990 and 1991 alone, the number of person-offense cases increased 9 percent, from 239,800 to 260,300. Person-offense cases accounted for 19 percent of the delinquency caseload in 1991, compared to 16 percent in 1987.

Criminal homicide was a charge in 2,700 of the cases in 1991. There were 4,700 cases of rape, 8,600 cases of other violent sex offenses and 30,000 cases involving robbery.

The total number of cases against persons was equal to 10 for every 1,000 juveniles over nine years of age and potentially under juvenile court jurisdiction in the U.S.

I'll say we've got a problem, but I think the source responsible for much of that problem is liberals, not tattoos.

Liberals who refuse to face the hard, cold fact that as long as society is willing to give young punks who prey on society and consume our resources all the rope they want, chances are real good they won't use it to hang themselves.

What they will do is push, push and continue to push the envelope in an effort to see just how much they can get away with.

I have often heard California referred to as a land of fruits and nuts. To that, I would add that it is a place with an army of politicians of gall and guts.

The facts more than speak for themselves. Decades of unbounded liberalism and permissiveness preached to American families, practiced in the public schools and made law in our courts have reaped the only harvest they possibly could: a crop of completely unchecked juveniles, supported by simpleminded politicians, all of whom appear to be resistant to the obvious—that liberalism has failed.

If we hope to redirect this new generation of youthful superpredators back into the fold of civility, we had better be prepared to do it the old-fashioned way, by reestablishing and enforcing the values of respect for human life, personal dignity and accountability to oneself and one's community. I am talking about the kind of respect founded on striving to earn the right to be addressed as "sir."

If the California punks that Belgard and Mello are fussing about were really serious about earning that respect and turning over a new leaf to land decent jobs, they'd be out collecting and selling empty soda pop cans and old newspapers to get their own money to clean up their epidermis.

Gun Legislation
Borders on Ridiculous

First published October 1998

I love it when law-abiding citizens who are quickly frittering away their Second Amendment rights to keep and bear arms realize they have been manipulated by the gun grabbers out to disarm every American.

An excellent case in point concerns the plight of military veterans of the United States who reside in the Commonwealth of Massachusetts. Recently, they had such a jolt when they realized they hadn't read the fine print as their state voted in one of the country's most restrictive gun-control laws.

After the new legislation went into effect, the veterans' groups learned that the law banned them from bearing arms at parades.

A big oops indeed.

According to the Associated Press, buried in the complex and quite comprehensive legislation is a restriction saying nobody can carry in "any public way an unloaded rifle or shotgun, unless such person is engaged in hunting and is the holder of a valid license . . . or unless such rifle or shotgun is enclosed in a case."

The old soldiers can't seem to fathom the lopsided reasoning of legislators' passing a law that would ban a privilege, that of military marchers and honor guards from being properly outfitted with shoulder and sidearms—a tradition every American ought to revere.

Acting Governor Paul Cellucci penned the bill, then proudly referred to it as the toughest gun-control law in the land, on July 23. Violators of the regulations can be arrested and fined from 100 to 1,000 bucks.

Sure the Commonwealth has its share of problems with criminals, but it isn't as though Massachusetts were a lawless frontier state with out-of-control residents packing guns and felony-menacing one another.

Citizens willing to abide by the old laws already were compelled to apply for a permit to carry a firearm—concealed or open-holstered.

Residents even were required to appeal to the state—by applying for a permit—to possess a firearm at home or at work.

A gun owner's identification card or firearms-purchase approval permit was required to buy a handgun.

Apparently, just to be sure there wasn't a second incarnation of the historic Boston Tea Party, Massachusetts residents then were required to register their guns with the state police or the firearms registration bureau.

Those rules already read like the regulations of some tyrannical alien nation which no red-blooded American would live beneath passively.

So how could it get even more restrictive in Massachusetts? The answer is obvious.

The men and the women of the Commonwealth of Massachusetts voted away their Constitutional rights after being wooed and cajoled by gun-grabbing liberals who promised them a perfect community if they would just go along with the program.

Well, now the fact is the law is the law. Once in place, it must be undone one vote at a time.

Cheryl Jacques, the leading State Senate sponsor of the bill, told AP, "It was never the intent of this bill to stop our veterans from celebrating."

Reacting to the pressure from venerable veterans, Jacques and the State House sponsor, Paul Casey, are trying to restore the right for veterans to parade with their guns under a separate licensing bill for "environmental" police—whatever that is.

Meanwhile Representative George Peterson, Jr., who opposes the new gun- control law, seized the opportunity to block immediate action, saying he wants to compel a public hearing on the entire flawed legislation.

I contend nobody—including the vets—should be surprised at all this legal mess. It's bound to occur when trusting citizens give small-minded politicians the ability to dally with rights guaranteed by the founders of our nation and the framers of our Constitution.

Liberal Teacher Standards Cheat Students

First published July 1998

Once again, I must comment about an academic fiasco that occurred recently in Massachusetts.

It began when 59 percent of four thousand applicants testing to become certified New England classroom teachers verified—per the miserable results of their test scores—that they were ill equipped to cut the academic mustard.

By now, that humiliating fact is common knowledge among the local politicians whose academic policies apparently spawned these would-be educators. In fact, word has spread to a lot of literate Americans across our nation that the Massachusetts teachers' examination, implemented to test the knowledge of a new crop of English and mathematics teachers, proved too much for a majority of the would-be educators.

But instead of scurrying back to crack the books, it seems, some of the poorly prepared teacher wannabes are not learning much from their academic shortcomings.

For instance, consider the small-minded arrogance of Justin Whitton, a graduate of Northeastern University, who took the test when it was given to a second group of 2,500 prospective teachers.

According to the Associated Press, Whitton had been a student teacher who taught social studies in Boston's inner-city schools.

While test results were not available at this writing, it's obvious that Whitton even lacked the smarts to keep his mouth shut and benefit from the possibility that he may not be as bright as he thinks himself to be.

Quoted by the AP, Whitton arrogantly labeled the teachers' test "garbage."

And then, as if he hadn't pushed his foot far enough into his own big mouth, he added, "You had to write an example of an interrogative sentence. I was at a loss. I'm sure 99 percent of Americans would be at a loss."

The AP reported that Whitton believed such obscure facts concerning English grammar aren't relevant in schools like his, where he and his students have to put up with sewage smells from a hole in the classroom floor.

"It makes me so angry," Whitton said.

"Young teachers are out there. We don't have any advocates. We don't have any solidarity. I feel skewered by the politics."

Unbelievable?

No, not really. As I continually point out, I have yet to meet a dyed-in-the-wool, know-it-all liberal who was willing to admit that he or she was in error—so they can't see even the possibility that their education system might be flawed. From the liberal socialist's perspective, their blunders always are attributable to others' trying to sabotage them.

Still, I do take these befuddled liberals at their full face value. I don't doubt for a single moment that they are serious and sincere when they say they want a revolution in our way of life.

They just haven't convinced me they have a workable alternative to our old-guard system of public education, much less to liberty and democracy.

Judging by his own words, I can only assume that Mr. Whitton, in his infinite wisdom, has concluded that because inner-city kids attend class in dilapidated Boston public schools, he isn't obligated to rise to the challenge of being a fully qualified entry-level teacher.

But I contend that black or white, rich or poor, no American student attending classes in a public school deserves a classroom teacher who can't get a passing score on an examination of his most basic qualifications.

Would-be teachers like Whitton with half-baked notions about what is and what is not important for ghetto kids to study, in my mind, is just another example of a liberal with supposed compassion and excuses for failure. Poor kids in Boston's public school system, or in any other school system, shouldn't be subjected to that kind of compassion or failure.

Every American kid is entitled to a chance at a good eduction.

In this case, it represents their best rite of passage out of a sewer-smelling ghetto.

FIVE

Race

Sweet Revenge from a Fight Worth Waging

First published October 1997

Knowing when and how to take a stand in situations of racial bias is a strategy I preach on a regular basis from the bully pulpit of my talk radio show.

I can't count the number of times I have talked to black callers who were thoroughly convinced they had been casualties of racial discrimination and wanted the legal system to act on their behalf.

My immediate query is always:

"How do you know you were treated poorly because you are black?"

And almost always, they respond:

"I just know. You just know when you're black. You can see it in a white person's eyes. It's like you're not there; they look right through you."

But I persist:

"How do you know that white man or woman was singling you out in particular? How do you know his life isn't coming apart? His wife isn't cheating on him? His kid doesn't have cancer?"

"See, that's what I mean about you," comes the reply. "You never stick up for black people because you think you aren't black anymore. You'll learn one day, though, that white folks don't care any more about you than they do about any other black guy."

I'm dumbfounded by this unique insight that hypersensitive black folks think they have concerning matters of race. More important, I'm amazed at how willing they are to jump into any fray when they feel the least bit offended.

I am not insensitive. I know that discrimination abounds. Would that I could share some of the slings and arrows that have been directed at me.

But be the victim black or white, male or female, I encourage the offended not to swing blindly, but rather to pick battles carefully and then to fight the good fight.

A stellar example of picking the right fight against bigotry was reported recently in an Associated Press article concerning the outcome of a lawsuit brought against the Fort Washington, Maryland, outlet of the Eddie Bauer clothing store chain.

The litigation concerned the ill treatment in 1995 of three black high school students, who accused Bauer of "consumer racism." The young men were detained on suspicion of shoplifting, and one of them was forced to remove the shirt from his back.

An indignity, to be sure.

But in spite of that outrage and more, the boys ought to be commended for keeping their cool. In the end, they were amply compensated for the affront against them with $1 million in damages, awarded by a jury comprising four whites and three blacks.

The incident occurred when a security guard demanded to know whether one of the boys had bought the shirt he was wearing. When the lad couldn't produce a receipt confirming that he indeed had purchased the shirt the day before, the security guard told him to take it off.

What would I have done?

First, I would have asked the security guard—in my most polite tone—if he was certain he wanted to humiliate me by having me disrobe. If he insisted, I would have complied, just as the young man did.

Why?

Because it is by such prudent judgment on the part of the wronged that lawsuits are won.

Much to the embarrassment of Eddie Bauer and its management, the black teenager accused of shoplifting returned the next day with a receipt for the shirt that had been stripped from his back.

The plaintiffs didn't get the $85 million in damages they sought, claiming they were unnecessarily stopped and held by security guards solely because they were black.

But I'd say $1 million and an apology from Eddie Bauer officials still add up to sweet revenge—and a costly reminder of what can happen to a business when one of its employees foolishly misjudges a book by its cover.

I'd also say it was a selected fight well worth waging.

We Must Acknowledge
Progress

First published December 1996

An African-American Southerner named Dan called my radio show to express his ire over the beating and the intimidation of a black boy. Furthermore, he was angry with me for not raising enough of a ruckus about the occurrence.

The boy in question was nine-year-old Dwight Miller. A white South Carolina couple had tied him to a tree, beaten him, held a shotgun across his face and fired to make an example of what happens to "little niggers" like Dwight who steal from a white man's truck.

No healthy American could possibly deny that the assault against this boy was indicative of the most racist, ignorant behavior imaginable. That kind of crude and potentially deadly assault against a child clearly has no place in a civilized society. To that end, Dan had every right to be inflamed, as most Americans would be.

Because Dan was sixty-plus years of age, the assault against the boy by the white couple must have been sadly reminiscent to him of a time in America, particularly in the South, when blacks were frequently the target of attacks like this one.

But it was also clear to me that Dan was spoiling for a fight, and

I wasn't going to be his fall guy. Our conversation went something like this:

"How come you never talk about things like that on your radio show?" he began.

"Things like what?" I answered.

"Things like when black people have bad things done to them by whites."

"How did the case turn out?" I asked.

"They only got two years. That wasn't enough."

"How old are you, Dan?"

"I'm sixty-four years old," he said resolutely.

"Then you are old enough to remember when a white person wouldn't even have been questioned by the sheriff, let alone charged, tried and convicted for what happened to that black boy."

Dan answered with a reluctant "Yes."

I asked Dan whether he had seen the white couple on television groveling before a white South Carolina judge, a judge who had turned a deaf ear to their beseeching not to be locked up.

He answered yes again, then added quickly, "They should have gotten more time. Two years wasn't enough."

"Come on, Dan," I said. "You can ignore it if you like, but you have to admit you've lived long enough to see white folks go to jail— even in the South—for intimidating a black boy."

"You should have said more about it, though," Dan persisted.

"Why?" I shot back. "Justice was served."

That said, Dan grumbled a few more words, hung up and melted back into the sea of faceless voices I communicate with every day.

But indeed, justice had been served. And a powerful message had been dispatched with it.

Although many blacks might prefer to discount it, what came forth from that hallowed South Carolina courtroom was another powerful confirmation of the truth and justice that I deem to be at the core of our American way.

What came forth was the gospel that life, liberty and the pursuit of happiness will be protected for blacks in the United States today, just as they are for everyone else.

It is a powerful message consecrated by the blood and the struggle of every American—black and white—who fought, and in some cases died, to make justice a reality for a black American boy in a Southern courthouse.

Sadly, though, not all of the men and women who fought to make Dwight Miller's day of reckoning a possibility recognize the sweet scent of success. And I believe that Dan was one of those men.

There is an adage that says one should never judge a man until you have walked in his moccasins, so I don't pretend to know exactly what Dan may have suffered to make him so resistant to accepting change—even change for the good—in America.

But after listening to him, I realized that the impact of white racism has exacted a very heavy toll on him.

The question remains, however, whether America will indulge Dan's inability to accept the truth that real progress has been achieved between the races.

If we do, I fear it will be the Dwight Millers of our America who will have been cheated in the end.

Southern Tragedy Spawns New Level of Race Relations

First published November 1994

The entire nation held its breath, hoping all would end well, after Susan Smith, a young white mother in Union, South Carolina, reported to authorities that an African-American man brandishing a gun had hijacked her car and kidnapped her two boys with it.

When the nation learned that it was Mrs. Smith, not the mythological black man she had invented, who was responsible for the disappearance and murder of four-year-old Michael and four-teen-month-old Alexander, the deep sorrow and concern in the little town of Union was replaced with profound anger.

But what did not occur, at any time, was a reemergence of the historic call for mob retaliation that once was commonplace in the South when a black man was accused of committing a crime against a white person.

There were reports of some isolated cases of griping from thin-skinned blacks who took Smith's secondary misdeed—accusing a black man—as proof that white racism still exists.

But for the most part, blacks and whites in Union pulled together as a community to mourn the loss of the two youngsters.

In retrospect, the entire ordeal says something about the relationship between blacks and whites in the American South today—something a lot of new black separatists probably will never concede. But it is something, I believe, that speaks to a new harmony between the races.

Only the most jaded observers would deny the coolheaded professionalism with which Sheriff Howard Wells handled his investigation into the complaint that an armed black man had kidnapped two white kids.

Contrary to the old liberal myth of the potbellied redneck sheriff, this Southern cop appeared to work diligently without prejudice for nine days to resolve the mystery of the missing Smith boys. His reports to the public were evenhanded and noninflammatory.

The sheriff took the lead in reacting to the reported incident with concern for the children, not race baiting. There were no reported incidents of hooded night riders terrorizing the black bottom or calling for a lynching.

All in all, every American—especially the black and white Southerners in Union—can be proud of this aspect of the aftermath of a tragedy.

Of course, a sad note to Smith's accusation is that based on contemporary crime statistics, her story was reasonably plausible. Who else but a black man would this mother—desperately looking for an alibi to cover the murder of her two children—have accused?

Certainly her story would have been less believable if she had named a Chinese man or a Hindu as the assailant. Asians and Indians don't fit the stereotypical profile of vicious criminals most likely to waylay, rob and steal your car in America today. Sadly, young urban black men do.

Whatever Smith's tragic failing, she was describing the perfect profile of bogeyman who would frighten the folks she needed to convince that her story was true.

Was Susan Smith acting out of racism? I don't think so. She had but one thing on her mind—hiding her horrid deed. Nothing more, nothing less.

The tragedy, of course, is that despite a town united first in sorrow and then in outrage at Susan Smith, it will never again be possible for Michael and Alexander to romp and play among living souls.

But the upside—if any can surface in this sad affair—is that the people of Union rose to a new level in race relations when confronted with the trite accusation that a black man stole a white woman's children.

For that, we who believe in the ultimate triumph of the human spirit offer a salute.

My Personal Victory
in Memphis

First published January 1998

Memphis International Airport was a fuel stop en route to West Palm Beach, Florida, on my family's recent holiday trip to the Bahamas. This was a special trip because it was my six-year-old granddaughter Olivia's introductory expedition to the islands. It was the culmination of a year of planning.

After I landed on Runway 9–Right, ground control cleared me to taxi to the fixed-base operator.

The lineman, a young white kid who appeared to be in his early twenties, skillfully guided me to park my twin-engine airplane. Then he blocked the nose wheel, laid out the traditional red carpet of welcome and greeted me and my family with a gracious Southern smile as we exited the airplane.

As my son and I walked toward the building, a white man in a Civil Air Patrol uniform sporting the rank of major approached me with a smile, extended his hand and said, "Excuse me, but are you . . ."

"Yes," I said taking his hand. "Pleased to meet you, sir."

He, my son and I talked together on the ramp for a few moments about how much he enjoyed my talk radio show and my book, *Pick a Better Country*.

When the conversation was over, my son and I continued toward the building and he said, "Dad, isn't this the same place where you had some problems with a woman behind the counter?"

At first I couldn't imagine what he was talking about. A problem with a woman behind the counter?

Then my memory kicked in and I was transported back to September 7, 1980, more than seventeen years earlier, when he and I had landed at Memphis International Airport to a reception very different from the welcome we had just experienced.

The episode he was referring to came about when a white female employee, who either was having a very bad day or, dare I say it, had an ax to grind with colored people, insisted that I show her identification before she would sell me fuel for my airplane.

It became an incident.

I said no to ID—based purely on principle—and the woman behind the counter exploded into a tirade.

I still can't imagine what impact the situation was having on my son as I matched her tirade utterance for utterance.

Whoever heard of such a thing? Demanding identification from me before she would allow me to pay cash for my fuel. The more I thought about it, the more enraged I became. Ultimately, the manager interceded and cooled the situation by telling her I didn't need ID to pay cash for aviation fuel.

To his embarrassment, she persisted, wanting to know why the rules were different for me. It indicated clearly, at least to me, that someone on the management team had given her a green light to put Negro aviators in a category separate from our white counterparts.

I got her message, didn't like it and irately stood my ground.

Seventeen years later, however, the woman behind the Memphis counter greeted me with all the graciousness of a white Southern belle. While we were chatting, two more white pilots approached to say they also listened to me on the radio.

I boarded my airplane—*American Dream*—thinking how lucky I have been to live long enough to see the South in the late 1990s.

I also thought about the fact that I haven't changed much at all. Back then, I firmly believe, I was standing up for what was right. And likewise today I am proud to stand up with the courage to acknowledge that America has changed for the better.

Cleared for departure from Memphis, and with Olivia in the back seat primed for the next leg of her holiday trip, I concluded that unlike some others, I didn't have time to reinvent racist scenarios, especially since I had stood my ground to slay them.

Racial Hatred Knows No Boundaries

First published November 1997

Common sense tells us that it is not good to judge a book by its cover. Likewise, you would be foolish to judge a person by the stereotypes of the region where he or she resides. But we all do so nonetheless.

Take, for instance, the long-standing stereotypes about the men and women who reside in the American South. Color notwithstanding, we Northerners and Westerners still today tend to view them as somewhat dim-witted, crude, lethargic and inbred.

Northern white liberals and their skittish African-American sidekicks also attribute a natural proclivity toward bigotry and racial hatred to white Southerners, Southern white men in particular.

The ignorance of that kind of simplistic reasoning was brought home to me recently by the juxtaposition of two events:

The first was a visit to Charleston, South Carolina, where I was invited to be the keynote speaker at the sixth annual banquet of the Hundred Club of Greater Charleston, held to honor police officers for their heroic service to their community.

Charleston has a long and colorful past—including a time when slavery was an acknowledged social and economic institution. The firing on Fort Sumter in Charleston's harbor ignited our Civil War.

The climate in Charleston is mild, but it pales next to the warmth and hospitality of today's Charlestonians, both black and white alike.

Of course, as I said, Charleston is home to ghosts of a great many negative milestones in the history of race relations in the United States. And those ghosts undoubtedly contribute to the stereotype that Northerners—especially blacks—maintain about Southerners in general today.

And that's why I found it ironic that during my visit there last week, I was approached by many of those white Southerners who wanted to know: "What on earth is going on in Denver?"

Denver—perceived by most as a modern city open to all who employ the ethics of hard work and good deeds—has been my home of the past two decades.

The majority of law-abiding Denverites first were astonished by the murder of Denver police officer Bruce VanderJagt on November 12 by an assailant identified as a skinhead. Then, on November 20, another Denver police officer was fired upon by an assailant who was described as a white male armed with a fully automatic weapon. He too was thought to be a skinhead.

Soon after that, Oumar Dia, an African immigrant, was approached at a Denver bus stop by Nathan Thill, nineteen, a skinhead and a self-styled warrior for white supremacy.

According to Thill's own affidavit, he verbally accosted Dia, demanding to know: "Are you a nigger? Are you ready to die like a nigger?"

Thill, quoted in a Denver newspaper, said, "I remember when I asked him as I pointed the gun at him, was he ready to die and I remember him saying yes, he was."

Thill pulled the trigger.

Next Thill—in his apparent battle at the bus stop for white supremacy—turned his weapon on Jean VanVelkinburgh, a thirty-eight-year-old single white mother of two.

Why?

Because she had intervened by speaking up in support of a black man. Thill, a far cry from the honor among men in the West and the twisted little coward that he is, shot VanVelkinburgh in the back. The bullet severed her spine, and doctors believe she will never walk again.

Today the national media refers to Denver as a metropolis under siege—despite the fact that many of her citizens represent a generation of Americans who enjoy thinking of themselves as progressive, diligent whistle blowers in the war against racial inequality.

Most Americans would say the recent murder of a police officer, the attack on another, the assassination of a man because his skin was dark and the shooting of a white woman who sought to protect him are events that are simply not supposed to occur way out West.

Those atrocities supposedly are reserved for the South, where rednecks are accused of subtly signaling their lingering racist attitudes by flying the Confederate flag.

I must admit that as a black Coloradan, I found it odd and ironic to be talking with genteel white Southerners about murder, racism and hatred in the wide-open American West.

But I realized that hatred—just as love—for one's fellow man knows no boundaries.

Proof again, if any were needed, that one cannot judge a book by its cover.

Liberals in Denial
About Black Racism

First published December 1995

A couple of weeks ago I wrote a column cautioning that black people are the last ones who should indulge in the type of bigotry and hate mongering speculated to have been at the root of the arson attack on Freddy's Fashion Mart in Harlem.

The alleged perpetrator was a black man. He died in the fire, along with seven innocent people. Prior to this tragedy, there had been protests by black community leaders against this Jewish-owned establishment.

I saw a direct correlation between the hateful rhetoric against Freddy's proprietor, characterized by African-American activist Al Sharpton as a Jewish "interloper" on Harlem's 125th Street, and the actions of this black man who had been one of many street vendors banned from 125th Street for not paying taxes.

My comments resulted in an invitation to talk about hate speech on PBS-TV's *The News Hour with Jim Lehrer*. Also on the panel were Nadine Strossen, president of the American Civil Liberties Union, Judge Robert H. Bork and Wilbert Tatum, who is the publisher and editor-in-chief of New York's *Amsterdam News*, an African-American community newspaper.

After the show, I concluded that Strossen and Tatum not only espouse the epitome of white and black liberal dogma, but that they are in complete denial about a very dangerous force of evil—black racism—in America today.

When asked whether he thought that the anti-white and anti-Jewish rhetoric spouted by Sharpton and Morris Powell, another local African-American activist, had any impact on the attack on Freddy's, Tatum replied flatly, "No."

Tatum then tried to reduce the incident to little more than a landlord-tenant dispute that got out of hand.

How, then, pray tell, did a black street vendor get so embroiled in this business controversy?

According to Tatum, it was Mayor Rudolph Giuliani's fault.

He said it was the mayor's decree to remove the illegal vendors from 125th Street that provided the impetus to this demented man's deadly actions. I wonder why he didn't burn down the mayor's mansion, then.

Strossen pushed liberal permissiveness to the ultimate limits in her exchanges of legalese with Judge Bork. According to her, yes, the hate speech leading up to the incident at Freddy's was abominable, but we could not be sure that it caused the incident, so it was protected by the Constitution.

Let's review the course of events.

African-American leaders rant and rave, spouting anti-Semitism and white racism, in front of a Jewish-owned establishment. A black man apparently believes his oppression was fostered by this Jewish merchant's success, so he burns the place down.

Is it not common sense that one act led to the other?

I said on the television show and I will repeat it here. The good people of America are being encouraged by black apologists and white liberals to bury their heads in the sand while the expanse between black and white, Christians and Jews in this country is being deliberately exploited by self-serving African-Americans.

Eight people are dead in Harlem because men like the Reverend Al Sharpton declared open season on Jews. What happened was ugly, hideous and shameful.

But like the German people who tried to absolve themselves of responsibility for the atrocities against the Jews in Hitler's Germany, African-Americans in Harlem are doing everything in their power to disavow themselves from having ignited the fever of the mob.

Here's how I responded to their denials on the Lehrer show:

"Won't we ever step up to the podium and take responsibility for our actions? I'm talking not just about the black community, but I'm talking about the media and all Americans—black and white—who accept this type of rabble-rousing by a select group of black people that goes back as far as the Korean merchant situation in

Brooklyn. We have allowed a precedent to accept this kind of hateful rhetoric to be established.

"The liberals and the black apologists can try to scrub it up, try to deny it all they want.

"But the bottom line is that there's a monster of anti-Semitism and racial hatred growing in this country. Mindless black people were led to stand up in broad daylight on 125th Street in Harlem against some mythological encroachment of the infamous Jew. And the result was death in the heart of New York City.

"We have pogroms being committed again—this time in the United States of America. And they are not being committed by white Aryan, goose-stepping Nazis.

"This time, they are being committed by the sons of former slaves who should know better than most what racism and bigotry and hatred have wrought against us as a people. The people who will not speak out against this are nothing more than apologists, and I will not let them off the hook.

"Deny it all you want. But unless we dig our heels in now and say no, we are going to be a country torn asunder."

Paying Homage to the Notorious B.I.G.

First published March 1997

One of the best displays of the culture that I have labeled black trash occurred recently when residents from my old stomping grounds in Brooklyn congregated in a funeral procession to pay homage and bid adieu to one of their fallen cultural heroes, rapper Christopher G. Wallace, a.k.a. Biggie Smalls and the Notorious B.I.G.

In his short-lived and pointless life, Notorious B.I.G. managed to collect millions of dollars for belting out loutish grunts that he asserted to be artistic expressions of his—and other black men's—struggle to survive on Brooklyn's mean streets.

Like a lot of the base gangsta rappers of his day, Notorious B.I.G. claimed to be offering hope for the disenfranchised. But I question how much better a lifestyle is that glorifies disrespect for women and disregard for children spawned, or that is built on racial hatred and disdain for authority—all of which are exalted in rap music like that of the late Notorious B.I.G.

Furthermore, I'm willing to bet that not a single penny Wallace earned (either from his early years selling crack or from his later years performing rap music) went to assist one black kid to escape the old neighborhood he claimed to deplore.

Nonetheless, from the generally liberal perspective of the media, the homage the rabble paid to Wallace was portrayed as deep and profound sadness—the kind of mourning due any icon struck down before his time.

The New York Times did, however, report some degree of cultural hostility on the part of Wallace's followers toward authority in general, and the police in particular.

"The procession itself was marred by a brief clash between the police and several dozen people, which erupted around the corner from Mr. Wallace's childhood home in Fort Greene," the *Times* reported. "The incident began when a group of teenagers jumped onto several parked cars and a Dumpster and began dancing after Mr. Wallace's motorcade passed by."

The Associated Press reported: "Fans lined the block where Wallace once lived, leaving candles, flowers, pictures, empty malt liquor bottles . . ."

Am I the only person in the media who saw the dichotomy of this man's purportedly uplifting message and the culture it ultimately championed?

For me, the life of Notorious B.I.G.—not to mention the heightened coverage of his death on TV and in a cover story in *Newsweek* magazine—depicted a classic example of today's black trash culture and its negative impact on all American society.

In my book *Pick a Better Country* I wrote:

"By sanctioning some of the anomalies of today's black trash and their perverted welfare culture as possibly being on a par with mainstream American values, we have opened the door for black gangs and gangsta wannabes to elevate their common street violence to the status of guerrilla warfare for social justice.

"These black thugs, these street punks and predators, have been allowed—in some cases, encouraged—to believe that their acts of violence against innocent people and property are merely blows for justice, blows for black liberation and black sovereignty. They envision themselves as the point men leading the fight against the unfair system of the white man.

"The fact is these boys are a far cry from social crusaders. These boys are empty vessels. . . ."

White liberals, black apologists and social outcasts like Wallace can claim they are merely commiserating about the plight of poor blacks trapped in ghettos like Brooklyn, New York.

But the fact is they are fostering a culture with values diametrically opposed to mainstream America's and then demanding that that culture be recognized as just as legitimate.

The *Times* reported that many African-American parents took their children to view Wallace's memorial. I can't help but wonder what kind of a message those inner-city black kids got from a memorial that included a pile of empty malt liquor bottles.

Additionally, I am curious to know how many of the parents who dwell along the path of Wallace's funeral procession had the insight to collar their children and impart the fact that if they strive to be like Notorious B.I.G., they too should be prepared for a predictably untimely expiration.

Jocks Play
the Race Card

First published January 1997

It wasn't too long ago, perhaps two decades or maybe three, that liberal civil rights organizations sought to uphold the standards of education for all.

Specifically, their goal was to stop the exploitation of black athletes, many of whom were believed to be inherently dense when it came to their studies off the playing field.

These groups were distressed over the fact that many black jocks were recruited, usually by white talent scouts, only to shoot hoops, sprint or tackle for the heretofore all-white schools. Their academic education ignored, these athletes frequently walked away as dense as the day they had enrolled, and civil rights advocates concluded that something needed to be done.

They closed ranks, brought the appropriate amount of pressure and ultimately won the battle. The cry for equality and academic justice was heeded across the land, and black student athletes—some white athletes as well—benefited.

All athletes, including the foremost star black athletes—often stereotyped as drowning in an academic environment where the watermark was high above their heads—would be held to an academic standard. If they failed to meet it, they would not be allowed to compete in college sports.

This was considered among the more positive achievements of the American civil rights movement for black students of the day and for those as yet unborn.

Unfortunately, though, this essay doesn't concern the legacy of a civil rights accomplishment. It's about the modern-day betrayal of young black athletes who, because of their academic shortcomings, are being exploited by a self-serving assembly of liberals.

The assembly in question is the Washington, D.C.–based Trial Lawyers for Public Justice. Ethical-sounding indeed. But you best not judge this book by its cover, for the goal of these liberal lawyers is to challenge an important and hard-fought-for academic regulation of the National Collegiate Athletic Association.

According to a report from the Associated Press, the solicitors petitioned the U.S. District Court to issue an injunction against the NCAA on behalf of two 1996 black graduates of a Philadelphia high school.

Further, they are asking for a ruling on behalf of hundreds of young black athletes they claim are suffering because the NCAA uses SAT scores to decide who can play in college sports.

According to the AP, the plaintiffs, who graduated fifth and twenty-seventh in a class of 305 and who currently are attending Wheaton College and the University of Miami, originally were recruited for track teams at numerous NCAA Division I schools.

But according to a spokesman for the Trial Lawyers for Public Justice, "The overtures stopped after they received low SAT scores."

"The NCAA emphasis is wrong," says Tai Kwan Cureton, one plaintiff in the case. "And it is hurting hundreds of athletes like myself. I decided to sue the NCAA because I don't want others to go through what I've been through."

I am curious what Mr. Cureton and the army of lawyers who have rushed to his side think they are protecting the next wave of black students from.

Not surprisingly, they say they want to protect them all from racially biased tests.

I wonder, though. Could they really be trying to shield him, and hundreds of other black athletes with low SAT scores, from a hideous truth? The truth that the administrators and teachers assigned to educate them don't do them any favors when they sell them short on their ABCs in favor of sports?

In my day, the NAACP and every ethical lawyer of color would have been there to hammer out a deal that would have assured that the hope of the race—our black college students—understood that real power was vested not in one's muscle but in the power of a person's capacity to learn. We would have questioned why these students with supposedly good grades failed to measure up in an important test like the SATs.

We would have searched for and demanded answers, because we have always known that a mind is indeed a terrible thing to waste.

Honest, It's Not So Bad Being Black in the U.S.A.

First published June 1996

Promise Keepers founder and former University of Colorado football coach Bill McCartney and other white members of the Christian organization have decided they must give a million bucks to help rebuild some black churches that have been set aflame in order to combat "the sin of racism."

Frankly, their pledge turns my stomach.

I believe McCartney is a man who is forthright and sincere in his effort to link himself with goodness and grace in the eyes of God. But his organization's newest promise is—by his own admission—based on the pain, the suffering and the dismay that he associates with being Hispanic or black in America.

According to the *Denver Post*, McCartney said that white America is oblivious to the pain of minorities.

"I had no idea myself," he said, "and it took me years to find out that most of us don't have a clue."

It's as if a spook, rattling chains and all, visited McCartney in the dark and compelled him to ponder how tormented his own existence might have been if God had condemned him to spend his life in a black man's skin.

Well, I'm sorry for you, brother Bill, because someone has sold you the wrong bill of goods about how most of us colored folks feel about being black in the United States.

While it's true that not all African-Americans—as some prefer to be called—are happy about their lot here, the hearty majority of us know enough about the plight of blacks and whites struggling to survive outside the borders of the U.S. to count our American blessings.

So this black American will have to say thanks, but no thanks, for your pity.

The last thing my people need is you and your organization reinforcing the notion of how difficult it is to be dusky in the United States.

We don't need a white male army of God's angels on earth rushing to our aid, overcome with missionary zeal to liberate us from the hellishness of being black in America.

What we need is to be dealt with as equals, as fully vested Americans.

To that end, the professional African-American victims whom you apparently have gathered around you need to be informed that the madness of tabernacle burnings that seem to have afflicted our nation are but components in the mosaic of disappointment and suffering of Everyman.

As for the Promise Keepers' pledge of $1 million to rebuild burned black churches, I think that's a swell Christian commitment.

But I also happen to believe that it would be a much more fitting Christian charity if the organization didn't forget that other churches, churches that don't belong to blacks, are burning too.

McCartney conveniently overlooked the fact that both black and white church burnings have been occurring in the United States.

A June 12 report from Scripps-Howard News Service quotes the Bureau of Alcohol, Tobacco and Firearms as having 123 church arsons on record over the last five years—and only thirty-eight were in black churches.

Those numbers don't exactly add up to a scourge on black people.

But McCartney's position, as recounted in the *Post*, is that "the black church in America has been under siege for years. And we stood by and did nothing."

Not exactly true, brother Bill. A whole army of good Americans—black and white—said no to that practice in the South during the 1960s.

But according to the *Post*, McCartney contends that the "sin of racism is insidious and ingrained in the fabric of our society. It comes from a notion of white racial superiority—and the sin lies in that we do nothing about it."

Sorry again, brother Bill. I hear from hundreds of white Americans every day and week, all across this great land, who have rejected the pedestal of racial superiority and the sin of racism and who want to move on hand-in-hand with all Americans.

Perhaps you don't know about them because you haven't taken the time to come out from behind the bulwark of your multilayered organization.

But life in my America—where it isn't cool to loathe a person because of the color of his skin, because he's a Jew or because he is gay—isn't nearly as miserable for minorities as the African-Americans you apparently have been talking with say it is.

I'd urge you to open your heart to the millions who already have dealt with America's period of racial exclusion and are ready to embrace our country's diversity.

May God watch over you and our America.

Ghetto Withdrawal
a Killer?

First published March 1998

The politically slanted federal Center for Disease Control and Prevention in Atlanta has unleashed a new report concerning an increasing incidence of suicide among African-American teenagers.

I call the CDC politically slanted because I have long believed that this agency's perspective frequently goes well beyond the realm of medical research and disease control. I first suspected the CDC was an obliging ally of the left when it concluded in another study that guns might be considered a national health hazard because they were used to kill an increasing number of people.

I think the agency's suppositions about causes in this newly discovered upswing in black teen suicides is no less politically motivated.

But first let me say that it is a tragedy when any young person—be he or she black or white—becomes isolated and misguided
enough to feel the only option is suicide.

Furthermore, I think it is a matter of great concern to all of us
when a disproportionate number of suicides can be tracked to any
group of Americans.

And in this case, the study reported that the rate of suicide for
black youths aged fifteen to nineteen more than doubled, to 8.1 per
100,000 in 1995, from 3.6 per 100,000 in 1980. Likewise, there were
increases among black youths aged ten to fourteen years.

Suicide, according to the report, has become the third leading
cause of death for African-Americans fifteen to twenty-four years
old. The leading cause of death for black youths continues to be
homicide.

But I remain suspicious of the possible reason being put forth
by the CDC for the increase in black teens killing themselves over
the past two decades.

According to the CDC's study, the root cause of the trouble may
be associated with the pressure of "moving on up"—that is, making
the transition to the American middle class.

How can that be?

Why in this time of opportunity and plenty, a period when
African-Americans are more emancipated than ever before in the
history of our great nation, are the benefactors of the struggle for
Negro emancipation murdering themselves in greater numbers?

By the logic of some CDC researchers, more and more middle-
class black teenagers appear to be killing themselves because of the
stress and pressure the upwardly mobile black family may experience in a new social environment.

Do they mean pressure like adapting to a new social environment that doesn't consider jamming rap music on the stereo until
two or three in the A.M.? Do they mean pressure arising as a result
of being separated from the black trash inner-city culture of drugs
and street crime?

Or plain and simple, is the CDC suggesting that the children of middle-class black folks are killing themselves because of the stress of being separated from the ghetto?

I guess the solution to the notion that assimilation into the American mainstream may be detrimental to colored people can only mean one thing: Stay put in your own inner-city communities.

After all, the study came very close to concluding that black teens who killed themselves were more likely to be from a better socioeconomic bracket than blacks in the general population.

The meaning is clear to me. Black people who aspire to better homes, communities and public schools—among many other things—have long been denounced in the ghetto as race traitors.

Now the liberal CDC appears to be presenting the real possibility that if you are black, the American dream can kill you.

Who benefits from this convoluted logic? White liberal politicians and their minority minions, that's who—those politicians who thrive on the misguided notion that the inner-city districts under their command have declined because middle-class blacks have abandoned them, and certainly not because of their lackluster political and economic leadership.

The suicide of any child is a devastating experience for any family to try to understand. But let us not begin peddling the idea that more black kids have begun killing themselves because their parents are successful.

The long and the short of the situation is that biased notions like those contained in the CDC's suicide report are not designed to benefit anyone but isolationist inner-city opportunists—certainly not young and ambitious black Americans.

King's Legacy
Wasted on the Bitter

First published January 1998

I must concede I wasn't surprised to see an article concerning the conflict and turmoil confronting the Negro people in our country today published on the front page of this newspaper on this, the eve of what would have been Dr. Martin Luther King's sixty-ninth birthday.

This year's sorrowful rehashing of the bigotry that colored people like myself supposedly suffer was headlined:

"Civil Rights Struggle Continues."

One would think that since I am a fifty-seven-year-old colored man, my experiences and recollections concerning the dehumanizing ordeal of white racism and discrimination would be of interest to and carry some clout with my white liberal colleagues in the press.

But alas, such is not the case.

Because when white liberals feel compelled to bleed from the muscle in their chests, it's no cliché to say "there's no stopping them." So, as is par for the liberal journalistic course, this year's reminiscence of days long past featured the experiences of a black former Denver schoolteacher and her friend, who founded Denver's chapter of the Congress for Racial Equality.

The article, which was punctuated with an editor's note reminding readers that "The birthday of Martin Luther King Jr. will be observed . . . with speeches, parades and reflection on the civil rights struggle that marked King's life," delved into a historic account of the bad old days.

The story began with the teacher's recounting of an incident in 1951, a time in Denver when colored folks were restricted to certain sections at the cinema.

It went on to describe her friend's parallel incident when he was refused admittance to the Brown Palace.

Thank goodness my memories aren't so lastingly bitter. I have lived to enjoy a new day. Unfortunately, though, this article failed to mention how far black and white race relations have come since 1951.

And sadly the black woman whose experience of forty-seven years ago the story touts didn't seem particularly interested in our progress either. The story reports that she and her friend lamented that "after years of hard-won gains, the civil rights pendulum is swinging backward."

"I think this whole thing about affirmative action has to do with white people saying, 'You niggers have gone far enough,' " said the teacher.

What a sad commentary on four decades of progress.

Sad for all the obvious reasons.

But also sad in a way she may not even realize.

The story reported that the two were dismal because "some young African-Americans don't seem to relate to the trials of their slave ancestors or, even more recently, the struggles of their grandparents that spawned figures like Rosa Parks, King and Malcolm X."

From where I sit, words like those speak to wounds much deeper than the injustices white folks committed against the Negro people.

I think they speak to a greater sadness: that four decades later, after a life of fighting for equal rights, the progress that two elders helped to make has been squandered away by a generation of indifferent blacks and opportunist politicians gorging themselves at the trough of opportunity, the same opportunity they say doesn't exist.

And I think it speaks to the squandering of the great words of a man like King, who spoke of forthrightness and strength of character. Qualities that even the vice president of our nation recently denounced and described as the equivalent of a hunter's duck blind that bigots utilize to hide behind.

Truth is, King's ideal has been squandered by a generation of blacks reluctant to step up to bat and continue our historic struggle for social progress. I suppose that's easy to do when the white liberal media continues to reaffirm how bad it still is for us.

Sometimes I wonder if one sits very still, it might be possible to hear the stir of Dr. King turning over in his grave.

Sadly, Some Stereotypes Are True

First published January 1998

I had the pleasure of being included on a panel talking about race relations on the *Montel Williams* television show, which aired this week on Martin Luther King's birthday.

Specifically, the topic was about an objection by some white people in Riverside, California, to calling a new high school in their community Martin Luther King Jr. High School.

Also on the panel was former mayor of Atlanta and ambassador to the United Nations Andrew Young, who was a personal colleague of King's during the civil rights era, and a white woman from Riverside attempting to defend her racially mixed community from accusations of racism.

The debate was over the fact that some people in Riverside believe that naming their majority-white school after Dr. Martin Luther King, Jr., would hinder their children's chances for college because their middle-class kids—black and white alike—would be perceived as having attended a low-income, low-achievement school with a majority of African-American students.

Considering the push for strange new academic programs like "Ebonics" in some majority-black California public schools, if I were a middle-class California dad, I'd be skittish too.

And, of course, I said as much on this national TV show.

Dozens of young minority high school students from the New York metropolitan area were in the audience, and as would be expected, some of them had a bone to pick with me for expressing what they considered to be my racist disregard for a man as great as King.

But stereotypes can be a reality.

It's one thing to start out your life and struggle beyond the odds to excel in an inner-city school called Martin Luther King Jr. High School. To score high on college entrance exams in spite of lower-than-average academic standards during your high school years.

It's quite another thing to strap thousands of graduating seniors with the need to explain on college applications how "their Martin Luther King Jr. High School" was indeed mainstream and that their academic record from that school was on a par with those from other mainstream schools.

Based on that, I think white—and black—Americans have every right under the sun to express displeasure with their children's school board for naming a new school after King.

While some of their displeasure may well be racially motivated, I believe there also is some other valid basis for their objections.

Some liberals in the audience groaned with disbelief when I asked the kids to consider how they might feel if white folks campaigned to name a public school in honor of Louisiana representative David Duke, a repentant former Grand Dragon of the Knights of the Ku Klux Klan.

Naturally, they failed to see their own pat objections as racist.

Because I was included in the broadcast via satellite from Denver, I didn't have the pleasure of meeting Andrew Young—who was one of my heroes of the civil rights struggle—in person.

I would have liked to shake his hand for his past accomplishments and for supporting my message to the teens in the audience that day that our United States of America has come a considerable distance in improved race relations since men like him and King championed the civil rights cause.

I also would have liked the opportunity to speak one-on-one with some of those young people in the audience. Had I been able to do so, I would have told them I understood why they were incensed by me.

I would have told them I was probably the first person to have told them that life is a play-for-keeps competitive game and that some of them—the majority, in fact—were going to lose at the game of life.

And similar to their parents, when they lose, they're going to want a scapegoat to symbolically carry the blame.

In many instances the scapegoats for some of the losers in school today will become the hardworking students with them in high school today. Like their mothers and fathers before them, they will ostracize the good students instead of praising them for their success.

They will accuse successful graduates of being responsible for their own personal failures in life. And when they become better at laying blame for the deficiencies in their life on other people, they too, like so many before them, will discover the ultimate scapegoat of them all.

The fact that some long-gone distant relative was a slave and that secretly in their hearts white folks don't like colored people.

And when all is said and done, they too, similar to their parents, will have spent their lives boiling in the same emotional stew responsible for confining the generations before them to the eternal encumbrance of the 'hood.

American Dream
Only Cure
for Black Offenders

First published September 1998

I recently had the heart-wrenching experience of wading through an essay published in the September 7 issue of *Newsweek* magazine headlined "Lost Behind Prison Bars," by David L. Evans, a tutor at Boston's Charles Street AME Church and a senior admissions officer at Harvard University.

The essay asked the question why African-American men, who

constitute just 13 percent of the U.S. population, represent 49 percent of our nation's prison population.

In the prophetic words of Mr. Evans, the figures are "apocalyptic."

"A generation of young black males is at risk, but this is more than a 'black problem.' It is an American problem, and African-Americans must play a major role in solving it," said Evans.

It would have been easy for me to allow the cynical side of my nature to dismiss the pleadings of this black and highly educated Harvard liberal with the simple conclusion that 49 percent of black men are in prison because they committed a crime. But I decided to read on.

I should have quit while I was ahead.

According to Evans, African-Americans are superachievers. He cites the achievements of blacks one hundred years ago and extols the more recent successes of General Colin Powell, the Reverend Jesse Jackson and former Secretary of Labor Ron Brown.

But Evans noted that these examples of success "will appear anecdotal if millions of young black men are ensnared in the criminal-justice system."

True to the liberal agenda and its eternal aspiration to dull the broad-based achievements of the growing black middle class, Evans carped:

"I think many black professionals might have become too comfortable in the last 30 years."

Sorry, Mr. Evans. But could it be that, as I have always insisted, blacks like you are guilty about your own economic achievement?

So guilty that you can never find spiritual reconciliation with yourselves for beating the odds and having achieved?

Could it be that black liberals like you will never be happy until, in that grandiose socialist tradition, the black lumpen proletariat, which has squandered its opportunity for prosperity, is comfortably seated at Harvard, or in jobs it isn't entitled to hold?

Men like Evans bore me with their endless philosophical whining about the inequities of life for black people.

They cry the blues while avoiding the hard truth about why

young black men are disproportionately represented behind U.S. prison bars.

They ignore the truth that these young men are there because they have been encouraged, in the name of anti-American cultural diversity, to thumb their noses at the American Dream, replacing it with some very misguided ideals about pan-Africanism.

They are instilled with the faulty, unchallenged values of America's ghettos that life on the street and in the penitentiary is infinitely superior to being labeled an Uncle Tom.

They would rather be behind bars than "Tom out."

In the world of the ghetto, laurels are bestowed on these young men for doing time, not for earning a high school or a college diploma. Being labeled an Uncle Tom in this environment is a crippling attack to survive. It's a slur that no black kid wants to face.

Why?

Because when they face it, they are all alone. There aren't any prestigious African-American men like the influential Harvard officer around to bolster and encourage the right path: fulfilling the inquisitiveness and desire to get ahead that comes with youth.

Instead of fighting the good fight to defend fledgling American dreams and ambitions to reach for the moon, black liberals like Evans and the Reverend Jackson find it easier to take the path of least resistance in the community. They bow to the isolationist ideology of black racists like Minister Louis Farrakhan of the Nation of Islam and every other two-bit crackpot poverty pimp with a design on supposed black power.

I'm sorry, Mr. Evans. But there aren't any shortcuts around the truth.

The truth is that undereducated jailhouse blacks who are tethered to the values of black trash, with a proclivity for rioting and a nurtured desire to dismantle the American Dream, must be told that "one monkey don't stop the show." They must be reminded that the opportunity train is leaving the station with or without them.

If you really want to make a dent in the disproportionate African-American prison population, you will have to step up to the plate and denounce the notion that the ghettos, illiteracy, Ebonics, and the "survivalist" lifestyles of street whores and pimps are superior to keeping your nose to the grindstone and pursing the American Dream.

Scary, isn't it?

Well, I never said it was easy.

Black Skin Not Enough
in Black Africa

First published April 1998

I am about to share a sad tale with you that in all probability you never read about in your hometown newspaper or saw on the television news, though it was printed in the *New York Times.*

It is a sad story about sad people, Americans, who are compelled to confront some truths about their native land—a land that is proving to be as elusive as the mythical fountain of youth.

According to the *Times:* "Charles T. Moses, raised in New York City and once Governor Mario Cuomo's adviser for black affairs, lives these days in the northern suburbs of Johannesburg, eager to make a contribution to the new South Africa."

Moses holds a master's degree in business administration. Because the new South Africa has a shortage of educated blacks and because it suffered an immense brain drain caused by fleeing whites after the first black government was elected in 1994, he thought he would pop across the Atlantic to lend a much-needed helping hand.

But alas, the best-laid plans of mice and men are indeed notorious for going agley.

For, like many naive black Americans in search of their ancestral roots—along with a renewed appreciation of the significance of their blackness—Moses was shocked to find that they are not accepted by today's native Africans.

In particular, the *Times* article noted that Moses and other members of the black expatriate American community were chafed recently by an op-ed article in an influential Johannesburg newspaper that suggested that "black Americans were taking jobs that would otherwise go to black South Africans."

It was reported in the *Times* as the final straw for Moses—the final bitter pill forced down in what was believed to be a black promised land.

Responding in a letter to the editor of the *Sunday Independent,* Moses wrote:

"While black South Africans say African-Americans leave something to be desired, some African-Americans can offer similar comments. Many of us have been lied to, misled and abused by our South African brothers and sisters, usually out of jealousy and ignorance."

The Moses letter prompted South Africa's equivalent of Oprah Winfrey, Felicia Mabuza-Suttle, to spend two of her one-hour programs tackling the subject of tension between black South Africans and black Americans who envision themselves pioneers coming to develop a prosperous promised land.

Mabuza-Suttle's guests, an academic and two business executives, didn't hold their tongues where the matter of black Americans was concerned. According to the *Times,* they said black Americans in Africa were "patronizing, socialized among themselves and believed they were owed something because of their efforts to support anti-apartheid boycotts."

Panelist Makaziwe Mandela, President Nelson Mandela's daughter and an executive with the government-owned rail company, said that tensions have gotten so bad between black Americans and South Africans that at least one company has decided not to send American blacks to South Africa anymore.

"A lot of the black Americans come here expecting to find their brothers and sisters. But they don't share a common language or culture or background. All they share is their black skin," said Mandela.

Her words confirm what I have said about xenophobic black

Americans for a long time—that life would be difficult for the best of them in a country where no points are given for the raven color of their skin.

Mandela added, "A lot of South Africans see the black Americans as false affirmative action and there is some resentment for companies that do it."

Could Mandala be suggesting that white-owned American corporations should keep their soppy black Americans at home because South Africa doesn't need or want them? I think so.

Another panelist, Peter Luvuyo Ntshona, an executive for Iscor, a leading steel producer, said black Americans come to the motherland with an offensive attitude.

"There is always a paternalism, a sense that we can show you the way. Now we have a nation and we want them to treat us with dignity, respect and equality."

In a kind of poetic justice, he dismissed talk by American blacks about their sacrifice in coming to a developing country. He told the *Times* that was a ludicrous notion, "since most of them live in the fanciest white neighborhoods and have maids and pools."

Ntshona said, "They have a wonderful life here; they are not suffering."

Mzimkulu Malunga, an editor at a weekly business magazine, was quoted in the *Times* as saying, "Black Americans are seen as wanting black South African partners to pave their way into the market here, only to dump them later. White Americans might do the same thing. But at least they don't come here claiming they are home."

The *Times* article concluded with a pathetic comment from Charles T. Moses:

"Where is the hope for us in America? We will never be in charge. We will always be 10 percent. We will always be fighting to keep some cop from shooting us in the back. But here it's worth the battle. You can win this here."

Come back home to America, Mr. Moses. This is your true home and where you belong. It's where your true opportunities lie to live a fulfilled life.

Draw Strength
from Our History

First published December 1995

For some time I have been saying that American black people need to move on from that ugly period in New World history when we were held in bondage. We need to move on to embrace the benefits we have won as fully vested American citizens.

My message to those African-Americans who insist on living in the past by including their ancestral origin in references to themselves and who continue to fight for reparations for sins of more than a hundred years ago has been "Get over it."

I believe we have much more to gain by moving ahead and using every man's opportunity to partake of mainstream America than we have to gain by looking to get more of our perceived past-due bill from the white man's system.

But my message frequently is met with resistance from these staunch African-Americans. They continue to sustain their martyrdom as if it is destined to be their permanent station in life.

It has occurred to me that many of the followers of African-American community leaders who preach this gospel of continued suffering may not know the long and complex history of slavery in the world.

So I consulted my electronic Grolier Encyclopedia and culled a few pertinent facts:

Slavery has been an institution throughout recorded human history. There has been slavery among societies at all levels of development and material culture, from the ancient Greeks to nineteenth-century America.

By definition, slavery is based on the ownership, the dominance or the exploitation of one human being by another. But there have been many variations of slavery, ranging from cruel enslavement for unimaginably hard physical labor to men literally selling themselves and their families into slave labor as a means to pay off a debt.

The poems of Homer reveal that slavery was an accepted institution of Greek society as early as 1200 B.C. The philosopher Plato did not approve of Greeks enslaving Greeks, but he regarded other bond servants as simply inferior beings. Aristotle thought that slaves were lucky to have guidance from their superior masters.

Slaves traditionally have been a product of the captives of war and have been of a different race, ethnic group, religion or political persuasion from that of their masters. Almost never have people been held as slaves by their own tribe.

Neither the Bible nor the Koran condemned the practice of slavery. Both confirmed its existence and urged humane treatment.

With the opening of the New World in the fifteenth century came a large demand for cheap and controllable human labor to develop and work this new land. Native Indians were used initially but proved unsatisfactory—one reason being their susceptibility to European disease.

And so we come to the period of black African slavery.

The trade of black African slaves to the New World began when Portuguese ships raiding the coasts of Africa met black tribal chiefs who offered to barter their black brethren for weapons, metal, liquor or trinkets.

Only recently have scholars in Africa and the United States begun to talk and write about the fact that slavery had been a common practice in Africa among these powerful African tribal chiefs for centuries.

Ultimately, the period of New World slavery grew into an integral part of an enormous industry supported by a triangular system of trade. Ships would leave England, stopping first on the west coast of Africa to exchange merchandise for African blacks.

The notorious Middle Passage of the triangle was the crossing to America, during which slaves were held under the most appalling conditions, resulting in a mortality rate as high as 20 percent.

The slaves were sold to plantations in the West Indies (the route my forebears took to America) and in the Americas. During this stop, the ships were refilled with plantation crops such as sugar before returning to England.

Over nearly four centuries, as many as 15 million black slaves were traded. They were the strong backbone of the New World's agricultural and commercial enterprise, a system from which they did not benefit.

But black Americans today are the clear survivors of this tragic American beginning, and most of us have prevailed over that inexcusable period of misery.

Unfortunately, however, for some African-Americans this history is too bitter a pill to swallow. It is an emotional trauma, an Achilles heel that persists in impeding the final step to mainstream American citizenship.

After all is said and done, I firmly believe that if black Americans hope to develop a truly viable social and financial foundation from among the opportunities that abound in our nation, we must draw strength from the inexhaustible courage that it took our ancestors to prevail. We must teach our children to grow and prosper from that circumstance of our history.

Modern-Day Slavery Elicits Mostly Silence

First published February 1996

Samuel Cotton is forty-one years old, a husband, the father of a twelve-year-old daughter and a black American of extraordinary character in every sense of the word.

Cotton is a reporter for the *City Sun*, an African-American newspaper in Brooklyn, New York. In 1994 his editor assigned him the excruciating task of confirming the authenticity of rumors that black Africans were being sold and kept as slaves by Arabs in Mauritania, a country in northwest Africa.

My encyclopedia describes Mauritania as a bridge between Arab Africa to the north and sub-Saharan (predominantly black) Africa to the south. Mauritania's southern neighbor is Senegal. On the southeast and east, Mauritania adjoins Mali, and on the northeast it borders Algeria. To the west, Mauritania has a 435-mile coastline on the Atlantic. To the northwest, it borders Morocco and the disputed territory of Western Sahara.

History records that the Mauritanians were converted to the faith of Islam in the eleventh century, and the Arab conquest of the country in the sixteenth century resulted in the adoption of the Arabic language and culture by most of the people.

I talked with Sam Cotton recently on my radio show, and he confirmed that he had readily accepted what he considered to be a plum assignment to Mauritania. It was his first trip to the motherland, the African continent, which is pathologically revered by some African-Americans as holding the salvation to all their problems.

Cotton—a thoughtful and sober-sounding American who describes himself as dark-skinned with kinky hair—said that he spent twenty-eight days living undercover with a black African family in Mauritania.

Although he said he did feel some concern for his personal safety from time to time while there, he spoke openly to blacks who claimed to have a lineage of slavery in that country dating back some five generations.

My heart grew heavy and my soul sank while he narrated some examples of the routine punishment a black slave might receive from his or her Arab captors for the slightest fault or infraction of the rules. They included "beatings, denial of food and exposure to the sun with their hands and feet tied together."

But those punishments paled next to what Cotton described as the consequences of "serious infringements of the master's rules."

These included the camel treatment. A slave is tied around the stomach of a dehydrated camel, and the camel is then given water to drink until its stomach expands and the slave is torn apart.

They include the insect treatment, in which bugs are put into the slave's ears, his ears are sealed with wax and he is driven mad by insects inside the head.

They include the burning-coals treatment, in which a slave is buried up to his waist in sand with legs spread apart and then a fire is set between his legs atop the sand.

Cotton said he learned enough during his trip to believe that slavery in northern Africa is controlled to a large degree by the governments of Mauritania and Sudan.

I asked Cotton how the experience had changed him and what his opinion was, as a black American today, of the United States. He responded without hesitation that he thought this was the best country in the world and then noted that many African-Americans are misguided in believing that racism and racist attitudes do not exist among Arabs, especially among Muslims.

He noted—sadly, I might add—that he believed those misguided beliefs are why the prominent role Arabs have played in the black slave trade always has been downplayed by American blacks. And that those beliefs are probably the biggest reason why there is such a heavy curtain of silence from the heretofore prominent American civil rights leaders and organizations like Jesse Jackson, the NAACP and the Black Congressional Caucus.

I asked Cotton how the experience had changed his life. As might be expected, he said that it had changed him considerably.

I asked him if he had been threatened and whether he feared for his safety here at home in America. He said that he had been threatened and warned about telling his story by some members of the Nation of Islam. They warned him that he was coming dangerously close to becoming another Salman Rushdie, the author of the *Satanic Verses,* who was accused of defaming Islam and thus had to go into hiding after fanatic Iranian Muslims allegedly put out a contract to kill him.

That a black American should find himself in jeopardy in the U.S. of A., after spending nearly a month living undercover in North Africa to confirm that Arabs still have black slaves, is beyond my comprehension.

I understand why the Arabs continue to trade in black flesh. They do so for profit.

I even understand the heartless indifference of Minister Louis Farrakhan to such a scurrilous prejudice being continued against his ancestral kin. He too is inspired by the profit promised him from the Arab slave masters' ponderous purse.

But what of black America? Where is the call for justice from the African-American throng that crowded into the mall in Washington, D.C., during the Million Man March?

The silence of these self-righteous men begs me to ask whether we have become such lapdogs of ignorance and denial concerning the human injustice taking place in North Africa today that we can turn our backs and shut our eyes while a man like Samuel Cotton must learn to exist in fear for jeopardizing Farrakhan's enormous lie.

Arab Africa's
Dirty Little Secret

First published February 1996

Unfortunately, evidence continues to mount, like the residue from a scuttled ship of dreams, that black slavery imposed by Arabs still, in 1996, exists in North Africa.

But old-guard civil rights activists like Jesse Jackson, practitioners of African-American ghetto politics like Representative Maxine Waters (a Democrat from California) and community leaders like the former executive director of the near-bankrupt NAACP Ben Chaves remain mum.

Now that the nefarious anti-U.S. relationship between Colonel Muammar Gadhafi of Libya and Nation of Islam leader Minister Louis Farrakhan has been let out of the bag, one wonders whether these pious African-Americans ever will take a stand to denounce this modern-day horror.

The relationship I refer to is, of course, the recent news that

Gadhafi has pledged a reported $1 billion through Minister Far-rakhan to American Muslims in exchange for an inside track to in-fluence U.S. politics—domestic and foreign.

Is it possible we also are talking hush money concerning African politics here?

Last week, Clarence Page, a syndicated columnist with the *Chicago Tribune* and an African-American I must admit I usually consider to be an apologist for the inept moral and political leader-ship of the black underclass today, was moved to ask this question as well.

After recounting what the Libyan news agency reported that Gadhafi and Farrakhan discussed as terms of their deal, Page wrote:

"What they apparently did not talk about was something Far-rakhan has been curiously silent about: Slavery."

Since his October show of strength with his "Million Man March" in Washington and now with his reported newfound wealth, apparently what Farrakhan decides to dismiss in order to maintain the myth of the perfect African homeland is just fine by traditional African-American leaders.

But despite their lack of character and faintness of heart when it comes to confronting this travesty, other respectable Americans—not all of whom are black—have seen fit to take up the cause of free-dom on behalf of the dusky Africans still on auction blocks on the Dark Continent.

One of those Americans is Dr. Charles Jacobs, a Jew and the re-search director of the American Anti-Slavery Group, based in Somerville, Massachusetts.

According to the group's letterhead, it has adopted the motto of John Fitzgerald Kennedy:

"When one man is enslaved, no man is free."

Dr. Jacobs has been a guest on my radio show twice, each time seeming to have the weight of the world embedded in his words.

He has spoken of the indifference shown to him and to the ef-forts of his organization to rekindle the flame of the American civil rights movement on behalf of black Africans being held in bondage by Arabs in Mauritania, Sudan and Libya.

That indifference was actually a complete dismissal by Farrakhan's camp on the basis that Jacobs was a Jew and therefore simply acting out of anti-Arab sentiments.

Despite rebuffs from other prominent African-Americans who seemingly would be most likely to champion the antislavery cause, the truth is beginning to emerge through declassification of State Department documents, groups like Dr. Jacobs's and a handful of black journalists and congressmen.

One such State Department document, obtained through the efforts of Representative Frank Wolf (Republican of Virginia), confirms "widespread human rights abuses, [including] credible reports of massacres, kidnapping and forced labor, conscription of children, forced displacement and Arabization, and other abuses."

From the moment I became aware of the fact that the slavery of yore—the slavery responsible for my ancestors' being brought across the Atlantic against their will—had black accomplices, I have been curious about what ilk of man could do such deeds.

Watching the conscious deception and deals with the devil of Minister Farrakhan, followed by the stench of silence from our community leaders of color, I'm getting a pretty good idea of who those men were.

So since it's highly unlikely that the African-American crowd ever will be interested in exposing and condemning Arab Africa's dirty little secret, here's one place you can weep while you learn truth:

American Anti-Slavery Group, P.O. Box 441612, Somerville, MA.

SIX

Affirmative Action

The Supreme Court
Still "Progressive"
for Black People

First published June 1995

True to the irrationality of contemporary liberalism, the *New York Times* printed an editorial with the headline "A Sad Day for Racial Justice" the day after the Supreme Court ruled against the excessive implementation of affirmative action.

The *Times* editorial bemoaned what its pundits obviously saw as irony: "The Supreme Court, a place where minorities once looked for racial justice, did what it could yesterday to halt the progress its own decisions once sparked."

As a black American who fought in the trenches for civil rights in the 1960s and who got a job as the first black photographer at the *Detroit Free Press* in 1969—clearly under an affirmative-action mandate—I wholeheartedly agree that the Supreme Court has been a progressive force for me and my people.

The difference I have with last week's *New York Times* editorial is that, based on the high court's latest ruling, I continue to salute its progressiveness.

The editorial also noted that the affirmative-action ruling—along with another which struck down a Kansas City school desegregation order—"ignores the reality that America is far from overcoming more than two centuries of bigotry."

Is that really the government's role—to overcome bigotry? I'd say that's an impossible task, given human nature and the reality of thousands of years of historical bigotry among people.

While I believe the United States is unique among nations, I stop short of presuming that any nation can ban bigoted thoughts and beliefs. It can only ban bad actions that may result from those beliefs.

The *Times*'s stance against the Supreme Court obviously missed the profundity of the majority and concurring opinions from Justice Sandra Day O'Connor and Justice Clarence Thomas.

Justice O'Connor wrote: "The Fifth and Fourteenth Amendments [of our U.S. Constitution] protect persons, not groups."

The bottom line is that any individual who is discriminated against in the job market because of race or gender can—with the full force of our U.S. Constitution behind him or her—fight back.

But even more profound, in my opinion, was Justice Thomas's comment: "These [affirmative-action] programs stamp minorities with a badge of inferiority and may cause them to develop dependencies or to adopt an attitude that they are 'entitled' to preferences."

Hear, hear.

With between two-thirds and three-fourths of black Americans established in the mainstream middle class and beyond, when do we let go of the notion that we, as a people, need special preferences to compete in school and in the job market?

Will the *New York Times* editors, and other like-minded liberals, never allow us to stand or fall on our own two feet? Are we never, in their minds, to be granted the true test of equality?

But isn't that the "progressive" thing to do now?

By its actions, the Supreme Court is willing to grant us the next evolutionary step in the valid struggle to become fully vested Americans.

Unfortunately, the *Times* either doesn't think we are ready to stand shoulder-to-shoulder with the best of them, or perhaps the editors there believe in their narrow liberal hearts that we aren't capable of ever reaching true equality.

This kind of compassion reduces African-Americans to the status of human pets, always needing the care of the "superior" and "dominant" race.

Whatever the rationale for its position, the *Times* continues to write quite effectively for its core readers—the white social workers and the black urban politicians. They, in turn, use the paper's hallowed words of woe to stir up trepidation among those Americans of color who are nurtured to believe that working hard to get ahead is futile because of rampant racism practiced against them.

And that, of course, promotes the belief that the world, and the IBMs of the world, owe them a living.

Self-Reliance
Could Catch On

First published August 1995

Confronted by the genuine possibility that affirmative-action programs as black folks have come to know and love them could become as extinct as the flightless dodo bird, the Black Caucus of the California Association of Counseling Development—an organization of elementary, secondary and university guidance counselors—is urging African-Americans to look to self-reliance.

Their message, which I believe is long overdue, came in light of the University of California regents' vote of 14 to 10 to no longer consider race and gender in matters of admissions and hiring.

According to the *Santa Barbara News-Press,* Michael Brown—an associate professor of education at the University of California at Santa Barbara—counseled a gathering of about twenty people and five panelists:

"If, out of the kindness of their heart someone sees the conditions you have dealt with and they want to help you, that's fine. . . . But if they don't want to help you, that's fine too. You should never put your confidence in affirmative action."

The caucus, obviously distressed about the public's growing backlash against the nation's policy of affirmative action, gathered at the central branch of the Santa Barbara Public Library to reflect on the dilemma of blacks being forced to compete equally with other Americans.

Wait a minute. Isn't that the opportunity we fought for and supposedly won back in the 1960s?

I guess the agenda has changed because Babatunde Folayemi, a resident-service specialist at the Santa Barbara County Housing Authority and a local youth-education advocate, said at the meeting that African-Americans need to "stop kidding ourselves that it ever was or ever will be a level playing field as long as the same people [are in power]."

Unfortunately, Folayemi's opinion that no African-American ever can or ever will get a fair deal in the white man's America is a notion that too many African-Americans cling to in the 1990s.

They use it as a crutch to justify their seeming inability to work, mingle and live among other human beings without getting the gnawing, crippling feeling they are being discriminated against.

Of course, Folayemi invoked slavery, claiming that the attack on affirmative action is just more of the same white oppression African-Americans have faced in American in the past.

He said this latest action against blacks should have been expected, based on the past.

Unfortunately, we've allowed men like Mr. Folayemi and a cadre of socially dysfunctional and anti-American black leaders to develop and cultivate a dreadful xenophobia that causes some blacks to look for any possible sign of rejection.

And unfortunately, they peddle it to many adolescent blacks who will need to turn the tide against the remnants of institutionalized racism.

Perhaps I'm missing the point. But I fail to see how urging black Americans to develop an attitude of self-reliance, while in the next breath implying that they can't live fairly under the white man's law, will inspire anyone to grow strong and prosper.

But then maybe the challenge for self-reliance was never intended as inspiration. Maybe it was intended as another scare tactic thrown at an increasingly isolated black community.

It could backfire on the black community activists and blacks enamored of academic quotas, however.

Because once self-reliance gets a grip on the human spirit and one samples the power that comes from the habit of relying on oneself, it creates a human force that is capable of reshaping the status quo into something that African-Americans who spend their time evangelizing against the merit of the American Dream aren't likely to be able to swat down with their usual rhetoric.

I suggest that the brothers from the community in Santa Barbara better be careful with their threatening rhetoric, lest a sudden wave of self-reliance take hold and they themselves become obsolete relics of their own communities.

The Predictable Occurs
After Affirmative Action
Ends

First published May 1997

As the old saying goes, the proof of the pudding is in the tasting. Unless, of course, you happen to be a sociopolitical activist whose prime objective is to level the human playing field at any cost.

Here's a case in point.

A dispatch from the Associated Press reports that in Berkeley, California, the number of African-Americans offered admission to the University of California's Boalt Hall law school dropped an alarming 81 percent in the first year without the liberal safety net that affirmative action had heretofore provided. Admission of Hispanics dropped 50 percent.

Desperate to authenticate the illusion that aspiring black and Hispanic law students require a government-supported edge to compete in a "racist" environment, the law school's dean, Herma Hill Kay, pointed to the falling numbers as a prime example of "precisely what we feared would result from the elimination of affirmative action."

Well, the sudden decline in acceptable applications from minorities only confirms for me that indeed there has been a complimentary ride given to lots of unqualified minority students, and now it's over.

Black UC regent Ward Connerly wrote the new policy, adopted in 1995, which eliminates race and gender from being factors in deciding admission to California schools of higher learning.

The policy takes effect with graduate students entering classes in the fall of 1997.

Jennifer Nelson, spokeswoman for the American Civil Rights Institute, which was founded by Connerly, responded to the low minority admissions this way:

"These numbers really show the horrendous magnitude of the preferences that we've been giving in the UC system."

The magnitude of the numbers aside, the real tragedy was that rather than using preferences to be certain qualified minorities had an equal opportunity for admission, the quota system was used to admit a certain percentage of minorities at any cost.

Now we know many must have been unqualified.

Other UC graduate schools haven't released their admissions figures, but Dean Kay announced that minorities made up 36 percent of this year's applicants, compared with 39 percent the year before.

But only 14 applicants qualified this year, as opposed to 75 last year.

Black, tan or white, the last thing our country needs is more inept, unqualified lawyers who never would have seen the inside of a law school—much less graduated—if it hadn't been for affirmative-action programs, which apparently functioned on the notion that almost any person of color should be allowed to become a lawyer or a doctor.

Let the record show, I am not in opposition to qualified minority applicants cramming graduate schools at UC Berkeley or any other college or university. I'd like to see them represent 50 percent of graduates if they compete fair and square on their merit.

Thanks to the good common sense of Americans like Connerly and organizations like his American Civil Rights Institute, at least in California only students with the highest academic ratings and a burning determination to keep their eye on the prize will be among the proud graduates.

Whether old-guard affirmative-action proponents like Dean Hill Kay are willing to admit it or not, the elimination of poorly executed affirmative-action policies will establish a win-win situation for everyone concerned.

By competing as equals, minorities will be better equipped to meet the challenges of school and a career as equals, instead of graduating as hobbled men and women always under a cloud of doubt regarding their true abilities.

Let minority enrollment plummet at UC Berkeley graduate school if it means we are weeding out the unqualified. In the long run, it can only develop a better-educated class of professionals. This nation ultimately will reap the benefits—and so will the students, knowing they've competed on their merits and won the right to be there.

An Open Letter
to Jesse Jackson

First published September 1997

Dear Jesse,

I watched you march across San Francisco's Golden Gate Bridge protesting Proposition 209, California's new anti–affirmative-action law, on the day it went into effect.

And you were wrong.

One might have thought you were protesting the repeal of the

Fourteenth Amendment to the Constitution of the United States, which says: "No state shall make or enforce any law which shall abridge the privileges or immunities of citizens of the United States."

But that's not at all what Proposition 209 has mandated.

This is what it says: "The state shall not discriminate against, or grant preferential treatment to, any individual or group on the basis of race, sex, color, ethnicity or national origin in the operation of public employment, public education, or public contracting."

Jim Crow and its racially discriminating laws were knocked down a long time ago, Jesse. Black Americans—including you yourself—worked hard to achieve those gains, and thanks to all our efforts, today it is against the law to discriminate against anyone based on arbitrary factors such as race and gender in our country.

If Negroes, African Americans, colored men and women can't fend for themselves in today's America, it's no fault but their own.

So I believe your protest last week was extremely harmful to the thousands of young African-Americans who have been led to believe that opportunities do not abound for them in our country today.

You and people like Representative Maxine Waters (a Democrat from California), along with groups like the Black Congressional Caucus and the NAACP, ought to be encouraging this generation of black America to take their rightful place in the United States of today.

Instead, you and the old guard are doing a dreadful thing to them by hanging on to ghosts from the past.

Shame on you, Jesse. And shame on your apparent self-serving motivation for personal gain.

Once you were a legitimate champion, an icon, a guiding light in the cause of black civil rights. Today, Jesse, you are little more than a parasite subsisting off the repulsive history of segregation's sordid past.

Get over it, Reverend. You've had your day in the sun.

Since you are an elder statesmen of the civil rights movement, it's time for you to take the lead and let the word go forth into the ghettos that it's safe and appropriate for black people to venture forth into the American mainstream.

I know you comprehend what that will mean. I know you understand that by doing so, you and your political cronies will be compelled to run at large for political seats just like your white counterparts. I know you know that funds earmarked for affirmative action and civil rights, funds that you heretofore have managed, will dry up.

But that is the price we all pay for competing as equals in the mainstream and becoming a part of the whole.

In San Francisco, you resurrected the memory of Dr. Martin Luther King and his dream that someday the American Negro would be dealt with as any man's equal.

Well, that is precisely the essence of Proposition 209. And I think you know that in your heart.

After years of struggle, it's sometimes hard to let go of the invigorating challenge—even to admit success.

But in 1997, it's time for you and your old guard to take up the new cause. Spread the word among the descendants of the heroes who marched with King in Montgomery and Cicero that the barricade of bigotry has been beaten down and now it is the duty of black America to field our champions.

We must let go of preferential crutches that only continue to cripple us. We must send our very best to fill the countless slots for doctors, lawyers and other professionals that the civil rights movement and Americans like you are responsible for creating.

"The state shall not discriminate against, or grant preferential treatment to, any individual or group on the basis of race, sex, color, ethnicity or national origin."

Those are powerful words, Jesse. And although they may be frightening to you, it appears that twenty-nine states in addition to California are ready to adopt them or their essence.

Continue to fret and protest if you like, but this dusky American thinks we've come a considerable distance, Jesse. And now I believe we are ready to take that next step toward becoming fully vested Americans.

SEVEN

Crime

The Snarl of a Bogus Lion

First published January 1995

His name is Shahid—"Shahid S."

Although he is eighteen, legally of age to be tried as an adult, the "S" was substituted for his real surname in a story in the *New York Times*. It seems a deal was struck with the reporter to afford Shahid the luxury of remaining an anonymous felon.

The *Times* article about Shahid, part of an in-depth report on juvenile crime, undoubtedly provided bleeding-heart liberals with another voyeuristic peek into the subculture of the urban underclass.

But for me, it was just another replay of an old story—a tale of good intentions and misguided compassion directed toward youthful predators.

The article recounted the struggle by penal and social agencies to deal with an increasing number of young offenders.

It related how Shahid was the fourth of six black babies born to a mother who sustained them all on—what else?—public assistance.

Uninspired and undermotivated to make disciplined choices in life, Shahid was portrayed as typical of other illiterate kids like him. He quit school in the eighth grade. It was the first of many bad choices that left him shipwrecked on the reef of life without the skills he needed to fend for himself in mainstream society. And so, quite predictably, he became a criminal instead of one of the good guys.

For those of you who feel that my dismissal of Shahid as no more than a predator is cruel or unkind, let me acquaint you with his criminal history as it appeared in the *Times*.

It was reported that, by his own account, Shahid snatched more than two hundred automobiles, robbed between fifty and sixty people and shot at least four more.

If those statistics don't tell who Shahid is, consider his philosophy on life, described in the *Times*'s report as "a blunt Darwinian philosophy."

"Deers eat grass," said Shahid. "Lions eat deers, and men kill lions. I'm the lion. The working people are the deer, the grass is the money and the men shooting the lions is the cops. You take one thing out and everything will get screwed up."

Nice kid, huh?

I recognized Shahid for what he was the moment I read his predatory survival-of-the-fittest theory. He reminded me of one of the unscrupulous thugs who used to amaze me forty years ago when I was growing up in Brooklyn.

Mr. "S" is, indeed, a seasoned menace to society.

He and those like him have existed for ages. But in the past, society justifiably spent little time or money to "cure" them. Instead, there were only efforts to contain them.

As far as my mother was concerned, boys like Shahid were the devil incarnate, and she cautioned me to stay clear of them. I did, despite my own hard years as a youth growing up on welfare.

Of course, today most liberals don't bother to factor in the possibility that black boys born into poverty still are able to make good choices.

They seem incapable of going beyond the dossiers of young criminals like Shahid. All bad boys—black boys, in particular—are diagnosed using dire statistics to perpetuate the myth that poverty and a tough upbringing, not voluntary choices and actions, are accountable for their misdeeds.

I'm jaded about guys like Shahid, because I hold them and the do-gooders who excuse them responsible for devouring the quality of life in underclass communities.

The Shahids are social duds, and our seeming preoccupation with their plight along with the dollars spent trying to save them takes resources away from young boys who, like me, listened and heeded the lesson of right and wrong from moms, aunts or grandmas.

We had all better wise up and face the truth that there are thousands of socially twisted young black men just like Shahid who may be beyond saving. We'd better realize that many of them, like Shahid, perceive themselves to be heroic lions, not bad boys, when they commit the vicious acts that shatter our lives, our families and our communities.

Life Is Predictable
in "Dark Town"

First published November 1996

"An uneasy calm prevailed . . . after a night of disturbances."

These were the words reported by the *New York Times* after a notorious criminal element, well known to the police, raised its ugly head to foul the image of law-abiding black people and to tarnish the image of the city of St. Petersburg, Florida.

Sadly, I wasn't surprised at the violence that broke out after a black teenager was shot by a white St. Petersburg cop.

I wasn't surprised when I learned from a St. Petersburg reporter, who was a guest on my radio show and who was on the scene at the disturbance, that the dead boy had been in a stolen car, stopped after a high-speed chase.

I wasn't surprised when I learned from the reporter that the boy refused to roll down his tinted windows or respond to verbal commands from the police.

Still, the cop fired into the car, he said, only after he stepped in front and it "lurched" forward.

I wasn't surprised because such encounters are almost commonplace in areas like this one in St. Petersburg, areas that I have dubbed Dark Town.

Dark Town, as people know who listen to my radio show, is any place where the residents no longer can freely use their streets because of the fear of random violence brought about by the drug dealing and prostitution taking place on the corners.

It's any place where a son or daughter might be brought home in a body bag, just because he or she wore a particular color of clothing.

It's any place where a mother feels it necessary to bed down her babies in a bathtub in order to protect them from random bullets that might come through the windows during the night.

Dark Town isn't limited to residents of any particular race or creed. It's identifiable by police statistics which point to a high incidence of senseless crime.

Here's how I described one of my first trips into Dark Town in my book *Pick a Better Country:*

"The first time I rode with the police gang unit through the inner city of Aurora, Colorado, it struck me that the people I saw there were not part of the twentieth century. Instead, they appeared to be living by standards of the Dark Ages.

"There was a lack of regard for the rights of other people— their right to peace and quiet, their right to property, their right to a secure environment—and a seeming lack of regard for the value of life itself."

I also described Dark Town as an area not likely to see mainstream businesses set up shop—mainstream businesses that bring good jobs and a tax base to support the community.

Unlike the contention of those African-Americans who went on a seventy-two-hour rampage in St. Petersburg, I insist it's not racism that keeps these businesses out. It's the likelihood that disturbances just like this one will occur with great regularity.

And that instability is bad for any business.

The moral and law-abiding black residents of this St. Petersburg neighborhood know what I'm talking about.

In spite of a 1993 report from an advisory committee to the U.S. Commission on Civil Rights that concluded that "the lack of respect in police treatment of citizens was cited as critical to racial and ethnic tensions," they knew that the greater problem was whether the new

Walgreen's drugstore scheduled to open in the area would go ahead with its plans.

They knew that jobs and industry were the real measures of the health of a community.

The *New York Times* article quoted Abdul Rahman, sixty-three, as he looked at a gutted furniture store: "These people who stirred this up are not looking for jobs. You just have bad seeds out there waiting for this type of thing to break out."

Stolen Carts Are Thanks for Inner-City Store

First published September 1996

Most of us have heard the resentment expressed by xenophobic inner-city blacks who claim that because of racism, their communities are devoid of mainstream businesses like restaurants and well-stocked supermarkets.

But seldom do they see fit to link the fact that their communities have been transformed into barren wastelands to the lack of character or antisocial behavior of some of their residents.

Nope. They just blame bigotry and the indifference of white corporate America.

In the end, I believe the truth of the matter usually can be traced back to their community's tradition of apologizing or making excuses for the behavior of the thugs who have a bold disregard for mainstream American values.

In a chapter entitled "Black Thugs" from my book *Pick a Better Country*, I write about the caustic culture and irrational urban logic of the gangsters in these communities.

I describe the values of these lost souls, whose only hope of real success in this world has been squandered, run aground by small-minded, irrational and immoral community leaders who allow their antisocial behavior to thrive.

A perfect example of this twisted value system is exemplified by a recent row in Atlantic City, New Jersey.

According to an article from the August issue of *The Press of Atlantic City,* City Council president Rosalind Norrell-Nance is up in arms over plans by Thriftway Supermarket to construct a fence around its property in order to stem the theft of its shopping carts.

Norrell-Nance has reasoned that the construction of such a fence by the supermarket would perpetuate an ugly stereotype about blacks being prone to steal, and that would constitute a slap in the face to the African-Americans Thriftway was built to serve.

Of course, if you ask me, Thriftway entered into the agreement to build a supermarket in Atlantic City's ghetto because its parent company ignored good business logic in the first place.

It got sucked into a deal involving $14 million in public and private funding to build a center called Renaissance Plaza in the city's poor black community.

According to the *Press* article, it was only the second supermarket to build in the inner city.

But Thriftway has been forced to come to grips with the fact that as thanks from the community, half of its shopping carts have vanished since the store opened in June.

Desperate for a solution, Thriftway executives decided they would build the fence to try to retain the remainder of their carts.

According to one company executive, "If there was a *Guinness Book of World Records* for this type of thing, we would have broken it."

It's obviously not a laughing matter, however, when you consider the cost of the carts—about $100 a pop.

According to the *Press,* Thriftway has been forced to order 200 new carts since the market opened for business. Routinely losing 200 shopping carts at $100 apiece means that Thriftway has to sell a lot of food to break even, much less show a profit.

After struggling for decades to find a corporation silly enough to invest in the ghetto, you would think that Norrell-Nance would have been savvy enough to encourage her constituents not to tarnish a good thing.

Instead, in the tradition of irrational inner-city black politicians, she has launched an attack against Thriftway, threatening to shame it publicly on the grounds that:

"This community will not tolerate being stereotyped. I'm sure this is not the way you want to be perceived in the city."

Corporate racism or foolish African-American politicians? Whichever is the case, one wonders how many more supermarkets will set up business in Atlantic City's black ghetto.

A Community Proves
It Can Say No
to Crime

First published September 1994

An eighty-one-year-old civil rights heroine named Rosa Parks was taken to the hospital and treated for facial bruises after becoming another victim of black-on-black crime in her Detroit home.

Parks is a soft-spoken, durable black woman who has been aptly dubbed the mother of the modern civil rights movement because she refused to give up her seat to a white man on a Montgomery, Alabama, bus in December of 1955.

According to Detroit police chief Isaiah McKinnon, Parks was upstairs in her home about 8:20 P.M. when she heard a noise. She went downstairs to investigate and saw that her back door had been knocked off the hinges. She saw a young black stranger who she said stank of alcohol. Parks reported that the man babbled incoherently about coming to protect her, then hit her in the face and robbed her of $50.

Detroiters were stunned when they learned that Parks had been attacked. Cliff Russell, a spokesman for Mayor Dennis Archer, said, "I don't know what to say about anyone who would do something like that to Rosa Parks."

The attack on Rosa Parks was an affront to the entire nation.

But it was doubly shameful to the blacks who reside in the inner city of Detroit. And so, as if attempting to redeem Motown from the criticism of the country, neighbors in Rosa Parks's community mobilized to search for a young black man who fit the description of the intruder. Shortly, he was arrested and charged with the crime.

First, let me say I am glad this suspect was apprehended and is in police custody today. But more important, I hope that the significance of the citizens' in that black Detroit neighborhood contributing to the quick apprehension of Parks's alleged attacker isn't ignored.

Their action means that the hokum frequently spouted by white liberals and black community leaders that poor African-Americans are trapped in the ghetto and unable to fight the criminals or chase away the whores, pimps and drug dealers is, in fact, a bunch of bunk.

I've been saying for a long time that if a community gets angry enough, it can reclaim the streets for its good citizens.

I grant the fact that the capture of Rosa Parks's attacker by the men of her community clearly represented more of a courageous act than a similar act might have been by the citizens of Grosse Pointe, one of Detroit's most affluent suburbs.

Still, I think this community uprising proves two things:

First, it proves that even in the worst ghetto or barrio, poor and deprived people will act when a certain line is crossed. But it also proves that the men and women who continue to endure the abnormally high rate of crime in the urban ghettos of our once-great cities apparently have made a choice to live with it most of the time.

Their having done so may mean that no amount of money or commitment by outsiders to alter their society and improve their quality of life is likely to make much of a difference.

What other conclusion can you draw from the lack of community indignation and seeming tolerance of Detroit's 205 motorcar hijackings during a twenty-one-day period in July 1991? Or the fact that there was no massive protest from the city's black residents when William Hart, chief of police under Mayor Coleman Young, was indicted in February of 1991 for stealing $2.6 million from the city?

As for Rosa Parks, evidently being beaten and robbed isn't a part of a lifestyle or culture she is willing to endure, because reports are she has decided to move to a safer neighborhood where black boys— who weren't alive when she said no to white racism in 1955—are less likely to mug her.

Liberal Experiments Produce Generation of Superpredators

First published May 1996

The nation was rocked to its core when it was reported that a six-year-old boy in Richmond, California, was accused of nearly beating to death a month-old infant while trying to steal a Hot Wheels tricycle. I dubbed the youngster "the demon" on my radio show.

Liberals yelped that the assailant was a mere child, too young to be institutionalized, and thus should be sent back to his mother's home. Nonetheless, the boy was taken into custody, and now the system is pondering what to do with an accused violent criminal so very young.

Pondering also are the broad-minded folks—those who routinely have branded all forms of discipline, including spanking, as oppression and violence. They are wondering what makes a child that young capable of such violence.

Certainly, this boy's case is shocking. But is it unusual? Apparently not, according to another front-page story in the *Denver Post*.

"A 10-year-old boy was being held . . . as a 'potential suspect' in the apparent brutal beating death of an 18-month-old girl at their Englewood home.... Jazmine Haen died ... from severe injuries she received while being cared for by the boy and a 19-year-old man in the house. . . .

"Police were tight-lipped about the details of the incident and the investigation.... But they said the 10-year-old boy, who was baby-sitting the toddler, was being held. . . .

"The baby's mother and the boy's family say he isn't responsible for the girl's fatal injuries, and said they wonder why the police have him in custody."

The eighteen-year-old mother of the baby said she had seen bruises on Jazmine before after she had been left with the nineteen-year-old, and siblings of the boy in custody said they have seen the child abused before.

Despite what most of us would love to believe, the secret of good and healthy child nurturing isn't transferred from one generation to the next through the miracle of genetics. Thus not every woman is a good mother, any more than every man is a good father.

Time and experience are showing us that genetics cannot overcome the toll being taken by a subculture where children see their fathers shot, or their mothers arrested for hooking and peddling drugs.

It doesn't surprise me that any child left to languish in environments like those learns quickly that life is a short ride, and you had better grab what you can.

Social workers and the police have warned us to fasten our seat belts to ready ourselves for the emergence of a colder and younger predator.

In Denver, it's still too early to tell why an eighteen-month-old baby may have died at the hands of a ten-year-old. But in California, we are learning the simple motive of a violent six-year-old.

According to prosecutors, the *San Francisco Examiner* reported, the boy didn't like the way the baby's father looked at him. So he decided to get even with the baby's parents.

I am frequently accused of shamelessly bashing liberals.

"Gosh," they say, "you can't blame us for everything."

Well, I wouldn't say for everything. But I definitely hold liberals accountable for eroding the cornerstones of our culture when it comes to a civilized social order and the nuclear family—a unit comprising a father, mother and disciplined children.

The social experimenters have had their day. Between the 1960s and the 1990s, they have dabbled in unimaginable new-fangled and unsound notions—like schools without walls run by unqualified administrators—which together have produced a generation with way too many illiterate children.

They have given in to the shrill cries of radical feminists who proclaimed that the need for men, especially men as fathers, was passé. Test-tube fertilization made them obsolete.

The experimenters have allowed babies to have babies, and then supported the state paying for unending numbers of them.

Well, the results of the experimenting, which threw out discipline and age-old standards, are coming home to roost—in the form of a young and ruthless superpredator.

I'm not confused at all about why a child only a decade old would prey on another who is younger, smaller and weaker than he is. Thanks to the unchecked notions of open-minded liberals, today we have living among us a human animal that hunts and seizes what it wants, whenever and from whomever it pleases.

The youthful superpredator is just one of the tragic outcomes I predicted would come to pass when the standards of decent behavior and civility were permitted to be disputed.

Kids
Without Moral Rudders

First published June 1998

Ever since the most recent incident of a Middle America schoolboy mowing down his classmates (in Springfield, Oregon) pop psychologists have been showing up on television and radio talk shows at a furious rate.

But I haven't heard one of them utter a fresh idea about how to prevent a rudderless boy like Kipland P. "Kip" Kinkel from running amok in his adolescence and murdering all the people he either dislikes or feels inferior to.

Kinkel, fifteen, is charged with murdering his parents at home, then driving to Thurston High School and opening fire with a .22–caliber rifle, killing two of his classmates and injuring twenty-two others.

While these pop shrinks, social workers and kiddie coddlers lack the honesty to acknowledge to us or themselves that they don't have a clue about how to head off problems with kids like Kinkel, it is obvious that the lax stance in the matter of overseeing and disciplining children that they have advocated, has not worked.

Case in point:

After Kinkel fulfilled his urge to murder, the people of Springfield learned from newspaper accounts that he had been arrested less than twenty-four hours before the shootings.

Arrested, but not detained. How can such a thing be?

It's easy, because in the ethereal world where liberals exist there aren't any bad seeds—simply misunderstood boys and girls who would benefit more readily from hugs and kisses than from hard-nosed discipline.

By that logic, Kinkel wasn't transported to a juvenile facility to be processed and detained when police officers found a loaded .32–caliber semi-automatic Beretta handgun in his school locker. Nope. He was just suspended from school and sent home to stew about his perceived persecution.

No doubt there are those among you who will consider my perspective—that a benevolent dictatorship is always best where children and adolescents are concerned—to be a primitive form of thinking and a classic case of Monday-morning quarterbacking.

Be that as it may, few of us can dispute the fact that with the escalation of violence in Middle America's schoolhouses, the time is ripe to have a come-to-Jesus meeting concerning whether the liberal notions about child rearing that the government has stuffed down the throats of U.S. parents is pushing us farther along the road of anarchy brought about by our youth.

The pop shrinks may be talking doublespeak about what to do with the Kinkels of America, but solutions abut what to do abound from the people who telephone my syndicated talk radio show.

"Ken, we need to put God back into the schools."

That sounds like a good idea to me. With American kids gunning one another down—first in the ghettos and now in mainstream American schools—what have we got to lose?

"Ken, it's impossible for parents to discipline their children today with the government telling them and their teachers what they cannot do."

That's true too. And the kids know it and play it for all it's worth. I call it the "you can't do nothing to me because I'm a kid" syndrome.

Take the case of one elementary school teacher in New York who was attacked and assaulted by four sixth-grade girls demanding to watch the *Jerry Springer* show on the classroom's TV. According to the police report, the forty-one-year-old teacher suffered bruises on her face, neck, back and legs. But she chose not to press charges.

Or take the case of the San Diego sophomore whose objection to reciting the Pledge of Allegiance is being championed by the American Civil Liberties Union. In her infinite wisdom, acquired during fifteen years of life, this student said she thought about what the pledge actually meant and disagreed with its message.

Kids aren't stupid. Given the opportunity, they will push the envelope to test their parents, their teachers and society's limits. It's what they are supposed to do. That's how kids become independent thinkers; it's how they grow up.

But unless society is willing to do its part by providing margins and guidelines, it's my decided opinion that killings like the one in Springfield are just the beginning of a burly chicken coming home to roost.

EIGHT

Cops

The Thin Blue Line

First published August 1995

There was a hurried phone call in the final moments of my talk radio show one day from a police officer named Jason in Columbia, South Carolina.

Jason was appreciative of my ongoing support for law enforcement, but curious about what had spawned that support.

The clock forced me to end the program before I could get beyond the point that obviously some of the support I express for American police officers—in fact most policemen and policewomen around the world—stems from the fact that my own father was once a member of the New City Police Department.

But had time permitted, I would have told Jason that my support for those who serve and protect is founded on more than the fact that my dad proudly carried a badge and a gun and was sworn to uphold America's laws.

I would have said that some of my support is to counteract the fact that we commission cops to enforce the law but then we hobble them when we permit white liberals and minority apologists to force them to coddle baby-faced thugs on the grounds that they are nothing more than poor misguided kids.

I would have told Jason I back cops—guys like him—because after all the romantic movies have been produced, and the reams of sorrowful stories have been published in newspapers across the nation about punks with guns and their heroic struggle to get ahead in the ghetto, it's the men and women of the thin blue line, not the social workers or their fashionable socialist pals in the media, who have to face these punks who place little value on life.

I would have said I support the cops because too few Americans do.

I defend the police because if we look beyond the uniform, we discover that the man or woman is some mother's daughter or some father's son, or a husband or a wife, maybe a father or a mother themselves.

I choose to support our police in this column and over the airwaves because it's the only logical choice. If you doubt that, consider the alternative by trying to imagine how quickly the street you live on, your neighborhood or your town would be reduced to the hellish violence you read about on the front page of this newspaper without police to stop it.

Most of all, I support the police because they need a voice in the media to confront the growing influence of anti-police sentiment, such as that portrayed in the gangsta rap music that defines and tags our police as targets to be murdered on our streets.

Real targets like Omaha, Nebraska, police officer Jimmy Wilson, Jr., who was discovered recently by residents who live in that city's violence-prone ghetto community still strapped in his seat belt, slumped over the steering wheel of his patrol car. Officer Wilson, twenty-four, had been shot fifteen times. His death was the first among Omaha's police in years.

One of the seven princes of the ghetto arrested and charged in Wilson's death, according to the *Omaha World-Herald*, was an eighteen-year-old who was wanted on an unrelated felony warrant for—you guessed it—another shooting.

Targets abound when you are a ghetto kid inspired to believe that the world hasn't the right or the authority to hold you accountable for your behavior because of the color of your skin. They abound when a pop culture of antisocial behavior and violence has won the right to be considered mainstream in the subculture of the 'hood.

When you consider that convoluted logic, it shouldn't surprise you—or any other normal person—to learn that the main targets of the thugs who prey on our communities have become the men and women with a badge and a gun to enforce the authority to restrain them.

That's reason enough for my support of those who stand on the thinning blue line between the thugs and me . . . and I should think reason enough for you to wave hello to the next flatfoot you go by.

A Perspective on Tragedy

First published April 1997

Like most of the country, I found that my attention was piqued when I awoke to the news last week that thirty-nine people had committed suicide in Rancho Santa Fe, California.

The Associated Press described the death scene in lurid detail:

"The bodies of at least 39 young men [it was discovered later that women were among the dead] lying side by side in matching dark pants and tennis shoes, were found scattered throughout a million-dollar mansion . . . in an apparent mass suicide."

It also became readily apparent they had done their collective deed in order to abandon their earthly form in pursuit of some higher level of consciousness in outer space.

It didn't take long for some overly sympathetic folks to conclude that the nonviolent departure of the "California 39," which I dubbed them on my radio show, was a human tragedy.

I, however, beg to differ.

I remain of the opinion that if a man, a woman or, in this case, an entire group of emancipated Americans wishes to concoct a parable about little green men waiting behind the glow of a comet flitting by our planet and then use that parable as a rationale to slip the surly bonds of earth, then so be it.

Flamboyance does not always a tragedy make.

Unlike the November 18, 1978, mass suicide in Jonestown,

Guyana, where authorities came upon more than 900 followers of the Reverend Jim Jones dead and bloated beneath a hot tropical sun, this group's suicide didn't include the untimely demise of a single child.

All thirty-nine apparently were consenting adults who, after assessing their probability for a gratifying and purposeful life on this earth, simply decided to ditch their mortal bodies in hopes of launching their souls into the great void of outer space.

Other than the pain their suicides undoubtedly inflicted on the people who loved and cared about them, the deaths of these eccentric folks are of little importance—very far removed from the status of an American tragedy.

In fact, after witnessing a videotape of one of the deceased talking about how unfulfilled life was for her on this globe, I would guess that if it were possible to bring them back, she and the others probably would opt for the big sleep again.

All of which leaves me to wonder whether those who are trying to feel their pain are lacking the ability to discern the difference between a real tragedy and a monumental act of selfishness.

Let me explain.

On the same day the story broke about the self-centered California 39, Denver newspapers also carried a story about a rookie cop named Ronald DeHerrera.

DeHerrera, thirty-three, was riding with his training officer, Victor Baca, forty-three, when their patrol car was broadsided by a stolen vehicle joyriding through city streets at 80 or 90 miles per hour.

The real tragedy that occurred in this case was that it was Officer DeHerrera's second day on the job, and that as of this writing, he is still fighting for his life in a Denver hospital.

The real tragedy is the possible loss of one robust human being, a man who felt he had everything to live for—the loss of one man whose lifelong ambition had been simply to be a good cop.

That's a real tragedy, and it overshadows the untimely deaths of any number of emotionally challenged daydreamers who simply decided to cop out of their allotted time on earth.

Encountering
the "Bad Actor"
Behind the Wheel

First published November 1996

A saga of racial unrest in the black ghetto of St. Petersburg, Florida, continues to reverberate across the nation.

And I am struck at how it has given the floor to dusky American opportunists who believe that complete destruction of mainstream police and legal authority would be in the best interests of the people.

Wacky and ridiculous, you say?

Don't kid yourself.

It appears that is exactly what is being championed by the self-styled revolutionaries who have threatened to assassinate St. Pete mayor David Fischer and Police Chief Darrel Stephens. They are protesting a grand jury acquittal of a white police officer who shot a black motorcar thief at the conclusion of a high-speed chase.

The American media almost always proclaims its objectivity in matters like the St. Petersburg riots, but an examination of articles written usually reveals subtleties that leave the Fourth Estate dripping wet with culpability.

A case in point is a November 18 story by Paul Shepard filed with the Associated Press. It reports that the National Urban League is calling for a summit on police conduct in light of the acquittals of police officers both in Pittsburgh and St. Petersburg after the deaths of black motorists in two separate incidents.

The reporter writes: "Both deaths followed routine traffic stops by the officers."

I question just how routine the traffic stop in Pittsburgh could have been since it concluded in the death of thirty-one-year-old Jonny Gammage. Or in St. Petersburg, where the traffic stop terminated in the death of eighteen-year-old Tyron Mark Lewis, alias Michael Tay Cox.

Routine? I think not—unless it was the reporter's intention to suggest that race relations between the black rabble on the streets of America and the police have deteriorated to such a low ebb that it has become routine for police to kill black people during traffic stops.

While some among us may cotton to such notions, this black American begs to differ.

According to the AP story, Hugh B. Price, president of the National Urban League, said, "Occasionally these incidents involve really bad actors but all too often they involve ordinary citizens in what should be routine interaction with police."

Well, let me tell you who the two St. Petersburg police officers confronted after they succeeded in getting Tyron Lewis to come to a stop after a seventy-mile-per-hour chase.

It has been confirmed, though seldom mentioned in the press, that Lewis was running from the police in a stolen motorcar. He had crack cocaine in his possession and, in all probability, was flying as high as a kite when the officers confronted him.

The officer said he shot him when the car lurched forward toward him.

Who was Tyron Lewis? I'd say he was an immature black man rushing to his death. The following was taken from his police arrest record. Scan it, and see whether you agree.

In 1987, when Tyron was nine, he was arrested for trespassing and grand theft.

In 1988, he was arrested again for trespassing on school grounds, obstructing a police officer and burglary.

In 1989, he was arrested for striking a police officer, using an alias, burglary and striking a teacher.

In 1990, he was arrested again for burglary and for grand theft auto.

In 1991, he was arrested for trespassing, retail theft, disrupting a school, criminal mischief, grand theft auto and burglary.

In 1992, he was arrested for cruelty to animals and burglary.

In 1993, he was arrested for possession of a controlled substance, possession of marijuana, grand theft auto and possession of cocaine.

On that fateful day when a St. Petersburg cop found himself lying across the hood of the stolen motorcar—Lewis behind the wheel—I'd say the officer had become little more than a pawn dealt the dirty hand of fulfilling the inevitable. The officer would be the innocent participant in closing the circle around another black punk who long ago had abandoned any thoughts of pursuing a main-stream life adhering to the tenets of right and wrong.

I believe Tyron Mark Lewis was a kid looking for a place to die.

That meant there was little that was "routine" about this traffic stop involving him. Unfortunately, what was too common about this encounter was the "bad actor" behind the wheel.

D.O.A. in the Dumpster

First published April 1998

Whenever the question of why I support the police arises from some flower-power liberal, I generally give the following answer:

"Consider the alternative."

The fact is it's a mean and predatory world, and in most cases cops represent the power that allows most of us to survive un-scathed.

But just supporting the cops isn't enough.

I am also a big proponent of civilians' accepting the standing in-vitation to ride along with their local police on duty. I believe we all can benefit from getting a closer look at the slimy underbelly of the communities we call home.

Recently I scheduled myself to ride with a detective friend and motorcycle pal of mine. Detective Steve Shott is assigned to the homicide division of the Denver Police Department.

It was around eight o'clock on a Thursday night when I settled into Shott's unmarked patrol car.

"We've got to get rolling," he said. "We've got a call."

It involved a newborn baby supposedly found in a Dumpster. I fastened my seat belt and settled back, wondering what the night would hold.

"Is it dead?" I said.

"I don't know," responded Shott. "The uniformed officers are still searching for it."

Just then, as if in response to our questions, the two-way radio in the car transmitted the answer.

It confirmed that at 1379 Lowell there was indeed a baby in the Dumpster.

As abruptly as the radio had come to life, it went silent without telling us whether the baby was dead or alive. The interior of the car felt uncomfortably close. Neither of us said much, while Shott pointed the car toward Lowell Street into the heart of west Denver's Hispanic barrio.

The two-way barked again, Detective Shott acknowledged his call sign and the voice on the other end reported what the two of us feared:

"Ah, ambulance is saying that's D.O.A. Um, just try and make it as quickly as you can and as safely as you can. You'll see all the cars. We're just west of the ambulance."

When we arrived at the scene, two uniformed officers escorted us through an alley and to the back door of the residence where the fourteen-year-old mother of the infant lived with her mom, her father, known to the police as an O.G. (old gangster), formerly with a local Hispanic gang called the Inca-Boys, an older sister and a younger brother.

The word was no one knew the girl had been pregnant. In fact, Mom reportedly fainted when told her daughter had given birth.

I still find it difficult to think of myself as being older than the cop on the beat, but many of the young uniformed officers at the scene were visibly shaken by what they had found.

Some, fathers with newborn babies at home, were given permission by more seasoned officers to step back from the scene to collect themselves and, I would imagine, to still their anger.

I followed Detective Shott to the Dumpster. At first it took a moment to sort the body from the trash. It was lying face down in a white garbage bag. I believe that to anyone looking at that tiny DOA, it was instantly apparent that the child had been deliberately murdered.

But the jury ultimately will have to make that decision. In my mind, though, the Denver district attorney certainly didn't shrink from his duty. The teen has been charged as a minor with first-degree murder—which carries a maximum penalty of seven in a youth detention center.

Predictably, Denver already has begun to divide itself on this issue along racial lines. Some columnists and talk-radio hosts have begun the process of milking the death, posing the question of whether the girl is getting a fair shake. Asking would she have been charged with first-degree murder if she had been white.

Meanwhile, those of us who were there on that chilly evening in April aren't likely to shake the memory of that little DOA any-time soon. A baby boy—whose only crime was that he happened to slide down the wrong birth canal.

Don't Make Cops
the Fall Guys

First published December 1995

For as long as I can remember, this country's men and women in blue have been used as fall guys in the fight against crime by liberal politicians who have to answer to an electorate.

More cops, better cops, cops who aren't racists—these solutions routinely are thrown in as the answer to a disproportionate growth in drug sales and urban violence in select political districts across the country.

President Clinton made an increase in police the cure-all in his

1994 crime bill, claiming funding from the new law would add 100,000 officers across the country. Meanwhile, he went about pursuing what I believe was his real agenda—gun control—by including a ban on nineteen models of semiautomatic weapons in the bill.

In the end, we learned that the new police hires might be only symbolic, because many communities would not be able to continue to support them after initial federal funding dried up.

But to me the whole issue of more cops or better cops may be moot in light of a new Department of Justice study that shows state and federal prisons reported record growth during the last twelve months.

The study revealed an increase of 89,707 inmates in the twelve months ending June 20. It was the largest one-year population boom in state and federal prisons ever recorded by the Justice Department, bringing this nation's inmate population to 1,104,074 men and women.

The combined state and federal prison populations grew by 8.8 percent, which is higher than the average annual growth of 7.9 percent calculated since 1990.

The report indicated that the state prison population increased by 9.1 percent over the same period the year before. The federal prison population increased by 6.1 percent.

State and federal prisons house mostly convicted felons serving sentences of a year or more, according to the Justice Department.

To me, it all seems pretty strong evidence that America's peace officers are doing their part to apprehend this nation's worst criminals.

Of course, the habitual whiners—the Reverend Jesse Jackson, for example—would take that accomplishment away from the cops by complaining that all the prison report proves is a disproportionate number of African-Americans are behind bars.

He's right about the statistics.

The Justice Department confirms that the number of black inmates in state and federal prisons, as well as local jails, has grown faster than the number of white inmates.

The report shows that black male adults are incarcerated at a rate eight times higher than that of white male adults. Likewise, black female adults are incarcerated at a rate seven times higher than that of white female adults.

As of June 30, close to 6.8 percent of all black male adults in America were in jail or prison, compared with less than 1 percent of all white male adults.

This is a tragedy all right. But it's a tragedy spawned for the most part by a permissive system of social coddling that has black ghetto thugs practically immune to old-fashioned standards of right and wrong.

It is not a tragedy—as some would claim—spawned by widespread racism among our American police.

I have said repeatedly that the Mark Fuhrmans of the world must be cut out of the force, shunned by fellow officers and stopped from their illegal and evil endeavors behind their badges.

But I contend that they are weeding themselves out—thanks to the morality inherent in American public opinion.

No, the real tragedy is that in light of especially high black crime rates, liberal politicians and minority community leaders try to use cops as scapegoats—claiming they are a big source of the problem of a growing criminal element in America.

They try to shift the blame to the cops when hard-nosed policies to back up the cop on the beat are the real answers to stopping the rise of black and urban crime.

But solutions like that require moral political leaders willing to take a stand to support the basic principles of right and wrong upon which America was founded.

For my part, I'd like to send a big thank-you to all the men and women in blue for a job well done. May God continue to bless all of you who have taken on the seemingly thankless task to serve and protect.

Police Put Their
Lives on the Line

First published July 1998

The recent murders of two police officers at our nation's Capitol momentarily heightened our awareness of the men and women who stand—quite literally in this sad case—between the killers and average American citizens.

But I wonder how many who mourned this high-profile tragedy consider that the Angel of Death reaches out all too frequently to touch the police officers sworn to protect us.

Every day cops, expected to give their all on a moment's notice, find themselves in situations that easily could result in the lives of their families, friends and colleagues being altered forever.

No doubt that has been the impact on family and friends following the heroic, yet tragic, deaths of Jacob Chestnut, fifty-eight, and John Gibson, forty-two, two members of the 1,250-person-strong United States Capitol Police.

Both of them joined the force eighteen years ago. Officer Chestnut was a veteran of the U.S. Air Force scheduled to retire in a few months. Both of them were family men—Gibson the father of three and Chestnut with five children and five grandchildren.

It may seem shocking to say—considering how dramatic their deaths were—but experience tells me that the names of Chestnut and Gibson soon will disappear from the public memory.

In spite of the reverence our nation is bestowing on them now—with speaker of the House Newt Gingrich and other congressmen and congresswomen being overcome by the emotion of the moment—I'm willing to bet that before long the media and the public will turn their attention on the killer. We'll hear every detail about the life and times of Russell E. Weston, Jr., forty-one, the Rimini, Montana, man who has been arrested and held accountable for the deaths of Chestnut and Gibson.

The sad fact is that almost every day a police officer dies in our nation.

While their families suffer the devastation, all too often public defenders assert that destitution, mental illness or racial victimization was responsible for the murderer's actions.

Constables on patrol perish in the line of duty all over America, while organizations like the ACLU work to prevent their killers from paying their debt to society.

I must admit I felt a hint of contempt for the cavalcade of politicians decrying the senseless murders of Chestnut and Gibson.

From President Bill Clinton—who, the media reported, continued his golf game while the circumstances surrounding the deaths of Chestnut and Gibson were unfolding—to lesser politicians, all seemed to respond in shock, as if such things just don't happen.

Well, happen they do.

I became aware of the frequent deaths of officers serving on the thin blue line years ago, when I began acknowledging them by name on my radio show.

These officers didn't die on the steps of the Capitol. They served and they perished without notice by the president or any of the other Beltway politicians.

We didn't hear from President Clinton, for instance, when Omaha police officer Jimmy Wilson, Jr., twenty-four, was killed, shot at least fifteen times on August 20, 1995, during a routine traffic stop.

Nor did a Washington statesman speak out for Officer Larry Johnson, forty-four, an eleven-year veteran of the Sparks, Nevada, police department, who was gunned down on May 22, 1995, by a parolee free on bail.

No national leader commemorated Brent Holloway, twenty-seven, with the Teller County, Colorado, sheriff's department, who died October 16, 1995, from a shotgun blast to the face while sitting in his patrol car at the site of an arson fire.

I'm no politician. I don't speak for any Congressional or Senatorial district. And I concede that last week's fallen officers struck close to home for Washington's politicos. But I still think the ease with which the media routinely overlooks the everyday deaths of our men and women in blue is a tragedy.

So I will continue to honor all officers killed in the line of duty by playing taps on my radio show whenever word reaches me that another cop has fallen. In a continuing effort to be sure that heroic men like Jacob Chestnut and John Gibson are not forgotten, I will continue to dedicate a section of my web page (hamblin.com) to them.

And when I hear people demean or dismiss police and their role in our civilized society, I ask them to consider the alternative. Consider a world—let alone the United States Capitol—without police standing guard.

Go with God, Jacob Chestnut and John Gibson. Go with God, knowing that you were loved, honored and respected. And like others before you, may you and your families rest assured that some of us know you have given your all to our republic.

Who Wants to Go Home to the Ghetto?

First published July 1997

In another one of his sweetheart gestures, as only he can dish out, Bill Clinton has been moved to address the plight of America's downtrodden, decaying cities.

The president's newest notion supposedly is designed to make it easier for hardworking families, particularly families of police officers, to become homeowners.

The new federal proposal would grant as many as two thousand police officers a 50 percent discount on ghetto dwellings currently owned by the Department of Housing and Urban Development.

As a further incentive, first-time buyers would be granted a whopping $200 discount in closing costs.

Wow.

Clinton calls it his "Urban Homestead" incentive plan, and he chose the U.S. Conference of Mayors shindig in San Francisco to unveil it.

I'm guessing that the liberal feudal lords in charge of our urban centers will be eager to snuggle up to this newest federally supported plan to try to salvage their decaying fiefdoms—or at least keep them from slipping further into the abyss.

What got my attention concerning Clinton's magnanimous "Urban Homestead" announcement was the "Officer Next Door" part of it. I was amazed that he and other bigwigs in government actually believe that police officers, who already spend their time on the job working on the mean streets of the urban ghetto, would actually be interested in calling those streets home.

Liberals like Clinton, along with myopic African-American mayors who hold sway in cities like East St. Louis and Detroit, always tend to overlook one basic fact.

Inner cities have been abandoned because some of the people who live there have been either allowed or encouraged to believe that their barbaric culture of dealing drugs, robbing and killing is socially and politically justified because they are poor, because they are a minority or because they had a bad childhood.

Validating a culture like this one produces neighborhoods where laissez-faire gun battles and open-air drug sales are deemed a rite of passage for disenfranchised black boys touted to be perpetual victims of white American racism.

This cultural anomaly adds a very dire dimension to a crime problem.

And I, for one, can't think of any rational person who would voluntarily move his or her family into a ghetto where street gangs operate with reckless abandon in that culture.

The last person I would single out to receive this special incentive to move into harm's way is the urban beat cop.

Frankly, I'm at a loss to explain what in tarnation—short of contempt for the thinning blue line of men and women who toil every day to hold back the urban thugs—would inspire the president to believe that once they achieved a middle-class salary and status to afford them a way out of the urban jungle, these cops would want to expose their families to the violence they see already all too closely.

In fact, when I heard about Clinton's "Urban Homestead" plan, it reminded me of something a police officer friend of mine once said.

This man, who had attained the rank of detective, was a seasoned, hard-nosed street cop with decades of experience on the job and an enviable reputation for getting his man or woman once he caught the scent.

"Ken," he said, "want to know how you stop a cop who is on your trail?"

I looked at him, thinking I was about to have my leg pulled. But then I noticed that he wasn't joshing. From the expression on his face, I saw that he was deadly serious.

"Yes," I responded. "Tell me."

"You threaten his family. If I ever thought that the bad guys I chase every day could get to my wife or my kids, I'd walk away from this job in a minute."

"Urban Homestead" incentive plan? "Officer Next Door"?

Sorry, Mr. President. I don't think so.

Cops in Ghetto Housing Good Only for Pols

First published October 1998

The Associated Press reported recently that more police officers across the nation are going to be eligible to buy homes for half price and possibly at reduced mortgage rates if they are willing to move into low-income neighborhoods. When I read about it, I laughed and immediately tagged it for what it was—a federally sponsored "Roast a Pig" program.

If you're naive and don't savvy exactly what the government means by low-income neighborhoods, the fed is talking about those inner-city communities where in most cases thugs, dope dealers and gang-bangers rule the roost.

More to the point, these are neighborhoods where Mr. Policeman seldom is considered a citizen's best friend, but rather an adversary intent on upholding the laws the rest of us think are a good thing.

It's an understatement to say the policemen and -women who put their lives on the line each day to preserve civilized society are generally despised in these communities. Even a lot of the law-abiding residents have been persuaded that the cops are racist because they try to maintain order and thus arrest the thugs of color.

Nonetheless, Vice President Al Gore used a White House ceremony not long ago to announce that the "Officer Next Door" program managed by the Department of Housing and Urban Development would be expanded to include a thousand more police officers in its second year.

The program was begun in 1997, and I denounced it then.

But supposedly, more than two thousand of the nation's police officers have taken advantage of the chance to purchase a house in America's ghettos at close to give-away rates. Not that I doubt what Washington tells us, but I have to wonder about this.

I have a lot of friends who are cops, and I find it difficult to imagine that the men and women who toil every day in the soft underbelly of the ghetto and the barrio would be willing to expose themselves and their families to the insecure, chaotic, dangerous lifestyle practiced in most of these urban neighborhoods.

Judging by the continuing reports of urban hooliganism and the continuing liberal tendency to coddle instead of punishing the bad guys, I think the vice president's claim that all those cops have taken advantage of the chance to purchase a piece of the ghetto surely must be misleading—if not an out-and-out lie.

Not only does such a claim weaken the effectiveness of our constables on patrol but, I suspect, it's also a roundabout technique to try to keep ill-informed blacks and Hispanics sold on the notion that ghettos are swell places to live.

Sound silly?

Not really. Not when you consider that barrio-based Hispanics and ghetto-based blacks traditionally vote as they are instructed—almost always for Hispanic and African-American liberals who have those districts locked up without serious political challenge.

Could it be a coincidence that the African-American voting bloc is the only one completely intact as the Democrats are torn apart by President Clinton's bad judgment?

According to the Clinton administration, the theory is that if a cop lives in a neighborhood, it's likely crime will decline in the area, and that, of course, encourages this xenophobic voting bloc to stay put.

Since the program is only a year old, there can't be any meaningful statistics to confirm whether cops embedded in ghetto communities actually help to reduce crime. But that hasn't stopped the White House from declaring the program a glowing success.

The whole thing just doesn't ring true to me, though, when you consider that we live in a society where thugs from these mean urban streets still gun down police officers sitting in their patrol cars.

What is apparent to me is that Gore and the rest of the Clinton administration are not above marketing the notion to the American people—in particular, to their last solid voting bloc, African-Americans—that, thanks to them, urban ghettos and barrios are on the mend.

As proof of that success, they contend that America's policemen and policewomen are willing to move their families lock, stock and barrel into the bowels of those sad neighborhoods. Sorry, folks, but my street sense tells me this program may be good for one group only—the politicians.

NINE

Justice

Even Cops Going
Soft on Felons?

First published March 1996

Last Saturday, I was pursuing my love of recreational motorcycling on my "hog"—an affectionate term reserved for the Harley Davidson brand of bike—with a group of friends, many of whom are Denver area cops.

On one of our pit stops, our lighthearted conversation happened to turn to the subject of felony-class criminals.

Between bouts of uproarious laughter and high praise for the quality of the day, one detective, who works for a metropolitan police department bordering Denver, spoke casually of a particular criminal whom he described as not being such a bad guy because he had been convicted of only one felony.

"Hold on," I said. "Just what kind of a garbage-can world do you guys live in? He's not a bad guy because he has accrued only one felony? Hey, guys, think about what you're saying. I've never been convicted of a felony offense. Neither have my friends or the people who work with me."

I passionately pleaded with them to remember that a felony offense on any one of their records would have prohibited them from becoming police officers.

They couldn't become a member of the Colorado or almost any other state legal bar association. Being a felon, they couldn't even get a job hauling the U.S. mail.

About then, someone said, "Don't let Kenny get on his soapbox."

I caught myself getting crazy on my day off.

"No, I'm not going to do that," I said. "But listen to yourselves. You guys have been ground down by a justice system that's become so liberal and permissive in favor of the bad guys that you can't see the forest for the trees.

"What do you mean, he isn't a bad guy because he has only accrued one felony? That logic epitomizes the guff spouted by the liberal prosecutors who won't ask for the death penalty and the liberal judges who put the bad guys back onto the street—sometimes before you finish the paperwork to process them."

My detective pal said, "Kenny may be right. I guess we are getting all screwed up about this. We've begun rating guys according to the number of felonies they've committed. If it's six, we think of them as bad guys. If it's three or four, we say they're jerks. If a guy's committed only one felony, we say he's not such a bad guy."

Someone else said, "Hey, no more talking business. This is our day to ride."

Whereupon the conversation returned to more important matters—like which way to ride next.

But I thought about my chat with those hard-core cops the rest of the weekend. And I am sad to say I believe it revealed the presence of a giant fissure beginning to spread through the tattered remnants of the thinning blue line.

Over the past thirty years, law-abiding Americans have witnessed, much to their horror, the flagrant liberalizing and thus the systematic dismantling of our institution of justice by white liberals and minority apologists.

Liberalism dictates, in the name of understanding cultural diversity and fighting oppression, that it may be okay for some Americans to aspire to be pimps, to sell drugs and to kill one another because their skin is dark.

It's unlikely that these bellowing minorities and their sidekicks, the bleeding-heart white liberals, ever will face up to the truth. The truth is that coddling habitual thugs—like rating them not so bad if they have committed only one felony—is a failed and illogical approach to stopping the growing mayhem on our city streets.

Today our entire justice system is under an attack rooted in permissiveness.

It is under attack because African-American apologists have reasoned that too many blacks are incarcerated.

And unfortunately, these ideologies and illogical premises are gaining a foothold—apparently even among those once least likely to succumb.

On my ride home last Saturday, I realized that I had inadvertently glimpsed firsthand a crack in the last line of defense against the liberal reason that declares people who steal, who do bodily harm and who kill to be just victims of a mean-spirited society.

Unfortunately, I realized that my friends—men who carry the burden of the uniformed beat cop, who wear the plain clothes of the robbery detail, the homicide squad and the FBI agent, those men with decades of police experience among them—are being polluted right along with the social work and court systems they used to be at odds with.

Baltimore Needs Sheriff Joe Arpaio

First published January 1999

Some time ago, Joe Arpaio, sheriff of Maricopa County, Arizona, was faced with an overpopulation of criminals and people awaiting trial and an undersized county jail. But he refused to throw in the towel just because liberal politicians resisted the idea of building a new prison facility.

Instead, he erected surplus military tents from World War II on the jailhouse grounds to accommodate the new inmates. And to stay within his budget, Sheriff Arpaio served military MREs (meals ready to eat) to the new residents of his expanded jail.

You might expect that the good sheriff would have won accolades for his brilliance in the matter of accommodating, feeding and watering his growing community of detainees and convicted criminals.

You might even expect he would have won converts to the idea that the judicial and penal system can and must find ways to expand to accommodate all those folks who run afoul of the law.

But in Maricopa County, the liberals took him to court, asserting that compelling people to live in tents and eat military rations was cruel and unusual punishment.

In his usual cool and collected way, Sheriff Arpaio won his day in court by arguing that if canvas tents and MREs were good enough for our servicemen and servicewomen serving in the Gulf War against Iraq, they were good enough for the bad guys and gals in his county jail.

In the end, Joe Arpaio's creative law enforcement won him the unofficial title of Toughest Sheriff in the U.S.A.

Unfortunately, there are not enough Joe Arpaios.

Consider another criminal justice story about how liberals tried and, in fact, did gum up the law to the benefit of the bad guys.

The case in point concerns justice thwarted in Baltimore in the murder of Shawn L. Suggs, twenty-one. According to the Associated Press, Suggs was murdered in October 1995, when he was ambushed and shot by Donte Spivey, twenty-two; William Harrison, twenty-one; Stacey Wilson, twenty-nine; and Jay Anderson, thirty. The four were formally charged with his murder.

But amazingly, last week the murder charges against the four defendants were dismissed .

Why, you ask?

Because, according to the AP, their trial had been repeatedly postponed, at least half the time because no courtroom space was available. Circuit Judge Roger W. Brown ordered the case dismissed because the delays, twelve in all, had caused the speedy-trial deadline for the four men to pass. Trials are supposed to be held within six months of a defendant's first court appearance.

Besides no courtroom space, the other half of the delays reportedly were caused by the unavailability of defense attorneys, prosecutors or witnesses.

And thus, in the truest broad-minded interpretation of liberal fairness—and the absolute letter of the law—four possible killers were cut loose from their day in court to swagger back onto the tough streets of Baltimore.

The AP also reported that a whopping 43 percent of all the cases heard in Baltimore in the first ten months of 1998 were postponed. Currently, there is a backlog of some 5,500 cases.

So is this release of four possible killers just the tip of the iceberg? I believe it well could be.

To which I say, God help Baltimore—and the multitude of other bastions of liberal justice in major American urban centers today.

Judge Brown's ruling was based on a recent decision by Maryland's Court of Special Appeals, which threw out the sex-crime conviction of one defendant because his case had been postponed nine times for the lack of a courtroom.

Although it isn't perfectly clear at the moment, Maryland prosecutors are wondering what the consequences of Judge Brown's ruling will be on other cases currently backed up in the legal pipeline.

Circuit Judge David B. Mitchell noted, "It doesn't take a rocket scientist to figure out what the possibilities are."

Meanwhile, according to a December 28 story in the *Washington Times,* Baltimore has recorded more than three hundred homicides a year for nearly a decade.

In the final weekend of 1998 alone, the *Times* reported:

"Dana Ellerby, 21, was shot and killed Saturday on Garrison Avenue around noon. . . . Later that day, a man was found dead of a gunshot wound on Edmondson Avenue. . . . Yesterday afternoon a body was found in Leakin Park off Weathervane Road. Homicide detectives did not know the exact cause of death yet."

One wonders how many killers in Baltimore know they might win the waiting game.

Would that Baltimore had a few good judges who were cut from the same mold as Maricopa County sheriff Joe Arpaio. A little creativity on the part of law enforcement and the politicians might have saved that city from the bleeding-heart liberals apparently bent on letting civilized society run amok.

Liberating the Candyman

First published May 1997

Recently the *New York Times* reported that a federal appeals court in Manhattan ruled that judges have a responsibility to require jurors to abide by the evidence and the law in deciding a case, instead of relying on their own values to determine a defendant's guilt or innocence.

The ruling was against a growing practice known as jury nullification, in which a juror might vote to excuse a crime and acquit the defendant for reasons such as his race or economic condition, ignoring the facts of the case.

Many Americans believed jury nullification occurred in the O.J. Simpson case when a predominantly black jury acquitted the defendant because they believed the L.A. police were prejudiced against black people in general. A Middle America backlash against high taxes and too much big government has led to other cases of supposed jury nullification.

Whatever the motive, jury nullification is in vogue among more and more Americans from all walks of life who feel for one reason or another that they have an ax to grind with this country's judicial system.

According to the *Times*, a three-judge panel in the appeals court took a strong stand against jury nullification in connection with this Albany, New York, drug case:

Jurors in the case complained to the judge that one juror— the only black member of the panel—was determined not to apply the law, believing instead that the defendants had "a right to deal drugs."

After talking with the jurors, the trial judge surmised that the African-American juror believed the defendants had a right to ped-

dle drugs in flagrant violation of the law because they "were in a dis-
advantaged situation," and "no matter what the evidence was," he
would not vote to convict.

The judge released the African-American juror from his duties,
and the eleven remaining jurors voted to convict.

Judge José Cabranes, writing for the unanimous three-judge
opinion, upheld the local judge's decision. He labeled the potential
jury nullification "a violation of a juror's sworn duty to follow the
law as instructed by the court."

He further concluded that "trial courts have a duty to forestall
or prevent such conduct" by admonishing or even dismissing jurors
who do not follow the law.

The sad fact is that the race card is played more and more frequently in our court system by African-American attorneys, community activists and so-called civil rights groups to absolve
themselves and the underclass black community of taking responsibility for the breakdown of civility in their downtrodden ghetto
communities.

But if the lawful residents of drug- and crime-ridden ghettos
are ever to gain the upper hand against the decay they face on the
streets, they—not just the courts—will have to speak out against the
reasoning of black jurors like the one in Albany.

Otherwise, we are attempting to maintain two separate societies—one law-abiding but groveling behind walled and barricaded
communities, and the other advancing the theory that black criminals can do no wrong because of historical crimes against them.

Jury nullification is a topic raised on my radio talk show from
time to time, and it is tied to more issues than race and the "disad-
vantaged."

Some folks who advocate using it perceive jury nullification to
be a legitimate tool to thwart a judicial system stacked with activist
judges who have abandoned the basic tenets of the U.S. Constitution
in pursuit of their socialist goals.

I'm not sure I can totally disagree with them about these judges,
but I can't totally commit to their tactics either. What I can say with
certainty is that we the people of the United States will be headed

down a slippery slope on the day we allow jury nullification to be used as a means of liberating the Candyman.

Give Felons the Vote?

First published October 1998

While Democrats busily argue that their national poll *du jour* proves that a majority of Americans are okay with the fact that President Bill Clinton deliberately lied under oath, it looks as though liberal opportunists are preparing to drop yet another shoe in their campaign to erode our nation's values.

This one's a clodhopper that will take us one more step down the path to the dismantlement of our justice system and the perpetuation of racial mistrust.

It's embodied in an alarming report, *Losing the Vote: The Impact of Felony Disenfranchisement Laws in the United States*, which is a collaboration between the Washington-based Sentencing Project and the New York–based Human Rights Watch.

"13 PERCENT OF BLACK MEN NOT ALLOWED TO VOTE," screamed the headline in my hometown newspaper.

That's the kind of report that catches my attention, and I immediately scanned the story, courtesy of the Gannett News Service.

How could it be, I wondered, that so many black men could be disenfranchised, especially after the four decades of turmoil our nation went through to protect the voting rights of her black citizens?

When I saw that the report in question was cosponsored by the Washington-based Sentencing Project, however, I suspected that there might be a catch. I'd crossed philosophical foils with this left-wing organization on my syndicated talk radio show before, and I knew their methods.

Sure enough. As it turned out, the 13 percent of black voters the Sentencing Project was whining about were convicted felons.

"An estimated 3.9 million Americans . . . have currently or permanently lost their voting rights as a result of a felony conviction," the report noted. "Of that number, 1.4 million are African-American men . . . a rate seven times the national average."

In the unending liberal game of pitting blacks and whites against each other, the report paid little attention to the 2.5 million felons who are equally denied the vote but find no vocal champion because they don't happen to be black.

Instead, Marc Mauer, the report's coauthor and a Sentencing Project assistant director, chose to further exacerbate the already combustible notion of discrimination that is prevalent among dysfunctional blacks, urban politicians, community leaders and the criminals themselves.

"Fifty years after the beginning of the civil rights movement," Mauer said, "it is tragic that every day more black citizens lose their voting rights. This is not just a criminal-justice issue, but one of basic democracy."

These claims of discrimination, however, don't stand up even in the context of the report itself, which justly notes: "In 46 states and the District of Columbia, criminal-disenfranchisement laws deny the vote to all convicted adults in prison."

Now, I certainly can understand why this would trouble white liberals across our nation and worry black politicians, especially those in the District of Columbia, where even the mayor is a convicted felon.

But it doesn't take an especially acute American to see what the liberals are up to.

"With as low a rate of voter participation as we already have, we should be doing everything we can to be inclusive," Mauer told the press. "Even if just 10 percent voted, that would be close to half a million more voters."

I dare say Mauer doubts that those enfranchised felons would vote Republican.

And there would be an extra benefit to the restoration of convicted felons to the voter rolls: the restoration of their right to sit on a criminal jury. Given the growing tendency toward jury nullification among blacks who already believe that there are too many black men doing time, that should appeal to Mauer at least as much as it alarms me.

Try to imagine the impact black felons would have on a jury pondering the guilt or innocence of black defendants.

On this basis alone, I consider the Sentencing Project report to be more than just another pile of liberal bunk. It is one more assault by left-wingers against the American justice system, an assault black students in our nation's law schools undoubtedly will be encouraged to join.

Mauer is either an imbecile, which I doubt, or a ruthless propagandist who is consciously attempting to mislead my people into believing it is racist to punish black felons.

Why would he do such a thing? As always, I believe that the answer comes down to political leverage.

I suspect that the liberals hope to use this new report as a political club with which to bludgeon into silence Republican opponents of an upcoming drive to give felons the vote.

TEN

Guns

D.C. Cop Challenges
Gun Control

First published April 1996

The National Rifle Association hit the nail on the head when it noted in a press release:

"In what must be a nightmare for Handgun Control, Inc., four members of the Metropolitan Washington, D.C., Police Department met with about 100 crime-weary Capitol Hill residents March 19 to discuss home security, including how D.C. citizens could legally own shotguns and rifles for home defense."

The force behind this radical move to disclose ways that law-abiding citizens can defend themselves against a growing tidal wave of urban crime in Washington was none other than Lieutenant Lowell K. Duckett. A twenty-eight-year police veteran and the president of the Black Police Caucus, Duckett currently is head of the Delta crime-fighting unit, organized to track down street thugs.

I talked with "Duck the Duckster," as he is referred to by his childhood friends, on my syndicated radio show. I took an instant liking to him and to the strong Christian values he uses to define right and wrong.

He was very straightforward regarding his opinion about results—actually the lack of results—brought about by Washington's 1976 gun-reform law, among the nation's most stringent.

"Today if you see a man with a gun in Washington, he's either a crook or a cop," Duckett told me and my radio audience.

According to an article in the *Washingtonian* magazine last August, the police in the District of Columbia's Seventh District are at war with the gang-bangers.

The magazine quoted Duckett as saying, "It's not unlike Vietnam, where American troops had a hard time telling the civilians from the guerrillas. Make a mistake and a cop can die."

Of course, cops aren't the only folks who must fear for their lives in the District of Columbia. Washington is infamous for its black-on-black violence. The fact is anyone who happens to cross paths with the thugs who have taken over the streets is at extreme risk.

Tragically, though, whenever law-abiding black or white citizens of our nation's capital muster the courage to speak out to demand that something be done to curb crime, they usually are accused of being insensitive. The predominantly African-American criminals who have frightened them off the streets of their city aren't really bad boys, the citizens are told. They're just the victims of white racism and poverty.

African-American role models like comedian Bill Cosby, filmmaker Spike Lee and an array of black politicians all have caucused unsuccessfully to try to find a solution to the fratricide occurring among urban blacks.

But the only significant action that has been taken is gun control.

And as Lieutenant Duckett bluntly told the *Washington Post,* "gun control has not worked."

Duckett points out that Washington has the strictest gun laws in the nation, yet one of the highest murder rates. He believes citizens have a right to defend themselves.

"It's quicker to pull your Smith & Wesson than to dial 911 if you're being robbed," says Duckett.

Pretty powerful statement from a black cop.

On the radio, Duckett explained that while handguns were banned by the 1976 Washington, D.C., gun law, the public's perception that all gun ownership is illegal is wrong.

According to the 1976 law, citizens can apply to the police to purchase shotguns and rifles and then must register them. Registered guns in homes must be kept unloaded and disassembled or locked.

That really evens the odds for some misguided pauper's son who has just broken into a law-abiding gun owner's darkened home.

Not surprisingly, Tanya Metaksa, the NRA's top lobbyist, supports Lieutenant Duckett's views.

"With the District's citizens terrorized by violent criminals, it's time the city's leaders recognize what police rank and file have long known. D.C.'s gun law turns honest citizens into easy prey for criminals."

Hearing a cop acknowledge that Americans have the right to keep and bear arms to defend their loved ones and their homes is extremely telling in our fight against urban crime.

I can't understand why liberals are so appalled at the idea of citizens' defending themselves from the criminal element skulking in the streets of our cities.

Some of the folks I talk with on the radio say it's because liberals like to use the out-of-control criminal element to frighten people into becoming more dependent on the government.

You'll have to decide that one for yourself.

In the meantime, I'd suggest we keep an eye on the next slick politician who promises to make the thugs disappear if you and I would only surrender our guns.

Armed Citizenry
Fight the Bad Guys

First published September 1997

There is no doubt in the minds of most avid defenders of the Second Amendment that a large number of liberal bigwigs in the national media stand foursquare against granting law-abiding citizens their Constitutional right to arm themselves.

Thus, it doesn't surprise me when the talking heads on television do everything in their power to put a negative spin on a story even if it is a clear-cut example of an armed citizen's successfully defending himself against a common criminal.

A good case in point was an NBC television promo of an up-coming story about an incident at Sam's St. Johns Seafood, in Jacksonville, Florida, where a would-be robber armed with a shotgun ambled into the diner and, with the flair of the wild West of yesteryear, proceeded to order everyone to hit the floor.

NBC's teaser went something like "Is the solution to criminal violence more violence?"

Well, here's the story as reported by the Associated Press. You can judge for yourself whether there was an excess of firepower.

It didn't seem to matter to the young gunman, Dervonne Marquise Moore, seventeen, of Jacksonville, that he was in Florida, one of the most progressive states in the union concerning the Constitutional right of the people to arm and protect themselves.

He soon found out about an armed citizenry, however, because as Moore was ordering a waitress to get cash out of the register, sixty-nine-year-old Oscar Moore drew his .22–caliber revolver and shot gunman Moore in the belly—quite an uncomfortable place to take a round, I might add.

But that wasn't all. Another armed customer rose to the occasion to back up citizen Moore.

Robert Guerry, eighty-one, pulled out his .22–caliber Derringer and fired at the young man, who by now was hightailing it out the door. Police arrested him later that evening when the teen arrived at a local hospital seeking treatment for the bullet in his gut.

Questioned by the media, armed citizen Moore, who said he always carries, commented, "That gun I didn't trust to try to go for a head shot. . . . If I'd another gun with me, I'd have gone for a head shot, taken care of it from here to eternity."

Instead of spouting the usual pap about the danger of having guns in his establishment, restaurant co-owner Sam Bajalia was smart enough to savvy the benefit of a couple of armed customers in the house.

In fact, Bajalia was elated that Moore and Guerry were there, because he feared the robber might have started shooting if waitress Amy Norton hadn't produced cash quickly enough.

My take is that the situation at Sam's St. Johns Seafood con-

cluded with a storybook ending. No one was hurt—save the bad
guy—and police said that citizens Moore and Guerry would not be
charged for coming to the rescue.

It was a classic example of two law-abiding men, legally autho-
rized by the state to arm themselves, taking a stand for the good of
the community, protecting property and innocent folk.

I say God bless them for having the strength of their convictions to confront a common thief in a society where it has become all
too common not to get involved.

But then, I can tell by their ages that Moore and Guerry are
men from a different time. They are from an age when people took a
stand to defend what belonged them and their neighbors. They are
from a time when right and wrong were clearly delineated.

The news staff at NBC, of course, didn't see it that clearly.

In spite of a crystalline example of the essence and intent of the
Second Amendment right to bear arms, they still want to contem-
plate the evil of an inanimate object.

Right to Bear Arms
v. Free Speech

First published September 1997

Let's hear it for actor Charlton Heston, who has what it takes to cut
the pie down the middle where our Second Amendment Constitutional rights are concerned.

Heston, first vice president of the National Rifle Association,
put the pedal to the metal in support of gun-owner rights when he
told members of the media at the National Press Club that the right
to keep and bear firearms is as essential today as it was in this
country's earliest days.

Quoted in a report by Knight-Ridder News Service, he said,
"The right to keep and bear arms is not archaic. It's not an outdated,

dusty idea some old, dead white guys dreamed up in fear of the red-coats. No, it's just as essential a liberty today as it was in 1776."

Then Heston hit close to home with his audience when he declared that the Second Amendment was more important than the First Amendment right to free speech.

I have no doubt that Heston's powerful words insulted and irked some liberal members of the press who were in attendance.

But I wonder whether they realize that the First Amendment freedom which they depend upon to do their jobs would be no more than meaningless words without the Second Amendment rights to back it up.

Electing Charlton Heston to the office of first vice president may be the best thing the NRA has done in a while.

His strong stance certainly helps to eradicate some wishful thinking by Second Amendment opponents who declared the NRA had run its course, that it had spent all of its political clout and thus lost all of its ability to influence gun votes on the Hill.

Dismiss them as old dead white men if you like, but the men who gathered in 1787 to draft our Constitution recalled very vividly the British attempts to keep Americans disarmed as part of their efforts to halt American independence.

Our forefathers reckoned if this republic was to become a reality, if it was to survive the aggression of Great Britain or any other nation that might try to suppress its dreams of a fruitful future, its citizens must have the Constitutional and moral right to be armed—unlike the unarmed, powerless peasants of Europe.

Today, it seems, any man who stands up to speak out against that which he considers to be oppressive policies of the government in Washington, D.C., runs the risk of being dubbed a nut or a kook, a disgruntled member of society who simply does not want to pay his fair share.

But think about it. Today criminals abound, and thus crime threatens all law-abiding citizens—not just middle-class Americans, but the poor who dwell in this nation's ghettos. If ever there was a peasant class in the United States, the latter represents it today.

And all of us are being treated like the peasants in feudal Europe, systematically stripped of our Second Amendment right to defend our hearth and home.

Heston hit the nail on the head.

If free speech was essential to the citizens of the new nation, then the means of defending that free speech also was essential.

True liberty, in my book—and in Heston's—takes both free speech and the right to bear arms.

During his speech, Heston attacked the liberal press for trying to undermine the Second Amendment, for working diligently "to denigrate it, to degrade it, to readily accept diluting it."

He was right.

I can't begin to count the members of the press I know who have no trouble calling for the elimination of the Second Amendment from our Constitution.

When questioned about it—if they choose to respond at all—their answer is something like:

"There is too much crime in the city" or "Fewer guns would help curb the anarchistic and racist activities of militia groups."

Clearly, they fail to get the point.

What Heston was saying to these liberals in the media was that, like it or not, the founding fathers saw to it that every citizen would be protected from the whim of some intellectual in power who decides that the people can best be protected—and handled—if they are unarmed.

Well said, First Vice President Heston. And thank you for breathing life back into an essential organization.

ELEVEN

Capital Punishment

Challenge to Visit
Killers Accepted

First published June 1997

There comes a time when every man must put his money or, in this case, the strength of his conviction where his mouth is. And I'm about to do so.

As a forceful proponent of the death penalty for capital offenses, I talk about capital punishment quite often on my talk radio show.

Predictably, my stance attracts an abundance of people who dub themselves advocates for the rights of the condemned. They argue over and over that the government has no legal or moral right to execute unfortunate and misguided people who kill.

This is a very popular liberal stance, one that even some of the most highly visible journalists and commentators are comfortable espousing. For instance, according to a 1995 article in the *Houston Post*, ABC's Ted Koppel spoke out against the death penalty while visiting the state prison in Huntsville, Texas.

Koppel was airing a two-part *Nightline* program on capital punishment, and according to the article, he was worried that society doesn't even take notice of executions anymore.

"We're executing a lot of people in this country today," Koppel said. "If we ever become so blasé about people, in our name, killing other people, then I think we've lost touch with one of the important aspects of civilized society."

By his comments, I think, Koppel—like a lot of liberals speaking on behalf of the condemned—showed limited compassion for the victims and their anguished families.

He showed himself to be hand-in-glove with an array of bleeding-heart politicians, religious leaders and inconsequential activists whose sociopolitical agendas demand that they make excuses for the street violence of killers rather than hold them ultimately accountable for their heinous actions.

I've endured the rhetoric of these liberals with only part of the story for more than a decade from my perch every day on the airwaves.

Recently, though, I heard a new twist in the debate. An anti–death penalty proponent challenged me to visit the death house in Huntsville to see, feel and smell for myself the horror of being restricted to a cell, counting the days before being executed.

The caller's perspective was that this punishment is nothing short of barbarism, and he felt confident that once I went there, I would return to my microphone an enlightened man. Once enlightened, of course, I would publicly denounce the death penalty.

Well, I have taken the challenge.

I'm scheduled shortly to visit this nation's most gruesome death row in a state that executes more killers than any other state in the union—twenty-four so far in 1997.

I think it is highly unlikely that I'll develop a compassion for killers like Irineo Tristan Montoya, a Mexican national who was executed at Huntsville this month for the 1985 murder of John Kilheffer, of Brownsville, Texas.

Montoya confessed that he and a friend stabbed Kilheffer twenty-two times. Then they dumped his perforated body into a grapefruit grove next to the Rio Grande near the Mexican border.

Their defense?

A simple one, according to this killer. Kilheffer had picked them up while they were hitchhiking near the border and apparently insulted their sense of machismo when he invited them to have sex with him at a local motel.

Well, this conservative American—and obviously the men and women on the jury who convicted Montoya—believe that was a pretty poor excuse for killing a man.

Another recent Texas execution was that of Eddie James Johnson, found guilty of the 1987 slaying of three people, including a ten-year-old girl and a boss who had been promoted ahead of him.

Only time will tell if my visit to the front line of arguably America's most extreme legal punishment will alter my stance on the death penalty.

I'm guessing it won't, but I'll keep you posted.

Still Pro–Capital Punishment After Trip to Death Row

First published July 1997

Well, I took the challenge from one of my radio show callers and visited death row in Huntsville, Texas. The caller was against the death penalty and sure I would join his ideological ranks once I saw the conditions of a death sentence and the real people subjected to them.

I assure you I remain a steadfast supporter of capital punishment. But I must admit that my visit had a profound influence on me.

Being pent up—sometimes for decades—in a tiny, two-man cell without air-conditioning for twenty-three hours of every stifling hot, humid Texas day, knowing you are waiting only to die, is ugly.

Few of us deserve to live under those conditions—certainly not you or me, Mr. and Mrs. America.

But then, we're different, aren't we?

We're different because we have not killed another human being.

We are different from Robert Wallace West, Jr., thirty-five, who is the next Texas inmate scheduled to die, specifically after 6:00 P.M. on July 29, 1997.

He has been on death row for fourteen years for the 1982 murder of a twenty-two-year-old waitress. He broke into her room, stripped her, bound her, strangled her and then beat her to death with a wooden club.

Why?

Because West, who admitted the murder when he was arrested, said he believed the victim had been indirectly responsible for the death of one of his friends.

I met West in the visitors' room, where he sat across from me, locked up in a tiny cage. He was full of jailhouse bravado, apparently enjoying talking with anyone from the outside, primarily, I'm guessing, because it afforded him an opportunity to leave his cell.

"Is the death penalty fair?" I asked him.

"No," he replied without hesitation or emotion.

"If you were free, would you kill again?"

"No."

"Are you telling the truth?"

He only smiled.

Emerson Edward Rudd was convicted for murdering a twenty-three-year-old fast-food restaurant manager. He was eighteen and a high school senior in the fall of 1988 when he and three accomplices demanded money at gunpoint. After the manager surrendered $800, Rudd shot him in the gut.

Rudd's pals got twenty, fifteen and ten years for murder and aggravated robbery.

Rudd is an excellent example of what becomes of young black boys who refuse to live by society's rules. His extreme rebelliousness has left him living in a hot cage with only one way out.

If prison has taught him anything at all, it's to hustle anyone in the media who will give him an ear.

We talked for an hour, during which he wove the usual tale of how he, not the victim, is the real casualty of this situation. He painted himself a victim of institutional racism, of a paltry education, of incompetent lawyers, corrupt prosecutors, indifferent judges and a biased jury.

He confided in me—as I am sure he has in many others—that he has become a reader of philosophy and how he now understands that the black man is oppressed.

I asked Rudd what he saw when he looked from his cage at me—another black man, who in spite of whatever oppression, wasn't locked up waiting to die.

Did he perceive me to be an Uncle Tom, a sellout?

Not sure how to respond, he seemed to try to stroke me.

"No, I don't see you as no Clarence Thomas or nothing like that," he said finally.

He only smiled and fidgeted with his fingers when I continued to probe him: "Doesn't it bother you for me to see you in that cage?"

He was less forthcoming than West about his crime.

"Did you kill that manager?"

"I ain't saying, 'cause I'm still making my appeal."

"You've been on death row for eight years. Suppose you were released, given fifty bucks, a bus ticket and the pledge of a job, and that job didn't materialize. Would you do the same thing again?"

"No, because I've prepared."

"But life doesn't offer any guarantees. If it didn't pan out for you, would you get a gun and do it all over again?"

"No, because I've prepared."

Prepared for what, I wondered. Rudd never did tell me what eight years on death row had prepared him for in the outside world.

Maybe that's because he, like most killers who seek to solve their problems with a knife, a gun or a club, still may not be prepared to do much else besides kill. The men I met on death row certainly hadn't prepared themselves to take responsibility for the people they already had killed.

And that fact alone allows me to remain an adamant proponent of the death penalty and all the inmates' suffering that goes along with it.

Freedom, Sweet Freedom

First published July 1997

The dictionary defines freedom as "the state of being free or at liberty rather than in confinement. Exemption from external control, personal liberty. . . ."

Freedom. Americans tend to use the word lightly. It's a concept easily taken for granted by countless generations of U.S. citizens.

About the only time we hear about freedom with any depth of emotion is from Americans who have lost and then regained freedom after being held as prisoners during World War II, Korea, Vietnam and most recently during the Gulf War.

Then they speak of freedom in flowing and romantic terms. They tell us about their lives prior to their confinement, when they seldom gave their freedom a second thought, taking it as lightly as the truth that the sun would rise at dawn.

I've always been fascinated by such people. I think they have a lot in common with folks who claim to have had near-death experiences. Having recovered from their ordeals, both groups seem to spend a lot of time talking about seemingly very esoteric things.

Like the beauty of a rose or the sweet smell of freshly cut grass. They claim to have a deeper understanding of themselves, in some cases even a fuller comprehension of the meaning of life.

While I would never put my recent visit to the death house in Huntsville, Texas, on par with having been prisoner of war or with having a momentary glimpse of life after death, I do believe that having stood next to the gurney in the death chamber has given me a greater appreciation for the value of life.

I reassessed my own freedom the moment I left Huntsville. When I was seated behind the controls of my twin-engine airplane, its nose pointed upward into a blue Texas sky dotted with towering clouds, the open sky came to depict the nectar of my liberty.

That moment became symbolic of my reward for following the rules, for doing the right thing and obeying the law. It was my reward for toiling to consummate my dreams long before there was even a light at the end of the tunnel.

Climbing away from the overbearing Texas heat and humidity below me, the gloom of the death chamber, the warden's dispassionate description of how a condemned man is prepared to die, climbing away from men none of us "square citizens" would want to meet on a dark street, I enjoyed the sweet sensation of my own freedom.

My mind drifted to what before had seemed inconsequential

musings. I skimmed the aeronautical chart, noting that Florida was here, California was there, and that I was free as a bird to point the nose of my airplane whichever way I so desired.

I pondered the luxury of being free to swig a cold beer when I got back home to Denver.

I thought about being free to write and talk about my personal impressions of death row and the men I met there.

Since my trip to Huntsville, often while I routinely prepare for my daily talk radio show, the shadowy image of one of the death row prisoners comes back to me. I remember him squinting out of his cage at me, my freedom making me a species of man apart from him.

I am far from going soft on convicted killers. They committed murder, and their rap sheets confirm that in the grand majority of cases, they were deliberate in their deeds.

But still, I ponder the tragic lives of the more than four hundred "dead men walking" in Huntsville. And I wonder why it takes a stint as a POW, a near-death experience or a trip to the death house before we truly appreciate and husband the precious freedom that most of us take for granted.

Mail from the Death House

First published August 1997

Shortly after my recent tour of the Texas death house in Huntsville, I received a letter from an inmate awaiting his well-earned appointment to have the state induce the big sleep.

He was quite annoyed about my stance in favor of capital punishment—a position, I might add, which I held both before and after my visit, during which I spoke at length with two other death row inmates.

My trip made me no more or less convinced about the social, ethical and religious pros and cons concerning the right of civilized people to condemn another person to death. But it did make me certain of one thing:

After talking with the condemned, I realized that being sentenced to death for the murder of another human being apparently doesn't change the self-centered opinion they have of themselves.

A good example is the case of the author of the letter to me, Texas death house inmate No. 999163, Nanon McKewn Williams. Date of birth: 8–2–74. Race: black.

Williams and co-defendant Vaal Solomon Guevara were convicted in the robbery and murder of nineteen-year-old Adonius Collier on May 14, 1992, in Houston. Guevara was sentenced to ten years in prison, and Williams was sentenced to death for his role in the murder.

Before I tell you more about that brutal killing, let me share some excerpts from Williams's letter to me, in which, predictably, he stands morally against the death penalty.

"Recently you visited two inmates here on Texas death row and you wrote an article pertaining to those visits, more so, exactly why you support the death penalty. But that brief judgment you made touched thousands of readers and they could have been easily influenced by your own ignorance concerning [the] death penalty."

It appears to me that Williams, like a good many capital offenders, is unwilling to concede that it is he, a killer, not I, a columnist, who is responsible for the greatest influence on the public's opinion about this issue.

He does little to change that public opinion by maintaining his attitude of "forget the victim and focus on me because I am the real casualty in this situation."

His letter went on: "When I first learned of your visit I only hoped you would look beyond the subjectivism that most people are placed in."

I can only suppose he hoped that I, like many journalists with dusky-colored skin, would prove to be a bleeding-heart liberal who would not focus on his misdeed but on his victimization by society.

Which brings me back to his misdeed. According to his rap sheet, issued by the Texas correctional authorities, Williams and Guevara lured the victim into a deserted section of Herman Park, in Houston, under the pretense of scoring a large amount of cocaine.

But instead of doing the drug deal, Williams pulled a .25 caliber pistol and shot Collier and another man in the head. The second victim fled, which prompted Williams to fire a shotgun blast into Collier's head.

Williams wrote on: "It is unfair, but more so it is even cruel because of the simple fact that you can reach many minds, but not in the capacity that could make positive changes, or at the very least, something pertaining to the facts surrounding the death penalty. You allowed your perception of two individuals towards you to dictate your frame of mind, not the mitigating circumstances that place people on death row.

"You asked Emerson Rudd [the black inmate I interviewed and wrote about] did he perceive you as a 'sellout,' or an 'Uncle Tom.' . . . What does that have to do with the death penalty? Just because you are a successful Black man in America wouldn't define you as an 'Uncle Tom,' unless you are self-conscious about your own misdeeds toward your race of people."

I thought it was interesting how Williams characterized me as unfair, cruel and "self-conscious" about my "misdeeds."

At no place in his three-page, typewritten, single-spaced dispatch to me did Williams ever mention his own unfairness or cruelty toward his victim. He did not express remorse for the brutal murder he and Guevara committed on that night in 1992.

And that cold-blooded act of street violence, Mr. Williams, is what continues to make me an advocate for your execution.

Williams concluded his letter by asking me to "please check more into the death penalty, and all its facts before you are so quick to conclude that human lives are meaningless."

Human lives meaningless?

No, 999163. I think you conveniently choose to miss the point—the point being your obligation to society for your own rush to judgment and your lack of compassion for human life where your victim was concerned.

Reinstatement of Death Penalty = More Executions

First published October 1997

The well-earned execution by lethal injection of Gary Lee Davis took place last week, and no one can convince me that God in his heaven paused one moment to shed a tear.

Davis had been convicted of the brutal rape and murder of farm wife Virginia "Ginny" May, a neighbor of his on the eastern plains of Colorado. His death sentence was the first carried out in that state in three decades.

Aside from eliminating a natural-born predator of unsuspecting women, the Davis execution also served the purpose of breaking the anti–capital punishment log jam, which had derailed the wishes of a majority of the residents of Colorado for thirty-some years.

According to a recent *New York Times* article, Colorado is among a number of states that have moved to settle the score with its capital offenders of late:

"Within the last year, Oregon and Kentucky have conducted their first executions since 1962. By the end of next year, Connecticut, New Jersey, Ohio and Tennessee may also hold their first executions since the 1960s, according to the Death Penalty Information Center."

The *Times* article noted that at present only twelve states and the District of Columbia outlaw the death penalty.

"Of the 38 states that allow it, 29 states have had executions since 1976, when the Supreme Court reinstated the death penalty.

"With 59 people executed this year, executions are at a 40-year high. The nation has not seen so many since 65 people were executed in 1957."

The stats make sense to me. Did convicts and their anti–death penalty cohorts think killers would somehow slip the hangman's noose after the death penalty was reinstated?

Still, after the execution of Davis, some anti–death penalty supporters wanted to know whether those of us who had demanded our pound of flesh for the hideous crime in which Davis and his wife kidnapped, raped, tortured and murdered Virginia May eleven years ago were satisfied.

The answer is decidedly yes.

I think the world is a safer and a better place because one fewer sexual predator is alive. So far as I am concerned, even behind prison bars, Davis was a threat to society. We would have had to live wondering about the real possibility that someday a bleeding-heart liberal on the Colorado Parole Board might have deemed him rehabilitated and let him loose.

And so, to that end, the world is definitely a safer place for some unknown mother's daughter, because Gary Lee Davis is dead.

I'm not among the many who argue that capital punishment is a deterrent to others. Frankly, I don't care if the execution of Davis doesn't deter another single killer.

What I care about is that Davis has paid with his life for the horror, the terror and the suffering he inflicted on May when, in her final hours, he became the embodiment of evil for her.

The fact is capital punishment isn't about those who might kill one day. It's about punishing the man or woman who already has taken a human life. From that perspective, capital punishment was 100 percent effective on the thirteenth day of October in 1997 in Colorado.

In the end, muddleheaded liberals and convicted killers persist by arguing that execution is pointless because it won't bring back the person killed.

I would counter that allowing these killers to live out the rest of their lives—even behind bars and, I might add, at great expense to taxpayers—hasn't ever been known to resurrect the person they killed from a cold and premature grave either.

But by my logic, there is one undisputable result of Davis's execution:

The other convicted killers who shared space with Davis on death row in the Colorado state penitentiary must be taking their sentences a whole lot more seriously.

A Killer's Lasting Bequest to Feminists

First published February 1998

Texas death row inmate No. 777, whom the world knew as Karla Faye Tucker, is gone.

As ordained by the will of the Texas justice system, Tucker vanished from our world in the thirty-eighth year of her life at 6:45 P.M. (CST) on February 3.

Right up to the moment she was induced by lethal injection to take the big sleep, there was considerable chatter about whether the code of the Western world would permit administration of the state's will in this case involving a woman.

Nonetheless, Tucker was, in fact, executed for her role in the horrid murders of twenty-seven-year-old Jerry Lynn Dean and Dean's new lover, thirty-two-year-old Deborah Thornton, who was probably just in the wrong place at the wrong time.

It seems Thornton had met Dean only the day before.

According to the official report—and contrary to the way anti–capital punishment sob sisters have tried to soften it—this is how the homicides came about:

Tucker and her accomplice, one Daniel Ryan Garrett, cat-burgled their way into Dean's Houston apartment, supposedly to steal some motorcycle parts.

Tucker testified that when the two of them encountered Dean in the bedroom, Garrett began beating him on the head with a hammer.

When Garrett stopped clubbing him, Dean began making a "gurgling sound."

Allegedly irked by the sound, Tucker hefted a pickax and plunged it into his back.

That completed, Tucker, obviously getting into the swing of things, turned her attention—and the pickax—to Thornton, who was discovered cowering beneath a blanket.

When the coroner examined the bodies, each victim was found to have more than twenty stab or puncture wounds. The pickax was found embedded in Thornton's chest.

In the end, Tucker testified against Garrett and he against her.

Garrett testified that Tucker bragged afterward about getting sexual gratification every time she whacked Dean and Thornton.

Tucker denied getting any joy from her blows, claiming instead that she went at Dean with the pickax because he had defaced photographs of her mom.

If ever there was a cold cookie who deserved to be executed, I'd say it was Tucker. And indeed, Tucker was convicted and sentenced to death for killing Dean.

Garrett, who also was sentenced to die, cheated the executioner when he died from a liver disease in 1993, while on death row.

Meanwhile, as her date with the hangman approached, Karla Faye Tucker became a perfect poster girl for the anti–capital punishment movement in our country today.

She was an attractive woman—appearing dainty and petite even in her prison attire. She proclaimed her born-again Christianity and, along with it, her complete rehabilitation.

Her police record confirmed that she was a feral female animal when Texas authorities yanked her off the streets, but behind bars Tucker didn't fit the stereotypical profile of a killer.

And, of course, she was a woman—the first to be so near to Texas state execution in more than a century.

The anti–capital punishment contingent must have realized that if they could forestall Tucker's execution—on the grounds that she was a female—it would be possible to flood the courts with hundreds of anti–capital punishment pleas, based on the legal reasoning that the state of Texas applied the death penalty in a biased manner.

But thanks to the political mettle of Texas Governor George W. Bush, who refused last-minute pleas to intervene, their strategy failed miserably. And already, Tucker's name has begun to fade from the headlines.

For all of her effort, Karla Faye's only lasting bequest to the anti–capital punishment movement and the on-again-off-again feminist crusade may have been inadvertently to displace the glass ceiling from the dome of the death house in Huntsville, Texas.

Crime Isn't "Child's Play"

First published April 1997

In spite of the recent headlines saying that crime in America is declining, not even a Pollyanna liberal can deny that juvenile crime remains beyond the level that law-abiding Americans are willing to tolerate.

Every day headlines in the newspapers and stories on nightly television newscasts broadcast one horrible tale after another concerning the viciousness of today's youth. . . .

Pelham, Alabama: "A man, his girlfriend and her two young daughters were found dead in their home, and police were questioning the man's 17-year-old son." Associated Press.

Richmond, California: "He's a poster boy for three-strikes laws—burglary, theft, assault and finally the murderous beating of a tiny infant, prosecutors say.

"But he's only 6 years old, his legs too short to reach the floor from a chair in a juvenile courtroom. The youngest child in the nation ever charged with attempted murder has confounded juvenile authorities debating whether to punish or help the boy—and how." Associated Press.

In 1995, the U.S. Justice Department reported in what the *New York Times* labeled the "most comprehensive report ever assembled on crimes committed by young people": "If current trends continue, the number of arrests of juveniles for violent crimes will double by the year 2010."

And just last week, in another *New York Times* report—this one labeled "the most comprehensive study ever of crime prevention"—it was revealed that some of the most popular liberal crime-prevention programs for juvies, such as bootcamps and late-night basketball, aren't curbing juvenile criminal activity.

This story was based on a study done for Congress by University of Maryland criminologists.

So now comes Governor Pete Wilson of California, along with other conservative leaders in that state, suggesting that the time may have come to consider executing capital offenders as young as thirteen.

The *Chicago Tribune* reported that it was suggested the death penalty be used against young killers judged to be "hardened criminals" or who "may be lost forever."

Naturally, death penalty opponents—the same liberals who brought us the innovative ideas of midnight basketball and drug reeducation in drug-ridden neighborhoods and schools—have been quick to voice their displeasure and to denounce Governor Wilson.

Some called the Governor's idea "nutty."

But Wilson told the Sacramento Press Club last week, "What is needed is a juvenile justice system that teaches our youngest offenders that crime is not child's play."

He challenged his opponents with hard facts.

To illustrate juveniles under eighteen (the present minimum age for execution in California) who "may be lost forever," he recounted the instance of two thirteen-year-olds who recently stomped a sixty-one-year-old man to death in a Sacramento train station.

Authorities theorized that crime may have been part of a gang initiation.

The thought of strapping down and sedating a thirteen-year-old killer may be difficult for some to envision. But that's probably because you are fixating on your own sweet kid.

Furthermore, even a convicted thirteen-year-old probably wouldn't be executed until he was twenty-three or even thirty-three years old because of the long appeal process for those sentenced to death.

Governor Wilson may sound like a merciless barbarian for daring to propose that we execute our children who kill.

But I predict that if adolescent killers continue to rampage unchecked, the day will come when he will be cheered for having the political courage to cope with a scourge that must be confronted.

TWELVE

Immigration

The Gate's Open

First published June 1997

Washington politicians have packaged and fed the American people a supposed solution to the failing integrity of our southern border, a solution that carries the grandiose name "Operation Gatekeeper."

Operation Gatekeeper began in October of 1994 and cost $25 million to implement. It was supposed to showcase Washington's determination to regain control of our border.

In fact, to hear the Clinton administration tell it, Gatekeeper was the ultimate line drawn in the dirt to protect the overburdened taxpayers of the U.S. from the peasants of Mexico and other countries to the south who sneak into our country and usurp our government-provided services, everything from medical services to education.

According to a 1994 *New York Times* article:

"Dubbed Gatekeeper, the new Border Patrol defense is an intricate . . . quasi-military combination of fencing, high-intensity lights, additional manpower and increased use of high-tech radios, night-vision devices and motion detectors."

Sounds efficient. But I've heard the propaganda from Washington before.

So I took my radio show to San Diego for a week to see for myself whether Gatekeeper was working as well as claimed to cure the illegal immigration problem.

As a result of my visit, I can tell you quite assuredly something the agents of the U.S. Border Patrol and the San Diego police already know—Operation Gatekeeper is a bust.

It's just another Beltway scam created to hoodwink the American people. With the help of the silent media and the effective muzzling of malcontents in the U.S. Border Patrol, Gatekeeper represents an out-and-out fraud perpetrated against the American taxpayer.

Talk with the public information officers from the Border Patrol and the Immigration and Naturalization Service, and they'll offer the official word: Gatekeeper is a huge success.

But if you are willing to dig beyond that official message and take a minute to learn what's really happening, if you talk to patrol agents who are ducking hot Mexican lead fired at them across the border and to officers of the San Diego Police Department who patrol just miles beyond the frontier, you will learn quickly that Gatekeeper isn't all it's held up to be.

Not more than twenty-four hours after I arrived in San Diego, Border Patrol agents, city cops and average citizens in San Diego told me not only that illegals were still slipping through our border, but exactly where they were going.

"Of course, they're still getting in," said one San Diego businessman and friend. "They live in the canyons right behind my house."

After a couple of days in San Diego, I had a handle on where several campsites of illegals were supposedly located. I had specific directions to canyons with vegetation camouflaging worn paths off roads that dead-ended out of expensive suburban housing developments.

Before we left San Diego, my wife and I drove about thirty miles north of the city to see for ourselves. We found numerous encampments, the sites obviously currently occupied. Children's toys were strewn about. Small gardens of crops were growing. Signs of cooking and personal hygiene were evident.

A Mexican we met on the dirt road leading to the canyon paths told us through an interpreter that he figured the "residents" had gone to town since it was Friday, and thus payday.

How did we know they were illegal immigrants? When we asked the Border Patrol, the police and San Diego citizens, they just smiled and said if they were legal they would be at the local job service office, not standing on appointed corners every morning to be picked up for a day's work.

One frustrated border agent told me that the core of the problem with Gatekeeper is that his agency has been restricted to the immediate border area, prohibited from pursuing anyone who slips by their "line in the dirt."

In essence, Gatekeeper has reduced the Border Patrol to a single line of defense, and the illegals know it.

They know that once they make it past the bright lights, the high-tech motion detectors and the night-vision lenses, they are free to run north and into the arms of building contractors, farmers, horse breeders and California housewives looking for accommodating Mexican men and women ready and willing to shovel horse manure or scrub floors for the U.S. dollar.

Just Enforce the Law

First published February 1997

The U.S. Immigration and Naturalization Service has released a new report that confirms what millions of Americans have been saying for a long while—that the sovereignty of our nation is at risk from a flood of illegal immigrants who are pilfering the benefits of being U.S. citizens.

The INS report indicates that the number of illegal immigrants who live within our borders has increased to 5 million and is swelling by about 275,000 a year.

According to this newly released data, the INS estimates the illegal population has increased 28 percent in the past four years and illegal immigrants now represent as much as 2 percent of the U.S. population.

I suggest that this new data be accepted for what it is—evidence of the implementation of liberal policies in Washington aimed ultimately at doing away with U.S. immigration restrictions altogether, perhaps even doing away with the border between the U.S. and Mexico.

If that seems absurd, how else can we explain such a flagrant disregard for our immigration statutes?

The truth is that efforts to prevent illegal immigration have been reduced to little more than a recreational game of sociopolitical dodgeball between illegals and the sympathetic U.S. government.

The liberals who hold sway over the INS today don't always follow the law and stop or send back foreigners attempting to enter our country illegally. They are just as likely to send illegals—particularly those who fit into the romanticized category of the beleaguered Mexican poor—into the waiting arms of a human rights group that entertains the notion that Mexicans still have a legal claim to the southwestern U.S.

This absurd claim has been advanced into mainstream politics by a ragamuffin cadre of political activists.

Their stance would be humorous were it not encouraged indirectly by a generally liberal media bemoaning the circumstances of the runaway Mexican peasants—and by turncoat conservatives like former Housing Secretary Jack Kemp and bygone Education Secretary Bill Bennett.

Kemp and Bennett contributed to this extremist movement when they sided with the opposition to Proposition 187, a 1994 referendum put forth by overburdened California taxpayers trying to stop footing the bill to support illegal aliens flowing across their state's border.

At the time, the Urban Institute estimated that Californians were burdened with the support of some 15,000 illegals in their prisons. They paid another $166.5 million for emergency medical care and $1.3 billion annually to educate illegal immigrants' children.

The federal government refused to reimburse Californians for these unjust costs. Believing they had been betrayed and abandoned both by the federal government and by opportunistic politicians like Kemp and Bennett, California voters sought their salvation by overwhelmingly voting Proposition 187 into law.

The election was stolen from them, however, when both a state and a federal judge subsequently ruled that illegal immigrants could not be denied services and that their children could not be expelled from California schools.

It's no surprise that the illegal population in the U.S. continues to rise.

The INS report of ever-increasing numbers of illegals living in the U.S. also represents a glaring failure of the liberal Immigration Reform Act of 1986.

This grandiose plan granted amnesty to almost 3 million illegal immigrants living in the U.S. at the time. It was supposed to be an act of leniency and compassion that, by liberal logic, was intended to stem the flow of illegals, particularly Mexicans, slipping across the border from that time forward.

Once again, though, time has proven what the average American already knew and could have told the politicians in Washington, D.C.

Cruel as it may seem, the more lenient and kindhearted we become, the more illegals Mexico flushes north for us to support.

The proof is in the pudding—or in the latest INS report, to be precise.

According to a spokesman for the Center for Immigration Studies quoted in the *Washington Post:* "The illegal population has now reached the level that it was before the 1986 amnesty. The past ten years have essentially canceled out the entire effect of the amnesty."

The fact is we don't need any new political solutions. This is a matter of law. And the American people know—even if Washington politicians don't—that all we have to do is enforce the law.

The "Colorado 29"

First published April 1996

Let me say first I assume that most of my readers are law-abiding citizens. Based on that assumption, try to imagine yourself in the predicament of being an American pulled over by the police in a foreign country.

Unlikely though it might be, you would be the driver of a vehicle that wasn't properly registered. And as if that weren't bad enough, your bad dream would take place in a foreign country you had entered illegally.

Think that's a tough spot?

That's because you belong to what may be an ever-shrinking pool of citizens who still believe everyone should obey the law.

But unimaginable as such a situation might seem, a traffic contact exactly like it occurred in western Colorado.

If you are as fed up as I am with U.S. officials turning a blind eye and a deaf ear to illegal aliens overrunning the southwestern United States, the following account ought to heighten your blood pressure:

According to the *Denver Post:* "A van filled with 29 illegal immigrants was stopped on Interstate 70 in Grand Junction . . . but a lack of funds kept U.S. authorities from arresting them or their driver.

"Colorado State Patrol troopers and agents with the U.S. Immigration and Naturalization Service were able to interview occupants of the van but then had to send them on their way."

That's right. A van loaded with twenty-nine people believed to be from Mexico and in violation of U.S. immigration laws was stopped, given the once-over by the Colorado State Patrol and INS agents and then sent on its merry way.

Is it any wonder why so many illegals don't think twice about crashing our southern border?

The *Post* article said that troopers stopped the van because it had no visible license plate. How far do you think you or I would get without a license plate on our vehicle? Probably no farther than the local sheriff's office and then to the nearest bus stop.

But the INS told the *Post* it had no choice in this particular case because a specially funded push to halt illegal immigration into Colorado had run out of cash. All they could hope for, said the agents, was that another jurisdiction down the road would have access to sufficient funds to arrest and deport the van's occupants.

Agent Larry Hines said, "It's frustrating for us and for the state patrol who stopped them. Hopefully someone else will have the funds to handle them."

Pardon me. But when did the federal government run out of cash to detain and deport people in our country illegally—whether they come from Mexico or any other nation?

Did Agent Hines inadvertently signal the surrender of the government's effort to control U.S. borders, to protect and to defend our nation's sovereignty?

Ridiculous notion? Well, let's not forget this is an election year.

President Clinton hasn't exhibited any shyness when it concerns manipulating facts about crime, the public dole or the economy, if doing so might gain a few votes for him.

Why wouldn't he bend a little when it comes to the illegal immigration statutes? I don't think it at all beyond the president's men to put a bug in the ear of INS brass not to ruffle the feathers of Mexican Americans by detaining or deporting their relatives who cross the border as criminals.

Clinton and his campaign advisers might even be concerned enough about public opinion since the unfortunate beating of poor Mexican peasants in California to impose an unofficial moratorium on cracking down (no pun intended) on illegals.

The way liberals see things, so what if you break a few eggs—or even some laws—to make an omelet? After all, getting Bill Clinton reelected is for the greater good of the nation, and in their minds that may justify using any means necessary.

Meanwhile, word that twenty-nine of their countrymen entered the U.S. illegally, were stopped and sent along their way surely will reach the farms and cantinas where other Mexican citizens are weighing their chances for a new life up north.

In fact, we law-abiding U.S. citizens can't begin to imagine the flood of new illegal Mexican immigrants that little act of bureaucratic generosity near Grand Junction, Colorado, ultimately could bring to the welfare rolls of this nation.

Are Americans Stupid?

First published March 1997

A lot of liberals will tell you that only white bigots are in an uproar over the fact that Southern California has been invaded by a swarm of illegals from Mexico.

But Terry Anderson, a man who describes himself as a Negro American, is evidence quite to the contrary.

My radio staff and I produced a special *Ken Hamblin Show* that focused on illegal immigration across our southern border.

We gathered perspectives on the problem from a number of people heading up groups formed to fight illegal immigration.

The most interesting guest, however, was Anderson, an auto mechanic who lives in Compton, the South Central section of Los Angeles, and whose grandchildren attend L.A. schools. As a citizen, Anderson is enraged about the flood of illegal immigrants coming into his neighborhood.

"I don't know if your listeners know what South Central is," Anderson began on the program. "It's the ghetto, but it used to be a nice place to live. It's had its problems, but with the influx of these new people, it has exacerbated every problem we ever had.

"Our children—I'm black so I speak of the little black children—got thrown into school where they have to listen to everything that is said by the teacher translated to the Hispanic children. That leaves them a half a day's education, anyway you look at it.

"We go to PTA meetings, and everything is translated. Every billboard in my neighborhood is also in Spanish to facilitate these people.

"We can't get entry-level jobs in my community here in South Central for young black teenagers because these illegal aliens, thirty and forty years old, have taken the jobs that I had when I was fifteen, sixteen and seventeen years old."

I stopped Anderson and told him that he sounded like a middle-class American, like any guy, white or black, from any place across this country who was threatened about his neighborhood.

"Let me tell you," he continued, "my living has gone to practically nothing. Every time I give a price to a customer, they tell me the Mexican over here will do it for ten dollars. The body-and-fender business has been totally devastated. The bricklayers in my neighborhood can't find work."

I stopped Anderson again for clarification.

Was he telling me and my listeners that legal immigrants come into Los Angeles, go down to city hall, put their money on the table and purchase the proper licenses and permits to open up a business? And he was an angry American who couldn't compete in the free marketplace?

Or was he telling us that people not only come across our southern border illegally, but they then boldly set up body shops, do masonry work, build houses—all without the licenses and permits America requires?

"There is no legality here," said Anderson. "These people not only are setting up businesses. I have them living right next door to me, six feet from where I'm sitting right now.

"These people are illegals," he interjected. "Ask me how I know."

I did, and he told of this incident.

"They had a barking dog. I filed a complaint with the city, and they asked me for ID when I got there. I handed them my driver's license, and they took a picture of it for the record. You know what this man handed them as his form of ID?

"A video rental card. He looked at the woman and said, 'That is all I have.' And he said it through a translator. I'm telling you as an American I can compete with any other American or legal resident in this country who goes through the proper channels."

What Anderson clearly cannot compete against are a people usurping the benefits of his grandchildren's schooling, his hard day of work and his city and state services—all with no obligation to give something back.

He ended the interview recounting a conversation he had with one of his Mexican neighbors living in the United States illegally.

"He said Americans are stupid," said Anderson. "And you know what? He was right."

El Salvador Helps Citizens Flee to U.S.

First published November 1995

There must be a notion among our neighbors south of the border that we Americans are exceedingly easy and gullible when it comes to anyone perceived to be less fortunate than we are.

According to a recent report in the *New York Times,* the Republic of El Salvador has begun offering an unusual service: free help in filing claims for political asylum in the United States to its peasants living here as refugees.

That's right. The government of El Salvador is setting up offices here to help its own people flee on the basis of its own persecution of them.

Why would El Salvador do such a bizarre thing?

The *Times* reported that Salvadoran immigrants working in the United States—primarily as maids, landscapers and waiters—sent almost $1 billion back to their families in El Salvador last year alone.

The *Times* reported that amount may come close to El Salvador's earnings from its exports for that period.

Is it any wonder, then, that the Republic of El Salvador would be anxious to pawn off its, for the most part, unskilled *campecinos* on its liberal and naive neighbor to the north?

With that much money riding on the back of Central and South America's peasant class, it seems logical to me that we are going to continue to see nothing less than an all-out invasion of the United States from the south.

According to U.S. Immigration Department data printed last

week in *USA Today*, we deported 48,361 foreigners in the twelve-month period ending September 30.

It was also reported that of those, 31,244 were criminals, convicted of serious crimes, and the rest, 17,117, were sent back for "noncriminal causes such as violating immigration laws."

Pardon me, but when was sneaking across our border dropped from the list of criminal offenses against the United States of America?

That attitude from Washington, plus common sense, tells me that it is silly for the average U.S. Joe to expect the governments of Mexico, El Salvador and other Latin American countries to do much to try to stop the flow of illegals crossing our border.

Aside from the economic bonanza the expatriates send back into their homelands, it's especially silly to expect these governments to strictly prevent crossings from their side when the bureaucrats on our side seem to do little more than run a shuttle service back south when we catch these pitiful peasants.

The whole situation has reached the point that, as of late, some American citizens living near the border have taken matters into their own hands.

Last week another *New York Times* article said that assaults on illegal immigrants by U.S. ranchers in southern California are on the upswing.

The vigilantism has resulted in one illegal immigrant's being shot and another six being held captive by the ranchers.

A special representative of the U.S. attorney general's office tried to explain the citizens' actions to the *Times* by admitting that "crime against personal property . . . has increased" in East San Diego County, where many illegals now are coming across.

Perhaps these American citizens have crossed paths with the likes of the "Brown Avenger" from Oakland, California, who sent the following faxed message to my talk radio program when I was discussing the illegal-alien problem one day last week:

"You better get used to it, dude—we just taking back what the white gringos stole."

If the U.S. government truly is interested in stopping the modern-day Mexican stampede across our border, I have an idea—one I've been putting forth for some time now.

Instead of arresting and detaining illegals in holding cells for a matter of hours before they are bused home, only to start their illegal immigration all over again, why not keep them in jail here for six months?

A quick appearance in night court could surely give them due process before they were put on U.S. prison work duty for the period of their incarceration.

I'll bet the word would spread quickly that the gringos were no longer so easy and that we don't intend to give up our U.S. dollars— or our country—without getting in a few licks of our own.

Immigrants Caught DUI Need to Go

First published September 1998

Where exactly do you stand in the matter of dealing with folks who drive under the influence?

You know, the people who drive drunk. DUIs. Men and women who overimbibe and then attempt to beat the odds—usually at some innocent person's expense. Then they plead innocence, or ignorance, when they are ticketed and hauled into court.

Folks more gullible than myself argue that alcoholism is a disease and that its victims require all the sympathy and compassion that society can muster.

But I subscribe to the school of thought that people who insist on operating a motor vehicle while looped basically are selfish men and women who have developed a potentially deadly habit of thumbing their noses at the rules to which the majority of Americans subscribe.

That's why I am glad to throw my support behind a 1996 U.S.

immigration-reform law that allows our government to deport legal permanent residents who violate our driving-under-the-influence laws.

That law was enforced recently in Harlingen, Texas, when more than five hundred legal immigrants were processed for deportation in a roundup of aliens with three or more drunk-driving convictions.

A Texas law stating that a third DUI conviction constitutes a felony and a deportable offense under the law was upheld, based on the 1996 national law.

You would think any immigrant who legally migrated to the United States would be an eager beaver when it came to complying with our laws—particularly considering the social and economic benefits they stood to lose.

But, alas, such is not always the case.

I'm sure that most landed immigrants are committed to becoming good citizens. But there are always the few—just like the few of us who were born in the U.S.—who try to beat the system.

Since August, according to the Associated Press, in addition to those five hundred–plus, more than two hundred other legal immigrants in Dallas, El Paso, Harlingen, San Antonio and Houston have been apprehended for drunk-driving infractions and face being sent to their homeland by the U.S. Immigration and Naturalization Service.

I see it that hundreds fewer inebriated drivers will be behind the wheel in Texas.

But now enter the crybaby Mexican-immigration advocates, who predictably are lamenting that Hispanics are being discriminated against by the INS.

According to the AP story, immigrant-rights advocates are claiming that the arrests are unjust and break up families. They claim that the people detained are men in their thirties and forties who have been in the U.S. between six and ten years and are needed here to support their families.

Well, where is it written that immigrants between thirty and fifty, who have been in our country for up to a decade have the unique privilege to drive drunk?

Absolutely nowhere.

But that's not how the executive director of the South Texas Immigration Council sees it. Benigo Pena says his group isn't questioning whether driving while under the influence is a serious crime.

According to him: "What we're questioning is if this person went before a court, was tried, convicted, has shown remorse and it's time to pay back society—that's the American way of doing things."

I wonder how much better off we'd all be if immigrant advocates like Mr. Pena were to spend their energy convincing their clients to obey the law instead of fashioning one excuse after another for them.

But sadly, we can usually depend on them to dredge up the typical example of an "innocent" man just working hard to support his family. Such is the case of Eugeno Villela Torres, a fifty-two-year-old Raymondville grandpa who supposedly didn't drink anymore, but had a record with three past drunk-driving convictions.

Torres is hardly typical of some of the others arrested, many of whom had been arrested for drunken driving ten or eleven times.

The whole thing is just another example of how we've allowed our basic standards of right and wrong to be challenged, in the name of political correctness, in favor of the supposed underdog.

I think the Penas of this world are barking up the wrong tree when they try to defend any drunk driver—Mexican immigrant or anyone else—weaving along American highways.

Mothers Against Drunk Driving, which has publicly praised the INS campaign, don't buy their arguments. And neither do I.

Racing for the Border

First published April 1996

From beneath the pummeling blows of southern California police batons last week, an official poster child in the war to eradicate the border between the U.S. and Mexico has ascended.

It doesn't matter that the orphan from Mexico's socioeconomic storm not only crept into our country against the law, or that she lied about who she was when the angels of compassion and mercy saved her from the cruel clutches of the white man's law.

Initially, the Mexican poster girl presented herself as Leticia Gonzalez. Later she admitted to the *Los Angeles Times* and local television reporters that she had fibbed about her name.

Her real name was Alicia Sotero-Vasquez, thirty-two years old and from Xocheca, Mexico.

Sotero become the center of attention of many outraged and shocked U.S. citizens when she and a truckload of illegal Mexican aliens came to the end of their trail in Riverside, California, after an 80-mile chase by the police.

Clearly what happened next was way out of line. In fact, it was against the law.

Sotero and others in the fleeing truck, one of whom was identified as her common-law husband, were beaten by the frustrated cops they had tried to elude as a television camera hovering in a whirlybird high in the sky videotaped the action.

The offending officers have been suspended with pay pending a full investigation by the sheriff's department. Sheriff Larry Smith expressed shock about the unprofessional image of his men clubbing Vasquez and the other illegals à la Rodney King and has promised that there won't be any cover-up in his full investigation of the matter.

According to the sheriff, "No one is above the law." To be sure he keeps that attitude, the FBI has opened a civil rights investigation.

Meanwhile, the extremist political bottom feeders have gathered to try to strip as much flesh of opportunity from the carcass of the Riverside illegal Mexican beating incident as possible.

AFL-CIO Executive Vice President Linda Chavez-Thompson issued a statement condemning the "use of police batons to impose street justice."

According to the Reuters news service, L.A. lawyers from the Mexican American Bar Association and the Center for Human Rights and Constitutional Law have announced their intention to file a $10 million lawsuit against the two officers, Kurtis Franklin and Tracy Watson.

No one denies that despite the apparent wrongdoing by police, in the end this injustice will serve to champion the movement. And just what is that movement?

Well, some go so far as to demand that southern California be repatriated back under the domain of old Mexico.

Others are content to expose the forces of supposedly racist U.S. nationalism, which want to return to the days when Sotero and her pals applied to enter the United States, the land of milk and honey, legally.

I can assure you that in the coming days, weeks and months we will hear a great deal more about Alicia Sotero and thousands of others like her. We will read how difficult her life is. There will be features by compassionate journalists who will compare the relatively good life of average Americans to destitute lives like hers.

But don't let yourself be suckered into that liberal vortex. Keep your wits about you.

Try to remember also that Sotero for one probably will come out of the experience much richer than on the day she violated U.S. law by illegally penetrating our border.

It would serve us well to remember that every year tens of thousands of poor Mexicans not unlike Sotero filter across our border with Mexico.

They are coming to our land like a plague of locusts.

Despite what an assortment of sob sisters in the media and pro-Mexico Americans might want us to believe, try not to forget that similar to locusts on the march, wretched women like Sotero and her transitory companions in that truck crossed our southern border with every intention of taking whatever they could from our rich land—and try not to forget that they began their march illegally.

With the possibility of a $10 million purse being bandied about by the liberal lawyers, I predict that even more caravans of Mexicans in broken-down trucks who hope to strike it rich beneath the blows of an American policeman's baton will soon be racing for the border.

Viva La Raza!

First published September 1995

Like any sane and healthy person in this country, I found myself frustrated, disgusted and outraged after reading a story from the *Los Angeles Times* about a carful of kids being shot up by an estimated dozen gang members in a predominantly Hispanic part of that city.

The *Times* labeled the ambush in the Cypress Park section of L.A. a "classic urban nightmare."

The operator of the ill-fated vehicle and his passengers found themselves in the wrong place at the wrong time.

Timothy Stone, twenty-five, turned down a dead-end street and suddenly was at the mercy of the neighborhood predators, members of one of the Latino gangs indigenous to the area.

By the time Stone realized his mistake, it was too late. The gang members tried to block his escape from the alley and hurled trash cans at the vehicle.

From what authorities have been able to discern, just when it looked like Stone might have made good his escape from the clutches of the gang, they opened fire with handguns on the occupants of the vehicle.

During the barrage of gunfire, three-year-old Stephanie Kuhen received a mortal wound to her head. Joseph, her two-year-old brother, was struck in the foot. Stone was shot in the back. Stephanie's mother, Robynn, twenty-six, her five-year-old brother and the children's uncle, David Dalton, twenty-two, were not hit.

By the weekend, the LAPD had picked up four suspects in this slaughter of innocent citizens of an American city. But police also confirmed that Vincent Caldera, the first arrested, would not be charged because witnesses didn't identify him and family members provided an alibi for him at the time of the shooting.

The Cypress Park area is known to be plagued by conflicts between rival Latino gangs, but the cops reportedly were perplexed about why Stone and the occupants of his vehicle were attacked.

L.A. police detective Robert Lopez was quoted in the *Times:* "Clearly they could look into the car and see male and female Caucasians and not Hispanics. You can see a three-year-old and a five-year-old and you can pretty much figure they're not going to threaten your life. . . . I can't see a three-year-old flipping gang signs."

Trying to understand what bitterness and ethnic hatred could be powerful enough to cause barrio dogs, like these thugs in Cypress Park, to pepper a vehicle full of unarmed adults and kids with bullets just because they accidentally ventured into their neighborhood, I opened up the subject on my talk radio show.

I also invited Bette Hammond, director of United Citizens for Immigration Control, to brief my audience on the growing problems of illegal immigration control and ethnic violence in Southern California.

Hammond recited some disturbing facts about illegal immigration and crime. According to her group's research, approximately 12 to 15 percent of California prison inmates are alien felons; 9 to 11 percent of jail inmates are alien felons; and 8 percent of California youth-authority wards are alien felons.

Hammond also noted that Hispanic gangs, rather than black gangs like the Bloods and the Crips, are the dominant factor when it comes to crime in Southern California. They make up more than half of the estimated 60,000 gang members there.

While Hammond was making her point that a majority of the 800 gang-related murders that occurred in L.A. County in 1992 could be attributed to Hispanic gangs, my fax machine began to hum with protests, apparently from the same breed of punks who shot the babies.

One fax in particular helped me understand why the barrio dogs were able to kill as easily as they did:

"Yo . . . You should join your brown brothers, smash the white oppressor! You say barrio dogs [*perros*]. We say Freedom Fighters. We taking it back, dude—nothing to stop us. Viva La Raza! Viva Aztlan! Viva La Intifada Latina!"

Finally I got the picture.

You see, while the police may not admit it publicly, I'm convinced the people in that vehicle were shot for one reason that night—because they were simply the wrong color. They were white people.

A Flawed Argument
for Illegality

First published July 1998

The publication of a recent pro-immigrant report from Stephen Moore, an economist at the libertarian Cato Institute think tank in Washington, D.C., has concluded that immigrants contribute more to America than they cost.

According to Moore, whom I spoke with on my syndicated talk radio show, immigrants paid $133 billion in federal, state and local taxes last year and thus were a "fiscal bargain."

As the son of black immigrants from the West Indies, I say three cheers for them.

Moore's report confirms that these newcomers to America are not all deadweight—that is, a burden on the U.S. taxpayer. But most of all, it reaffirms to me that the American Dream is alive and working for them just as it has worked for me.

Unfortunately, I still find a serious flaw in this supposedly good-news report.

It's this: Moore drew his findings from more than two dozen other studies, which, according to the Associated Press, concluded that the nation's 25 million immigrant population, "spanning both legal and illegal aliens, provides a net positive effect to the United States."

Legal and illegal?

Sorry, but that's where this first-generation son of legal immigrants is compelled to draw the line. As other foes of illegal immigration have pointed out before me, how can there be any net positive result from an illegal act? How is it possible for a man who transports himself and his family across the borders of our nation illegally ever to respect the laws, much less the cultural values, of our republic?

In all fairness, on my radio show Moore claimed he isn't really trying to support illegal immigration. But then I say he should know it's irrational to try to sanitize the tsunami-like influx of illegal aliens with reports of the good they do for America.

Imagine, if you will, that you are in court listening to a public defender arguing on behalf of the thief caught in possession of your pickup truck. The defense might go something like this:

"Ladies and gentlemen of the jury: I don't dispute the fact that my client stole the vehicle in question. What I am asking you to consider is that while the truck in question was in my client's possession, he invested a considerable amount of his own money to repair the engine and the transmission. And he replaced all four tires.

"Yes, I will agree with the prosecution that theft is against the law. But please, please do not lose sight of the fact that the supposedly injured party in this situation undoubtedly benefited from my client's actions."

Sound too silly to be reasonably considered as a defense?

Well, in my mind, that is exactly the scenario the so-called pro-immigration movement in the U.S. is trying to peddle to us the people with reports like Moore's.

The Associated Press noted that the Federation for American Immigration Reform, a group opposed to any new immigrants to our shores, called Moore's findings "junk science."

I agree with the "junk science" label, but I am not proposing a total embargo on the acceptance of new legal immigrants.

I believe that any technologically competitive nation that hopes to remain economically, socially and militarily viable in the coming century ought to have learned a valuable lesson about the negative impact of fortification from outsiders, such as the Great Wall inflicted on China.

But short of the opportunists who feed like parasites on the sweat of their labor, who cares how much illegal immigrants contribute to the economic welfare of the U.S.? I certainly don't.

Not when the sovereignty of our nation is at stake.

Every nation has the moral right and the legal authority to secure its borders, and the U.S. is no exception. If the liberals in California, Texas and wherever else discarded Mexicans and Central and South Americans are battering down our border honestly want to lend a helping hand to these poor people, they should pressure politicians in Washington to "persuade" their fellow politicos south of the border to take more responsibility for their own.

One Country
Protecting Its Borders

First published January 1997

Once again my dedication to toiling diligently throughout the year has afforded the wife and me an opportunity to celebrate the dawning of a new year in a swell manner.

We were blessed to ring in 1997 as tourists in the British Virgin Islands, where the air is heavy with humidity, the night sky is cluttered with enough stars to quicken the pulse of a dealer in precious gems and the natives—unlike a lot of the visitors who come to their island—take life in an easy stride.

Yes, life in the BVI seems idyllic and unencumbered—that is, until you come across a tourist smitten with the desire to escape the complicated aspects of life in the Western world and run away to these sun-drenched islands.

In this instance, the daydreamer trying to liberate herself from her mundane European existence was a pleasant middle-aged British mother with an adult daughter back in England. I'll call her Lady T.

I had the pleasure of making Lady T's acquaintance when she became a welcome addition to our New Year's Eve assembly on Jost Van Dyke in the BVI.

The next day over coffee beneath an amazingly blue Caribbean sky on the deck of the 70-foot sailing vessel where we were guests, I learned that Lady T was residing and working in St. Thomas, the main island of the U.S. Virgin Islands.

While chattering about the beauty of the islands, Lady T said that, barring a minor hitch, it was her intention to resettle on the British side of the Virgin Islands.

When I asked what that hitch was, she told me the BVI had a law that gave first preference to the locals where matters of employment were concerned, and they were very diligent about it.

The law compelled every potential employer to make every effort to hire a native to fill any job opening before employing an off-islander. Specifically, an advertisement had to run for three consecutive weeks in search of the preferred BVI islander.

The law was a nasty little circumstance that was getting in the way of Lady T's landing a position of employment on the island of her dreams.

She seemed startled when I said—with considerable passion, I might add—that I thought it was a pretty good law.

I pointed out that without such a law, it wouldn't be long before off-islanders like herself would be owning and running the restaurants, the inns and whatever other enterprises attracted tourists to the islands.

That foothold acquired, friends of the new employers would follow, and it didn't take a genius to figure out who would have first choice at the best jobs. I pointed out that the islanders were only doing what was best for them and their children in the long run.

Eventually, while lounging on the deck of our sun-drenched ship, Lady T softened her view. And later that day, after giving our talk more thought, she conceded that the natives had every right to protect the quality of their lives.

Reflecting on our conversation myself, I wondered what the quality of life would be like in that tropical paradise if the liberals ever managed to infect it with the kind of loose thinking about immigrants that has managed to erode the U.S.'s sense of national sovereignty.

Oddly, the common sense that the government of the BVI

deems essential to the welfare of its people seems to have been sorely misplaced in the U.S.

When we departed from our island-hopping holiday, I watched the young boys working to free tourists from the burden of their heavy bags at the airport, the captains ferrying the boats and piloting the aircraft that connect the islands. I remembered the bartenders, the fishermen in the harbor, the bobbies and the customs officials, and I wondered how long it would take to tear paradise apart for these natives.

If liberal lawyers and organizations like the NAACP were allowed to promote their broad-minded ideals of quotas and affirmative action in the name of any and every immigrant determined to lay claim to his or her island in the sun, how long would it take to bring this paradise nation to its knees?

THIRTEEN

Patriotism

Modern-Day Paul Reveres?

First published May 1997

It doesn't take an especially insightful person to realize that the liberal media have been having a field day speculating about what they believe is an abnormal increase in right-wing patriots itching for confrontations with the federal government.

Their speculation is fueled, of course, by hard news such as the Oklahoma bombing trial and the recent uproar caused by a secessionist group calling itself the Republic of Texas, which hails from down Fort Davis way.

The Texas group was in the news after their members took a stand against the commonly recognized state authorities—a move that resulted in one secessionist's being killed in a gun battle in the Davis mountains.

I've noticed that often the way the media reports these incidents, it is insinuated that any American—especially one who is white, speaks out against the government and isolates himself from the benefits of today's mainstream, multicultural society—must be nuts, and racist to boot.

Those notions are easily propagated among the apathetic. They accept as fact that any disgruntled American, no matter how unfairly burdened he or she may feel as a result of the increasing demands of the federal government, must be a far-right racist wacko or at best a religious nut who deserves extermination by agents of the government.

But I am convinced that these extreme voices we are persuaded to dismiss aren't in reality the leading edge of a groundswell of hard-working Americans. Like the extremists, they are fed up with increasingly higher taxes, the decline of U.S. culture, the liberal tolerance of crime and a growing lack of morality among our political representatives—not the least of which is a seemingly total lack of scruples in the White House.

My analysis of the protests and the media coverage of extremist protesters has brought me to ask a question:

Do you think Paul Revere was a right-wing extremist and an unstable nut?

With public education as poor as it is today—not to mention the devaluation of U.S. history by some as just the stories of old white men—I'll assume some may not even know who Paul Revere was.

Revere was an American "patriot"—a word that evokes less-than-positive feelings in this day and age. Revere became a hero in the American Revolution when he rode from Charlestown to Lexington, Massachusetts, the night of April 18, 1775, to warn American revolutionaries of approaching British troops.

History records that Revere arrived in Lexington to sound the alarm that afforded John Hancock and Samuel Adams the opportunity to avoid capture by British troops.

Revere was a leader of the Sons of Liberty, a group of colonial patriots who I'm sure the British dubbed no less dangerous than the federal government sees the Montana or Michigan militia as being today.

Revere also participated in the Boston Tea Party, in 1773.

He was a heck of a rabble-rouser, and I'm sure that this nation's former British rulers would have given a pretty penny for his head served with their mutton.

But the fact is Revere was fighting for the principles embodied in the following words:

". . . That whenever any form of government becomes destructive of these ends [life, liberty and the pursuit of happiness], it is the right of the people to alter or to abolish it, and to institute a new government."

I am certain that when Paul Revere acted on that American

credo, King George III—not unlike the politicians and the media dealing with extreme protesters today—must have cast doubt on his words and dismissed him as a nut.

But he proved to speak for many Americans. And that's a history lesson that we would do well to preserve at any cost these days.

The Rage of Free Men
Is an American Legacy

First published April 1997

A considerable amount of tumult has been stirred up over the emergence of a letter that Oklahoma City bombing defendant Timothy McVeigh wrote to the weekly *Oklahoma Gazette* last year.

In the letter, McVeigh took the American public to task for allowing itself to be duped into believing the official spin from the government concerning the April 19, 1993, confrontation with David Koresh and his Branch Davidians near Waco, Texas.

It reads, in part:

"The public never saw the Davidians' home video of their cute babies, adorable children, loving mothers or protective fathers. Nor did they see pictures of the charred remains of children's bodies. Therefore, they didn't care when these families died a slow torturous death as they were gassed and burned alive at the hands of the FBI."

Excerpts like that recently published in the *Gazette* have unleashed a flurry of speculation that the letter represents proof of McVeigh's culpability in the Oklahoma bombing, which occurred on the two-year anniversary of Waco. Many say the letter will show motive to any jury.

Stephen Jones, McVeigh's attorney, however, dismisses the letter as immaterial.

I am of the opinion that McVeigh's letter simply confirms the discomfort he and a great many other Americans felt when they watched federal officers use excessive force to bring the standoff between them and Koresh to its fiery conclusion.

Don't misunderstand me.

I do not in any way condone revenge for this Waco atrocity. And if McVeigh is convicted of bombing the Alfred P. Murrah federal building in Oklahoma City, I think he should swing for his dirty deed. Certainly, such a deliberate act of terrorism against the 168 men, women and children who perished on that spring day deserves such just punishment.

But what about those men, women and children who died in Waco?

I believe a lot of Americans, myself included, could have written a letter similar to McVeigh's expressing concern about the government's heavy-handed involvement in the death of the Branch Davidians.

But while many could have, the majority of Americans who think of themselves as sensitive and caring people didn't write a letter or speak openly about it.

They found it easier to bury their heads.

Instead, as sensitive people, now they have pledged themselves to unraveling the riddle of Tim McVeigh. With the aid of government prosecutors who have a vested interest in having the events at Waco recorded their way, these good Americans are hard at work pondering, "What makes McVeigh tick?"

They have dulled themselves to the obvious as they ask what ever could have motivated him—or any man—to construct that awful fertilizer bomb and then leave it to kill all those blameless people.

They have chosen to ignore the reasons behind McVeigh's rage—reasons including the fact that he and many others perceive that Clinton, Reno and their minions behind government-issued guns are guilty of breaching their sworn faith to us and our American way.

I reiterate that the Oklahoma bombing was a cruel and vicious act. But try as we might, Americans cannot deny that the federal government has squandered its bond with the American people, and an ever-increasing number of us realize that.

The truth is that McVeigh's voice in this letter—whether we detest him or not—does speak for a large number of Americans. How many of them have been driven to the point where they are willing to plant bombs or take up arms against the federal government?

I'm not well enough connected to the extremely discontent, like McVeigh, to say.

I do know this, though. History has taught us that no amount of repression, nor any army of soldiers, can effectively still the rage of free men who believe they have been wronged.

Young men like Tim McVeigh who are willing to die if necessary for what they believe—in this case, his conviction that the pure hell of an oppressive federal government must be lifted from our necks—represent the spark whence revolutions come.

Mexican Pride Stops Where My American Pride Begins

First published March 1996

Last week I was greeted by an especially ugly sight on the front page of my *Denver Post*. It was a disgruntled Mexican-American student from an area high school trampling the American flag beneath his feet.

The article said that this student, Paul Romero, had chosen to denigrate America's colors while he stood swaddled in the flag of Mexico and sporting a headband declaring "Mexican Pride." He and an assembly of other young Mexican-Americans were protesting alleged acts of racism directed at Mexicans at another metropolitan area high school.

Nice shot, Mr. Romero.

But if you and the other disgruntled students truly believe that you can enhance pride among your people by denigrating the U.S. flag, you and your pals are very misinformed.

I think it's unfortunate that you, and many others of your generation, lack knowledge about the history of the flag you were so quick to trample upon.

I have a suggestion for you, Mr. Romero. It's something the white liberal socialists and the ethnic radicals probably responsible for stuffing your head full of anti-U.S. guff would never dare to suggest that you do.

I recommend—after the accolades you undoubtedly received from your teachers and pals have worn off—that you to take an afternoon out of your self-centered little existence and visit your local VFW post.

Walk in. Introduce yourself and ask to talk with the post commander. Don't do it as the Hispanic-American whose picture was published in the *Post* trampling the flag. Do so as a young American who is interested in discovering the names of the Mexican-Americans who have loved, served and died fighting for the colors you and your school chums so casually denigrated.

Young son, I am an American of color who can promise you this:

You will find thousands of names like Romero, Gonzalez and Hernandez identified with every branch of U.S. military service, from merchant marines who fought valiantly against German submarine wolf packs in the Atlantic to the leathernecks who died on flea-bitten islands in the Pacific.

I don't doubt that you and your misguided classmates thought you were helping to further the cause of Mexican-American pride by trampling on this nation's colors.

While I certainly think you are old enough to know better and that you should be held accountable for your actions by every American of any color who ever served this nation beneath that flag, I think it is important not to overlook the fact that your liberal educators and radical community leaders ought to share the blame for your patriotic ignorance. I think that they, perhaps more than any others, are responsible for convincing you that America has cheated you because your skin is brown, or because your name is Romero.

In my estimation, that makes you and your pals perfect suckers, first-class chumps. Wise up, dude. They are using you—using you to undermine all the opportunities available to you and all the other Americans willing to take the bull by the horns and vest themselves in the success available through their birthright as Americans.

Wise up, Romero. Look around you and think for yourself.

This is the U.S.A., not Mexico or Central America, where oligarchies and Latin bosses determine who will and will not rise above the level of tilling the land.

For decades your liberal teachers and the La Raza radicals have manipulated young minority kids like you. They do it every day in classrooms all across the country, by misdirecting you about the truth that in the U.S. you have total power to define what the quality of your life, and thus the lives of your children, will be.

Mr. Romero, I'll tell you what Mexican pride is about. It's about getting a top grade-point average in school. It's about being the best you can be no matter what the endeavor, because it will bring pride to your family, to your community and to your country.

Mexican or black, it makes no difference what color or sex you are, self-esteem can't be purchased or bestowed. The Mexican-Americans who came before you can't bequeath it to you. Like your father before you, you will have to earn it.

If respect for your Mexican ancestry means so much to you that you found pride in trampling the flag of a country where I'm willing to bet your ancestors struggled desperately to bring you, I think you would be well served to visit that VFW post.

After that, I'd suggest that you sit awhile with the old ones—*tu madre, tu padre y tus abuelos*. I'm sure that they will fill you in on the facts about what life would have been for a *niño* like you in Mexico.

History Rewritten
by Liberals

First published August 1995

Last week, we observed the fiftieth anniversary of the bombing of Japan at Hiroshima and at Nagasaki, marking the detonation of atomic devices over the homeland of one of the most tenacious enemies U.S. forces ever have had the misfortune of meeting in mortal combat.

I, for one, feel no remorse about the fact that we, instead of Germany or Japan, developed the atomic bomb first or that we used it to shatter the determination and vigor of an enemy that surely would have used it on us had time and technology worked in its favor.

As I think most citizens of this republic believe, I have come to reason that a strong defense tethered to the determination to prevail when our nation is threatened was then and is now a realistic and moral foreign policy.

So naturally I was irritated over the out-and-out bashing of the United States and the undue commiseration over Japan's defeat by many of the liberal intellectuals in the media during the anniversary observance.

All week, it appeared to me as if American pacifists, many of them remnants of the 1960s peacenik generation, were determined to spread only U.S. damnation and guilt over the fact that our atomic devices eclipsed the militarist and expansionist ambitions of Japan's rising sun.

It's been five decades since we defeated Japan. And over the years, these pacifists who have entrenched themselves in our nation's newspapers, television networks and museums obviously have achieved a considerable degree of success when it comes to portraying militarist Japanese as simply polite little people.

Few of the liberal-dominated TV networks or nation's newspapers revived the horrors of Japanese expansionism begun in the 1930s. Most failed to recount the stories of the babies of Chinese mothers and fathers in Manchuria being bayoneted for sport by the soldiers who represented the honor of Japan's emperor.

Instead, in that span of time, the insidious cloud of liberal extremism has transformed our nation into a country where our children are taught to punish themselves emotionally for breaking the back of Japanese expansionism. We probably shouldn't be surprised. This is the same nation where the great majority of our children no longer are even taught to honor our flag with the Pledge of Allegiance.

Only a small number of American students—and hardly any at all in Japan—are taught what the Japanese code of the samurai and Bushido, the way of the warrior, meant to the unfortunate souls who fell under the shadow of Japan's imperialist reach.

Thus, few understand today that the kind and courteous Japanese civilians we know are the direct descendants of an enemy who sent their imperial forces abroad to conquer the world in the name of Nippon and that their code of Bushido meant that it was honorable to look with disdain upon any opponent unwilling to fight to the death.

Today an ever-shrinking number of Americans comprehend that the way of the Japanese warrior meant giving no quarter to the Americans at Pearl Harbor on December 7, 1941, where 2,117 sailors and marines, 218 soldiers and 68 civilians lost their lives.

At Pearl Harbor, on Wake and Guam islands, in British Malaysia, Singapore, Hong Kong, the Dutch East Indies, Burma and Thailand and throughout the Philippines, wherever Japanese imperial forces sought to plant the flag of the rising sun, the ruthless practices of the Japanese warrior predominated.

Were two atomic bombs detonated over Japan because the United States had a grudge to settle with the Japanese people? Perhaps.

The death march of more than 9,000 American POWs at Bataan—a mountainous peninsula on the western side of Manila Bay in the Philippines—in the spring of 1942 certainly was reason enough for America to seek revenge.

Bataan was where Japanese soldiers adhering to the code of Bushido shot, beheaded, starved, beat or otherwise tortured to death thousands of our captured U.S. troops.

The atrocities recorded in the history of warfare among humans from all camps cannot be ignored. But in my opinion, neither should a hard-won and much-deserved victory over a tenacious enemy.

We must not allow the liberal historical revisionists to ignore the fact that in all probability the blinding atomic bursts detonated in the sky over Hiroshima and Nagasaki on those fateful days in August might well have been unleashed in due time over New York, Los Angeles or Washington, D.C., had we hesitated to use our advantage.

FOURTEEN

Parting Thoughts

"Greyhound Therapy"

First published May 1996

I have been predicting a backlash against the poor for some time. And based on a May 8 editorial in the *Birmingham News* in Alabama, there may be some hard evidence that backlash is taking shape.

It's no secret that taxpayers have been fed up with the irresponsible antics of the so-called hallowed poor for a long time. Now it looks as though someone, or some assembly of people in Birmingham, have decided to do something about them.

According to a recent editorial, headlined: "Greyhound Therapy," these mystery philanthropists are buying one-way bus tickets for homeless people in Birmingham and shipping them off to Huntsville.

The news called the endeavor: "Cold. Shameful. Shortsighted. Unneighborly."

Reading the paper's position, you would think these cherished homeless were the newspaper's personal property.

The editors were predictably stuffed with the usual liberal huff and puff as they ticked off the possible motives, including that business people who are concerned about losing consumers may not relish the presence of bums panhandling near their businesses.

Perhaps the why of the matter was simply that the homeless souls the *News* was lamenting were unsightly and annoying to people who are concerned about Birmingham's public image.

While I realize that to some, shipping undesirable bums out of town in the dark of night may not be considered the best way to save a town, it does get the point across.

It says, Hey, we community-minded folks are fed up. We are exasperated with feeding, clothing and sheltering a class of people who only seem to demand more, more, more. More of everything the majority of Americans have to work to get.

The liberal social workers in Birmingham seemed taken aback to learn that a portion of their homeless were being shipped out with a little pocket money thrown in.

Could it be their jobs depended on a "homeless count" in their domain?

I honestly think this proactive tactic to get the homeless "out of Dodge" actually caught them dozing and unprepared.

The homeless themselves, however, seemed unruffled. When questioned about how and why they had decided to relocate themselves to Huntsville, some told the *News* they were "given bus tickets and $10 cash to leave Birmingham. Others said they were picked up in downtown Birmingham, given $25 and taken to Huntsville by a man driving a van."

Naturally, Birmingham Mayor Richard Arrington has said the city isn't involved, and officials of a downtown business alliance have said that their hands are as clean as the pure driven snow.

Not sure of what else to do or say, the *News* editorial stooped to the only level left to them: that of trying to scold the culprits responsible for relieving the city of its bums.

"The problem, of course, is that shuttling away your homeless . . . who tend to be a drain on public or charity services isn't very neighborly to the destination city."

Whatever.

It isn't very humane, either, to encourage folks to linger at a certain level of poverty and homelessness to benefit from a socialist political agenda.

In spite of what the *News* wishes to hypothesize about the lack of neighborliness among folks in their town, fact is, working people in Birmingham and other cities are at their wits' end with the homeless.

The *Birmingham News* can call it what it wants. But compensating bums to get out of town is a far cry from tarring and feathering, lynching or shooting them. And that's probably a lot more than can be said for the next ill-fated person who will be carjacked or mugged in the section of town designated as hallowed for the homeless.

It's just possible that Greyhound therapy is an idea whose time has come. Unless, of course, you happen to live in Huntsville.

Reexamining Abortion

First published November 1994

I am pro-choice when it concerns a woman making up her mind about whether she wants to carry a pregnancy to term.

I became even more ardently pro-choice after reading an article in *Omni* magazine several years ago. It revealed that it was possible, at least in theory, to artificially impregnate a man by in vitro fertilization and then to deliver the baby by cesarean section—surgically delivering the infant through an abdominal incision.

The raging debate about whose rights superseded the other's, the fetus or the mother, was being waged as passionately back then in the 1980s, when *Omni* magazine published that astounding article, as it is today.

And I noticed then that although this scientific breakthrough made it seemingly possible for compassionate men of conscience or strong religious conviction to experience the miracle of artificial gestation and trick birth, none of these men—gay or straight—had volunteered to test the theory.

So after that, in protest against the selfish lip service and the overbearing pomposity of some men who seemed bent on riding roughshod over the reproductive systems of women, I restricted all dialogue on my radio show about abortion to women.

I banned husbands and lovers from crowing about the rights

guys had to determine whether their wives or girlfriends should carry a pregnancy to term. I stopped their self-righteous claims that any woman seeking an abortion was inherently unqualified to be trusted with God's gift of life.

Needless to say, since then I have taken a considerable amount of heat for that stance from more than one frenzied man who insisted they possessed some degree of legitimate authority to decide, even to force, if necessary, a woman to have a baby he may have planted between her legs.

Well, now let me tell you what has made me change my rules of abortion debate.

Certainly, nothing better evoked the love that the majority of people have for the miracle of children than the recent American tragedy of Susan Smith in Union, South Carolina, owning up to the murder of her babies.

Mrs. Smith's confession to the murder of her sons—three-year-old Michael and fourteen-month-old Alexander—struck a deep, profound and very personal blow to much of the nation.

It became an emotional topic of conversation that kept the fax machine and telephone lines to my syndicated talk radio show hopping for several days.

It seemed as if the hearts of every mother, father, grandma and grandpa had been torn open, leaving them exposed to a vile mixture of pain, bewilderment and rage.

But one particular fax, from Becky Airhart, of Salt Lake City, Utah, jolted me as profoundly as the *Omni* article did years ago. It began:

"Susan Smith's only crime was bad timing. If she had decided 3½ years ago and 20 months ago that her children would be an inconvenience, she could have killed them without any legal consequences.

"In America, it's legal for a mother to kill her children as long as her timing is right. And she can do it for the same reasons that Susan Smith killed her children: The boyfriend doesn't want the responsibility of raising the baby or she as a mother is not mentally or physically able to raise them or she just doesn't want a child right now.

"There are more parallels between this murder and the tragedy of abortion. I keep hearing people say that there are thousands of couples who would have been willing and eager, even desperate to adopt these children. I keep hearing that Susan Smith was so self-ish—thinking only of herself.

"When I listen to the outrage of this nation over the deaths of her two sons, I can't help but see the great hypocrisy we are guilty of. We as a nation allow hundreds of thousands, even millions of babies to be killed and think of it as a mother's right simply because their timing is better than Susan Smith's."

It may be unpopular for me to say so, but I must admit I'd have trouble living with myself if I didn't concede that Ms. Airhart's letter has given me reason to ponder my comfortable arm's-length stance on abortion.

I wonder whether those of us who weep for those little boys are capable of being as brutally honest about abortion and about the death of the Smith boys as this woman from Salt Lake City.

If we were, we'd have to admit that millions of cute little babies just like Michael and Alexander are terminated by moms not so unlike Mother Smith, simply because they couldn't be bothered by the inconvenience.

And just when does life begin? In light of the fax from Utah, it may be time for us all to rethink that question. I know I am.

The Airline Bullies

First published November 1997

Never let it be said that the business of writing a book is a task for wimps. I assure you it isn't.

After the euphoria you feel when your publisher accepts the final draft, and after you hold the first printed copy of your masterpiece in your hot little hands, the job of spreading the word about your masterpiece is just beginning.

This is a tiresome chore that can cause even the most unassuming author to lose his patience.

Recently, for a two-week period, I was on the road promoting the paperback edition of my book *Pick a Better Country*. I was compelled to pack my bags and fly the not-so-friendly skies of an array of commercial air carriers from Denver to the South, the North, the East and the West.

One would have thought I was being punished for some long-forgotten disobedience against my dear old mom.

Aside from meeting a lot of swell people in my destination cities, I found traveling excruciatingly strenuous and tedious.

In every airport I had to fight off the desire to approach the nearest skycap and present my suitcase to him to check. It was only a simple tote, purchased for the meager sum of $39.95 before wheels on suitcases were in vogue.

But in spite of harboring the hallucination of being able to walk free as a bird down the seemingly endless concourse that awaited me at every airport, I knew better. Commercial air travel in the latter half of the twentieth century has taught us all one common lesson:

"No matter what, never, never trust the airlines with your suitcase."

Particularly not if you have a long list of prescheduled television appearances awaiting you in each of your scheduled daily layovers.

Never check your bag. The airline will only lose it.

That has become the mantra of every seasoned traveler from the U.S.A. to Timbuktu—especially those travelers who have ever had to employ an apathetic airline employee to trace their missing luggage.

No, sir. I'm afraid that the days when a naive flying public believed that a commercial air carrier could be trusted to deliver its grips have long passed.

But back to my point for this essay.

Because of my recent travels, an article that told of a new proposal from the prima donna union of cabin attendants caught my attention soon after I got home.

It reported that the Association of Flight Attendants have concluded that carry-on bags are an increasing threat to air safety, and so they are demanding that new regulations be instituted to control what we the flying public can and cannot keep with us when we board.

United Airlines has taken the first step by planning to limit its discount-fare passengers at selected airports to one carry-on bag, while allowing its full-fare and first-class passengers to carry two.

Clearly, this is something we travelers should allow to go no further.

At least, not until the airlines guarantee every customer whom they bully into checking their carry-ons that they won't lose or destroy the bags. Not until they guarantee that paying travelers won't arrive at 10 P.M. with an 8 A.M. meeting—or TV appearance—and no clothes to wear.

Not likely to happen, you say? You bet it isn't.

Nor, from what I've seen, is the generally poor attitude of the cabin attendants toward the flying public likely to improve.

Sadly, the formerly proud career of providing top-notch service and courtesy, as an agent of the airline you work for, is a thing of the past.

One of the biggest public offenders, United Airlines, has tried to counter its poor service with a series of soppy TV ads promising a comeback to the old days . . ."United rising." But the ads can't dismiss the state of war that now exists between some cabin attendants and paying customers.

Commercial air travel today is a necessary evil, and the air carriers are hip to it. That's why I contend the flying public can't afford to give any ground to cabin crews who have come to perceive us as little more than flying chattel.

Recalling Why
I Live in Colorado

First published August 1993

My wife and I gave up on Detroit when the quality of life deteriorated to the point where we became afraid for each other's safety. We visited Colorado in 1975, and after that the mountains were all we thought about. A year later we moved to Summit County in the heart of Colorado ski country.

Before we realized our dream of Rocky Mountain residency, we scavenged every iota of information we could about the state. We savored every magazine article about the healthy quality of life, and on our frequent trips to Colorado we wandered—with the astonishment only a tourist can muster—through mountain towns with picturesque names like Frisco, Breckenridge and Montezuma.

In the year before we moved, we were like two birds flocking to a sanctuary the way we doggedly flew our twin-engine airplane on a regular basis over the expanse of Illinois, Iowa and Nebraska to visit our home-to-be. We circumvented spring and summer thunderstorms that turned the eastern plains of Colorado into a spectacular display of electrified fireworks. And we marveled at the bright sunshine in Colorado after years of gray skies in Detroit.

At Stapleton Airport, we rented motorcars and laughed at the locals when we realized how little they know about the weather just beyond Denver.

Then, seventeen years ago, we finally moved to Colorado for good. In those days, driving over a switchback on a high mountain pass or locking the hubs on my 4x4 before bouncing across a high-country dirt road were adventures to be savored and bragged about with friends who visited us in our new mountain home.

It may sound overly sentimental, but today when I'm cruising through the high country on my motorcycle, those memories are what skip through my head. By God, they were glorious days, those days when I was as inquiring as a puppy dog about what awaited me over the next hill.

Maybe it was my need to recapture those moments, to repeat the sensation of adventure and boldness, that heartened me to turn off I-70 and into the little town of Silver Plume as I crested the Georgetown Hill.

I've driven by Silver Plume dozens of times over the years in my commute between Summit County and Denver. But I don't recall ever stopping there more than two or three times.

It had been hotter than heck when I rolled out of Denver, and the turkeys who had been flooring their accelerators while demanding all the cooling they could get out of their air conditioners were scattered like a string of busted pearls along the side of the interstate.

But in spite of the heat and the steep grade in the road, my bike had climbed up to Silver Plume like a mountain goat holding its own.

When I pulled onto the town's narrow streets, it was as if I had stepped back a hundred years to the wildest days of the Silver Rush, for which the town was named. I parked my wheels and moseyed down Main Street.

My first stop was at the Sopp & Truscott General Store, which had a big sign "Bread" out front.

Proprietors Ann and Robby were a mother-and-son team who still embody the best tradition of the West: hospitality warmly extended to travelers. Not to mention that they bake that bread themselves fresh every morning using a sourdough starter nearly a century old.

I picked up a little something for the Mrs. at The Arts at Silver Plume, a delightful gallery housed in the remnants of an old chapel. Besides jewelry, which I knew would play well at home, it featured paintings and photographs by Coloradans.

The coup de grâce of Silver Plume was the KP Café—the closest thing to Alice's Restaurant we old relics from the sixties can possibly find. There, I met owners Chris and Ted, whose antiques and collectibles extended well beyond the walls of the restaurant to their upstairs living quarters.

It's been a tough summer in Denver, where we now reside full time. A good friend of my son's was shot down in cold blood and his wife brutally molested and beaten in the supermarket parking lot where my wife and I shop in our urban neighborhood. And these were only two among a string of unspeakable criminal acts of late.

But as the bodies pile up, I now think of the open road and the serenity of Colorado mountain towns like Silver Plume.

Silver Plume and the people who live there help me to recall what life is like when people aren't afraid to look one another in the eyes when they pass on the street. Silver Plume helps me recall why I moved to Colorado.

Despot Shunned in Death

First published September 1997

The headline in my hometown newspaper said of the man the civilized world holds responsible for bringing Zaire closest to the rim of the abyss: "Mobutu, shunned in death, buried quietly in Morocco."

Who cares? Mobutu was a black African despot of the worst kind.

A member of a moderately well-to-do family in the Belgian Congo who studied in Brussels and served in the Belgian-controlled colonial army, Mobutu ascended to the presidency of Zaire some years after a coup led in part by him in 1960.

I was a young man of twenty, and not particularly politically astute. But even today I still remember the coup. On the television set there was a black-and-white image of Premier Patrice Lumumba on his knees, sweat trickling down his dusky face with the sounds of the black African agitated crowd at his throat and the flash of clubs and knives in the background.

As I recall it, all the networks broadcast essentially the same version of this anarchistic event in a faraway land:

Premier Patrice Lumumba had been captured by forces fighting for true freedom and justice in Africa.

According to the report, U.S. advisers had helped to outmaneuver the Communists, and after a difficult battle, an essential player in the Red effort to take over Africa had been captured and taken into custody.

There he was on the television screen—bowed with his hands tied behind his back, eyes bulging, head turning to and fro like a wild animal's.

The newscasters' voices came across with an edge of excitement as they reported this high drama on the Dark Continent.

Tempers were running high in the former Belgian Congo, and the fates of Lumumba and other Red operatives in the newly independent African state were in question. The natives wanted their pound of flesh.

A short time later, the television networks reverberated with the news that Lumumba had been executed. According to the dispatches, it had been determined that he represented too great a threat to the new state (to be known as Zaire), to let him live.

The commander-in-chief of Zaire's new army was Mobutu Sese Seko. But that soon would change.

In those days, Mobutu's political tendencies leaned heavily in favor of the Western world, so the U.S. State Department found it easy to look the other way when he overthrew President Joseph Kasavubu in 1966 to become Zaire's president in 1967.

But by the early 1990s, it was clear to political camps throughout the world that the people of Zaire suffered greatly under the ominous dictatorship of Mobutu Sese Seko.

Mobutu's reign was conspicuous for its massive corruption, economic mismanagement, and human rights abuses and Mobutu's accumulation of a massive fortune for himself.

Mobutu was no piker. He ripped off his country and its people with gusto. After he was deposed earlier this year, the *Washington Post* noted that the Swiss found more Mobutu cash than they thought he had originally deposited:

"A Finance Ministry spokesman told Swiss media that the banks had found another $660,000 belonging to Mobutu and his family. In early June, the Swiss Federal Banking Commission declared the matter closed after it said a search of all the country's 406 commercial banks uncovered $3.4 million in Mobutu assets."

So in the end, a short article in my hometown newspaper reported that Mobutu was "shunned in death."

In the scheme of things, I guess it's really not important how many people make an appearance at your funeral after you've enjoyed a life of living off those people.

The media noted that a hundred police officers stood guard at Mobutu's funeral in Morocco. I reckon that's not a bad showing for a black African despot who had been ousted because of his human rights atrocities and modern-day piracy.

Cuba Sí

First published May 1993

I just spent a week broadcasting live from Havana to Denver. My time in Cuba was an amazing interlude filled with endless fiery political debate, tempered only by the warmth and beauty of the Cuban people.

The opportunity for this first live American-Cuban radio broadcast in thirty-three years presented itself when a boating buddy of mine who owns art galleries in Colorado asked me one summer Sunday, while we were both adrift on Lake Dillon, if I was interested in taking my Denver radio program to Cuba.

He had been back and forth to Cuba over the past year to arrange a special showing of Cuban artists in his gallery, and he understood the ins and outs of cultural exchanges between our two countries.

While our primary mission was a cultural exchange, it's impossible to visit Cuba without evoking strong political feelings. I had no idea, for instance, how my time there would harden my resolve against Americans who romanticize life in a socialist country.

Cuba provides a classic example of what life becomes when the state manages human incentive. No, I didn't see people begging or living in the streets of Havana as we do in the United States.

But the country of Cuba and the city of Havana are virtually crumbling because there is no money to refurbish them. While people are not starving, they are hungry. In fact, it's hard to imagine how the Cuban people can hold out much longer in this "Special Period" when Soviet support has ceased and U.S. exchange remains forbidden.

The scarcities of life in Cuba are apparent the minute you leave José Martí Airport and get a glimpse of the Avenue of Independence, the boulevard that takes you into Havana.

Gasoline shortages have forced the Cubans to store away their aging cars—if they still have them—and ride bicycles. Along the famous Malecón, it was common to see a man traveling with his wife and two children on a single Chinese-built ten-speed.

If they don't ride bicycles, they must travel on overcrowded buses called Wawas. Cubans without pesos for the Wawas are forced to walk or hitch a ride on any conveyance willing to pick them up. All official vehicles traveling with unoccupied seats are instructed to stop and pick up citizens on foot.

Food is severely rationed—the staples are limited to portions of six pounds each of flour and sugar monthly. Meat, chicken and fish have become nearly nonexistent.

But the Cubans I met don't want pity. In Havana, if the kids nail you for a tourist, they hit you up for Chiclets, not for food.

Cubans see the world by way of CNN from Miami. They know the good life is 90 miles north, yet the great majority of them willingly remain in Cuba.

Why they stay is an important question that I think the average American should ponder. And even after visiting Cuba, I'm not sure I'm qualified to answer.

Maybe they insist on backing Castro because we still insist on punishing them for it.

Why should Cubans be any different from the English, who refused to yield to Adolf Hitler when he tried to bomb them into submission during the Battle of Britain?

If the Cuban children are too young to recollect the sins of the oligarchy their grandparents toppled, at least they are wise enough to comprehend what their elders fought to overturn. This must be especially true for black Cubans, who before the revolution were forbidden even to use the beautiful beaches on the island.

I realize the world—even the U.S.—has changed a lot since Cuba's revolt. But with Cuban exiles frothing at the mouth to overthrow the Cubans in Cuba, it's understandable that native Cubans don't quite trust us yet.

Cuba isn't perfect. And in the end, the revolution still might be judged a failure if the old revolutionaries aren't keen enough to find a way to open Cuba to today's world.

The old men who drove the dons out of Cuba may still argue against such a move, but eventually they'll have to give way to the young Cubans who deserve more than what today's Cuba can offer them. Most important, I think my privileged glimpse inside Cuba has allowed me to go beyond the political agenda of Cuban-American exiles.

And that leads me to believe that a pax with Cuba may be ours for the taking—if we have the nerve to reach out with a dove instead of the muzzle of a gun.

Yes, Olivia, There Is a Santa Claus

First published December 1995

Question any child about what day this is, and he or she will say it is Christmas Eve, the day before Santa comes.

For some adults, the eve of the birth of the Christ child denotes the time each year to give thanks and pay homage to God for having sacrificed his only begotten son.

Of course, some among us argue that humankind has become obsessed with commercialism and Christmas spending, and thus we have drifted far from the spiritual profundity that Christmas represents.

Since I am not a cleric, I am hardly qualified to debate whether God on high is annoyed with those of us who can afford to string holiday lights, erect a gaily lighted tree and spread excessive gifts at its base.

So I think I'll continue to celebrate my personal joy of giving along with remembering my own very priceless joys of family.

Maybe it's a grandpa thing, but this year I find myself gazing longer at toddlers dragging their parents up and down store aisles laden with the playthings that, from the kiddies' perspective, their mommies and daddies are not bright enough to unearth on their own.

I have been studying these kids' anticipation of Christmas, including eavesdropping on the dialogue between Olivia Christine (my four-and-a-half-year-old granddaughter) and her Grandma Sue.

And I have concluded, without the least hesitation, that Santa Claus and his Christmas giving are good things.

I think the legend of Santa Claus, that jolly ol' man from the North Pole who dashes from house to house with gifts for little girls and boys who've spent at least the past few weeks behaving themselves and doing as they are told, is indeed a good tradition.

And if you'll permit me, I will go so far as to say that the spirit of God may even intervene in this Santa thing when absolutely necessary.

See if you don't agree. . . .

Last year, when Olivia Christine was just three and a half, I was immersed one Saturday morning in the excitement of packing her off to see Santa when, quite abruptly, she announced in a full-blown fit of defiance:

"Santa isn't real."

Needless to say, her mom, her grandma and her grandpa were devastated.

I kneeled to her level and said, "Where did you hear something like that, little girl?"

In a muffled tone, fidgeting with her little fingers, she replied: "He just isn't."

What a predicament for grown-ups about to escort their child on her first visit to Santa.

But, alas, not more than five minutes later, Grandma Sue called out from upstairs in a voice brimming with excitement:

"Olivia! Quick, where are you? Look through the window!"

Instantly, I heard the hurried pitter-patter of little feet as a curious Olivia rushed into the room. With childlike wonder and eyes as wide as saucers she exclaimed:

"Grandpa, look!"

Just beyond the window frame were several mule deer grazing, casually as you please, in our backyard.

"Don't move," I whispered, "or you'll frighten them away."

Slowly, a smile spread across my granddaughter's face as big and as broad as the expanse of the West.

"Do you know who those reindeer belong to?" I asked.

"No," Olivia replied in a tone of absolute innocence.

"They belong to Santa. They brought him this morning, so we can visit him."

She stared in amazement.

"Now do you believe Santa is real?"

She squeezed my fingers in her little hand and replied in the affirmative with a resounding "yes."

Was it divine intervention when a little girl most needed it?

I'll leave that for you to decide.

It did make me think that last Christmas might be the most special holiday I would ever have with my granddaughter. But I was wrong.

This year, Olivia delivered her special Christmas gift just as we finished decorating the tree. She stepped back, gazed with satisfaction and announced:

"This is the best Christmas I have ever had in my life!"

God bless, Merry Christmas and a happy holiday from the Hamblins to you and yours.